BORDERLESS LEADERSHIP

GLOBAL SKILLS FOR PERSONAL AND BUSINESS SUCCESS

BORDERLESS LEADERSHIP

GLOBAL SKILLS FOR PERSONAL AND BUSINESS SUCCESS

ZLÁTICA KRALJEVIC, PhD

CRC Press
Taylor & Francis Group
Boca Raton   London   New York

CRC Press is an imprint of the
Taylor & Francis Group, an **informa** business
AN AUERBACH BOOK

CRC Press
Taylor & Francis Group
6000 Broken Sound Parkway NW, Suite 300
Boca Raton, FL 33487-2742

© 2018 by Taylor & Francis Group, LLC
CRC Press is an imprint of Taylor & Francis Group, an Informa business

No claim to original U.S. Government works

Printed on acid-free paper

International Standard Book Number-13: 978-1-138-59149-3 (Hardback)

Visit the Taylor & Francis Web site at
http://www.taylorandfrancis.com

and the CRC Press Web site at
http://www.crcpress.com

Advance Reviews

"It took me fifty years of international travel to learn what Dr. Zlática Kraljevic summarizes in this book. The author shares valuable insights gained while she worked with C-suites and Boards throughout the world. Her five-step model illustrates how executives and companies can use new ideas and tools to increase awareness and understanding of their surroundings. *Borderless Leadership* should be studied, shared with colleagues, and blended into our corporate and personal lives. Leap years ahead of your competitors by instilling the principles outlined in this book. By internalizing and intentionally practicing these new concepts, individuals and corporations will have a winning strategy. These principles apply equally well when doing business in Beijing, hosting large receptions in the U.S. Ambassador's residence in Paris, or meeting suppliers in the interior of Brazil. They are successful in the corporate boardroom, with non-governmental organizations, and around the family dinner table."

— Donald E. Ellison
Board Leadership Fellow
National Association of Corporate Directors, USA

"*Borderless Leadership* is a well-written, fast-paced, and easy-to-read book that distills decades of global experience into usable and necessary guidance for today's interconnected business world. Kraljevic covers the globe, offering relevant examples on how to make a corporate move, develop global leadership skills, navigate potentially hazardous situations, and even relocate your family. She equips us with the latest thinking to help us manage in a global business environment."

— Regina H. Mayor
Advisory Industry Leader – Energy
KPMG, USA

"*Borderless Leadership* is a must read for anyone involved in international business. It enables beginners to avoid common pitfalls, and seasoned executives will recognize many of their own mistakes and benefit from the frameworks Dr. Kraljevic provides."

— Professor Sibrandes Poppema
President
University of Groningen, Netherlands

"I just cannot stop recommending this book to ever so many people—my academic colleagues, industry colleagues, friends in the government, former students, students, young CEOs of start-ups that I mentor, and my media friends. The book is very special, deep with several gems of ideas, told in absorbing narrative; neither a text book nor a cook book but a candid, sincere, and extremely effective set of real world lessons for so many global citizens. Dr. Kraljevic uses personal examples from across continents, in diverse industry settings. All I can say is this: Go, grab the book on a Thursday night, and you will have a wonderful weekend reading this amazing book."

— Professor S. Sadagopan
Director, International Institute of
Information Technology of Bangalore, India

"Everything I know about international markets, I owe it to Zlática."

— Sue Payne
Former ExxonMobil Area Manager
U.S. & Mexico

"As the global village rapidly expands, understanding borderless leadership becomes a prerequisite for international success in this 21st century. Kraljevic brings her vast and unique worldly experiences to open your mind with practical treasures, thoughtful how-to models, and conceptual insights. Find out about the human fractal on your journey to becoming a borderless leader."

— Lane Sloan
Former President
Shell Chemical Company, USA

Dedication

To Werner Artur and Werner Andrew
for their wisdom and invaluable support.
Love you both very much.

To all who sacrifice personal comfort
in the pursuit of global progress.

Related Articles Also by Zlática Kraljevic, PhD

Ten Checklists for Planning and Execution

Top 10 Blunders in Market Entry and How to Avoid Them

Strengthening Human Capital for Increased Revenues and Profit

Value Propositions—The Heart of Sustainable Alliances

Reinforcing Internal Workflows Helps Improve Profitability

Industry Assessment Plus Emotional Intelligence—Vital to Open New Markets

Available at www.andersfrontiergroup.com/blogs-updates/

Contents

List of Figures and Tables

Preface

I was in the finishing stages of writing this book when my son sent me a link to a fascinating YouTube video entitled *About Water*.[1] It had been created to graphically illustrate a commencement speech given by author David Foster Wallace in 2005. The video may or may not have followed Wallace's speech to the letter, but it was close. It highlighted the importance of being aware of our own surroundings and the advantages of stepping outside ourselves to connect with others and live a more fulfilling life.

The message relates so well to the content of this book that I decided to share my impressions, while also encouraging the reader to read Wallace's actual speech.[2]

In today's hectic environment, we all work long hours and interact with annoying situations; we suffer long commutes and endure heavy traffic day after day, year after year. It's no wonder that we're convinced that at times the world is a terrible place to live in and life is hard and unfair. We tend to believe that the inconveniences we suffer are directed at us; manifestations of bad luck or some kind of undeserved punishment; an injustice.

The parallel in the business environment, and particularly when we try to do business in emerging economies, is this: We're inclined to believe that global market conditions have turned against us. Although we know intellectually that there are significant growth opportunities abroad, we dread the moment we're commissioned by our companies to relocate and bring new and profitable business in, fast. Even when we recognize it as an opportunity, our lack of familiarity with other markets makes the situation look like an undeserved punishment.

The actors in *About Water* portray two young professionals, a man and a woman, standing in line at a supermarket. After a typical long day at the office, they're tired and cranky. They've grown increasingly frustrated as they face obstacles ranging from choosing a brand of bottled water among too many options to discovering most cash registers closed, causing long waiting lines.

While waiting, they suffer the annoying kid in the midst of a tantrum and the old, slow cashier processing customers at a snail's pace. The longer they wait, the more they think about the heavy traffic they will surely have to bear when they finally get to go home. They think about all the day's problems at the office and the new ones they'll face tomorrow. Their stressful situation is one we can easily recognize as way too familiar.

Again, the situation in the video parallels that of doing business abroad. As a number of executives in multinational companies can attest, doing business in emerging markets can be frustrating and annoying. Nothing seems to work the way they expect. The lack of physical and institutional infrastructure makes it difficult to get things done on time and cost effectively; they get frustrated "waiting in line" for things to happen while facing increasing pressure from headquarters to generate fast results.

And that's where the story in the video changes. It shifts the actors' perspective so they see that all these frustrations come from a need to believe that the universe revolves around them. In other words, things happen to us, not around us. Mr. Wallace suggests that we have a choice. Instead of complaining about delays in the supermarket line, we can choose to think about something other than our problems—possibly about the myriad possible scenarios that explain what to this point has frustrated us.

We could easily imagine that perhaps the senior cashier is slow because she works long hours to help her daughter pay for her kids' educations; instead of complaining about the unexpected traffic jam, we could think of the possible car accident ahead of us and the people whose lives may be drastically affected as a result of it.

We could also use that idle time to solve a problem we're dealing with at the office, or plan for the next day to alleviate stress instead of merely anticipating it. By shifting our perspective, we increase our empathy, becoming more familiar with strangers and better capable of managing a situation. At the same time, we increase our productivity and capacity to problem solve.

In business as in life, we desperately need to change the way we think. We need to get away from the "me" syndrome and see the world through the eyes of others. More than ever, we need to be aware of realities other than our own and understand why we are seeing what we are seeing.

Awareness about the people around us makes our life not only easier but more enjoyable. It's what helps us understand and be compassionate toward those strangers who populate our near and far-away world; those who seem annoying, intolerable, and even threatening, mainly because we don't stop for a moment to consider their realities and their lives' challenges.

Modern telecommunications make it almost impossible for us not to be exposed to what's going on in our country and the high number of global events that are affecting our daily life. Families and friends of professionals working in global companies and those dedicated to keeping us safe are directly or indirectly exposed to global events. And because we tend to believe that we are at the center of the universe, we get frustrated when we cannot understand and control how others think and behave.

Our current mindset creates a mental trap that causes us to live with constant anxiety, frustration, and a pessimistic view of the world around us.

When I decided to write this book, I considered several options as a central theme. As an international business executive with over 20 years of business experience spanning six continents, I knew I had a chest full of practical knowledge to draw upon. My business curiosity has exposed me to a rich and diverse set of circumstances, challenging business environments, and even life-threatening situations. But the more I thought about how to help others succeed in today's global market, the more I concluded that without a proper mindset adjustment any other advice is ineffective.

Our current business mindset is dangerously obsolete. Stuck in the 20th century, it prevents us from seeing and interpreting the significant changes that have occurred in the global market over the last two decades. This narrow view is sending too many companies down paths to failure as they attempt to conquer new markets.

Low profitability is showing leaders that change is necessary, but not everyone knows how to change or what kind of change might be effective. Until we adjust our way of thinking, our efforts to succeed will continue to disappoint.

A new mindset, one better attuned to the realities of the present, helps you see the world for what it is and guides you through the process of reconfiguring your role in today's global society and global market. Adjusting your view of the world is essential to managing human relations in business and social life across geographic boundaries.

Seeing the world from a fresh perspective allows you to acquire and interpret different kinds of information, insights, and experiences and helps you build the foundation you need to take effective action based on 21st-century conditions. At work, this new mindset will help you manage the wide range of risks associated with working in a global environment. Master these risks, and you will be a hero in your company and your family.

Borderless Leadership is about a mindset rearrangement. Its recurrent message is about ways to increase awareness of the world around you. It's about making mental adjustments and learning to succeed through collaboration with other people, particularly those who appear to be unfamiliar with and utterly different from your "norm." In the process, this mindset adjustment will help you manage the stress that an overwhelming global economy has brought into your life.

xxii Borderless Leadership

Borderless Leadership shows you how to acquire these skills through a simple five-step process. This process helps you build trust and develop the kind of relationships that allow you to achieve results beyond anyone's expectations.

I have helped my clients succeed over and over again by showing them how to work with and through foreign nationals in urban megacities and in remote, rural areas of the world. I have conducted business in over 30 countries on every continent (except Antarctica, but there is time), and in every case, I've been able to identify and do business with the right partners and associates. Equally important, I've been able to help clients recognize and walk away from business situations that would lead to trouble and failure.

One of the primary barriers to developing trust and rapport with foreign nationals is our lack of familiarity with other cultures and the apprehension and anxiety associated with the unfamiliar. Focused on our way of doing business, like the couple in the supermarket line, we seldom stop to consider that regular citizens anywhere in the world are just as interested in making a decent living and earning enough money to achieve their dreams as we all are.

All of us, regardless of origin, strive to provide food and shelter to those we love, pay for our children's education and health care, and develop our skills and talents for personal enrichment. We all seek out opportunities to be respected and be recognized for our efforts, to feel pride for work well done. The vast majority of people around the world want to live in peace in their communities and countries; they aspire and strive to achieve success so they too can benefit from the positive economic cycles and political stability that we enjoy.

What stands in the way of personal and business success today is an obsolete attitude, which carries over, subconsciously, when you travel abroad. It leads you to push aside unfamiliar societal characteristics and disregard the valuable contributions that foreign nationals can make to help you achieve your goals. Once you update your way of thinking and acquire new skills, no matter where you travel, you will be able to identify the right partners and friends.

Acting on the idea that our group or culture is better or more important than others—an ethnocentric viewpoint—is not intrinsically a bad thing; it helps us maintain our identity and draw on the advantages we may have over other societies. But we need to balance this view with an awareness of realities outside our world so we can incorporate different perspectives, come up with innovative solutions, and continue to grow.

In today's globalized world, a reluctance to listen and
embrace new perspectives keeps us as outsiders looking in,
rather than as effective leaders integrated into the new world.

Going back to the video scenario, imagine that a natural disaster strikes while you're feeling miserable standing in line. Almost instantly, those same strangers would run to help each other and would not hesitate to offer you the helping hand that could save your life. Now, imagine the same thing happening when you are traveling abroad, for business or pleasure.

Strangers you meet around the world, those you find annoying and difficult to tolerate, will also come to your rescue and offer you a helping hand. But for you to benefit from their willingness to help, you have to be receptive. A better appreciation for the realities of others will make you responsive to views other than your own, thus opening the door for making better decisions in your personal and business life.

Borderless Leadership is about achieving success with and through total strangers as you progress from awareness to understanding and from understanding to acquiring, internalizing, and applying new knowledge so you bring your approach to life up to date. Only then can you transform obstacles into unsuspected opportunities that will have a positive impact on your personal and business success.

There are more than seven billion people around the world with the potential for making your life easier, happier, and more successful. I invite you to embark on the discovery of an enlightened way to deal with today's complex but highly promising global market.

About This Book

Borderless Leadership addresses the need to develop a new personal and business mindset as a practice and a discipline. Our current state of mind and skills were acquired and developed over the last 20–40 years according to the rules and practices of a world that no longer exists.

This means that our traditional view of the world and the way we gather and interpret information is obsolete and out of alignment with current events. This misalignment is behind the significant anxiety and concerns we have about how globalization is impacting our personal safety, job security, and financial success. It's also the reason behind the disappointing results that corporations continue to show while operating in emerging markets.

Mindset adjustment is a strategic skill that can be acquired, practiced, and mastered by anyone at the individual and corporate level.

This book describes the five-step methodology that I have developed and implemented over years of working side by side with some brilliant leaders in Fortune 500 companies and their counterparts around the world. I have strategized, and more importantly, led the execution of strategies in the field while being exposed to and learning from a diversity of unexpected situations and challenges.

In my management consulting practice, I have advised corporate executives one on one, through management retreats, workshops, lecturing, and public speaking, and had the privilege of helping a good number of smart individuals with international responsibilities find solutions to business roadblocks while balancing the demands of work and family.

There are many "how to" books that focus on the tactical aspects of doing business abroad, just as there are many travel guides that help you choose the best places to visit in any country. This book is neither.

Borderless Leadership takes a fresh, novel, vitally different look at the way we see the world and aims to provide a tool that will allow you to identify and surround yourself with trustworthy people, no matter where you are on the planet.

Borderless Leadership is not an academic textbook. Instead, it's a practical guide that focuses on how to replicate throughout the world the normal day-to-day relations that you develop with co-workers and friends, which ultimately lead to your financial independence and a rewarding personal life.

Using real-life examples, this book illustrates how you can build trust and rapport with strangers across borders and establish the kind of relationships that help your business grow and make your life easier.

This guide is timely because the leadership role the West played so clearly and unquestionably in the 20th century is now challenged by emerging economies. Facing aging consumers at home, the Western world depends on fast-growing younger populations living in developing and emerging markets. This has significantly leveled the field, as more and more countries demand to be recognized as equal partners with the industrialized West.

Because personal relationships are at the heart of emerging market societies, the ability to build trust across cultures is a new business imperative. This guide analyzes the deficiencies of current tactics and proposes innovative solutions to help people develop global interpersonal skills. Until the human factor is properly incorporated into corporate strategies, companies will continue to bleed financially while foreign competitors become stronger and stronger.

Studies consistently show that partnerships among foreign nationals fail to generate expected results, at significant personal and corporate cost. The number one cause behind this failure is lack of trust among people at all levels within organizations. This book explores the disparity that exists between the ways we conduct business and how other cultures conduct business. It discusses, for example, how the Western preference for contract-driven business stands out against the relationship-driven approach used by citizens of emerging economies.

Borderless Leadership's premise is that if we cannot control the events or circumstances that surround us, then we can and must learn how to control our reactions to the new environment. Corporations desperately need to hire individuals who understand the world and feel comfortable traveling anywhere and interacting with diverse groups of people on the ground.

On the personal side, this book will help relocated families live an anxiety-free or at least an anxiety-controlled life as they learn to understand and manage their reaction to some of the momentous changes taking place throughout the world.

Whether you're a professional with international responsibilities or an individual with no international interest, chances are that in your lifetime you will be—directly or indirectly—affected by global affairs. Although you cannot control the future, you can take control of your reaction to the environment by fine-tuning your ability to anticipate, prepare for, and manage your reaction to global events.

Understanding and perceiving the interests and needs of those around you is the key to your personal and business success. If it seems an impossible task today, it is because you are still looking at the world in the old-fashioned way, with tools developed in and for the 20th century reality.

Companies are desperately looking for global experts and new millennium executives—who nobody is training. Because the need for global expertise is real and urgent, professionals today cannot and should not wait for educational institutions and corporations to catch up with the new realities. Success today requires pragmatism and bold actions.

The book is divided into five parts: Awareness, Understanding, Knowledge, Internalization, and Practice. Each part represents a basic ingredient in the process of updating our way of thinking, acquiring new skills, and learning how to apply new business and personal smarts.

- **Part I—Awareness** discusses how the far-reaching transformation of the global market in the last two decades has negatively affected traditional business. Through real-life examples, it illustrates the many challenges and lost profitability that Western companies have faced when entering emerging markets and outlines why we need to search for and adopt a better way to do business abroad.

  On a personal level, Awareness also addresses the phenomenon of today's information saturation, which clutters the mind and creates the kind of anxiety that leads to poor decisions or decision paralysis.

  Real-life examples describe striking changes rarely discussed in the news but that have a profound impact on our social life and business environment. Indisputably, personal and business success in a global economy requires that we rethink the way we see, collect, and analyze information about foreign citizens and foreign markets.

- **Part II—Understanding** describes how the world changed right in front of our eyes. To gain understanding of the world transformation, we take a look at the new demographics and migration patterns that helped shift the center of gravity and the balance of power from West to East and from North to South.

  Models for global interaction so successfully developed and implemented in the 20th century came crumbling down in the 21st. The entire world is in flux, making the definition of new models more difficult than anticipated by mega-corporations and governments alike.

  Trust across borders continues to be a significant barrier to world stability and progress, and studies consistently show that global partnerships continue to fail to achieve the desired level of success.

- **Part III—Knowledge** advances a radically new approach to seeing the world that empowers you with an updated set of decision-making skills. It's designed to accelerate the acquisition of relevant information about today's world in a practical and simplified manner.

  Because individuals, alone or in teams, are necessarily involved in all decisions from the boardroom to the consumer level, Knowledge deals specifically with the ubiquitous human factor that permeates all aspects of business and personal life.

  Decisions are intimately linked to personal knowledge, past experiences, and perceptions formed from a very early age, but these views are skewed toward the realities of the past.

  The new millennium has brought so many changes at so many levels that we need to retrain ourselves on how we gather new knowledge and interpret information. Doing business abroad requires that we—selectively—transform total strangers whom we meet in different countries into friends, acquaintances, and business partners.

  Awareness, understanding, and the acquisition of fresh knowledge about people's behavior around the world leads to better decisions, a more fulfilling personal life, and a more successful business career with financial success.

- **Part IV—Internalization** exemplifies how corporations and their employees can effectively apply their updated view of the world to achieve success and increase profitability when operating in the global market.

  Internalization highlights one of the most important applications of the updated mindset proposed in this book: The acquired ability to expect the unexpected and plan ahead of time for avoidable roadblocks that, if ignored, will wreak havoc in strategy and execution.

  This section describes classical business mistakes and proposes ten new tenets for business prosperity that I have developed and used to help companies gain business perspective, sharpen their survival skills, and prevent costly mistakes. It illustrates how smart executives use new ideas and tools to increase awareness and understanding and clear their minds to do more with less.

At the individual level, Part IV provides practical advice to help you build your own toolbox of international tricks and to be aware of what companies look for in future employees.

- **Lastly, Part V—Practice** describes a wide range of real-life situations that you may face while visiting or working in foreign countries. The stories are real and selected from personal experience. Unless otherwise indicated, names have been changed to protect individuals' identities. Each story is followed by a set of tips and questions designed to help you understand and put into practice the material shared throughout the book.

Why This Book?

The information shared throughout the book has been gathered while interacting with a wide range of people: From heads of state to ministers, senators, and diplomats; from board members to executives, professionals, administrative personnel, technicians, and field operators; from philanthropists and business entrepreneurs to social activists; from peers, families, and friends scattered around the world to all those anonymous individuals who have just been around in those places visited.

To write about trust building among the people of the world requires years of experience, observation, and practice. My familiarity with today's global market comes from more than 20 years of traveling and doing business abroad.

I grew up in the multicultural environment provided by pioneer families who included relatives from Western and Eastern Europe, Asia, and Latin America. Since childhood, I have been attracted to understanding people from different cultures, and as I grew up, it was natural for me to engage in international business, building relationships and developing alliances with diverse groups of people.

My passion for understanding the world and cracking the code of global business success has been the main driver behind my own professional career. When visiting other countries, I have sought to immerse myself in their cultures, seeing these places through the eyes of its local people and understanding their culture's impact on business.

I have systematically developed and fine-tuned my ability to read between the proverbial lines and interpret the subtleties of verbal communications and body language. I've consistently sought to learn and understand how people in each place think, behave, and operate. A long time ago, these observations led me to conclude that, while America is truly unique, the countries in the rest of the world are remarkably similar to each other.

Over the years I have worked with CEOs and top executives in multinational corporations in a wide range of industries and engaged in real-time negotiations with foreign officials in public and private institutions.

As a sounding board and hands-on adviser to CEOs and executive teams, I help manage strategy and operations risk in emerging markets, guiding the development of realistic strategies and proper execution of business plans that take into account the way people make decisions.

I work with individuals throughout the corporate hierarchies in Fortune 500 companies on how to conduct business in foreign countries, identify and connect with trustworthy and capable local people, build circles of positive influence, improve organizational performance in multiple countries, and deal with local leaders.

Last but not least, I help them act with confidence when confronted with unexpected environments and situations.

Familiarity with peoples of the world has helped me take precautions to avoid walking into dangerous situations, and when confronted with threats, to take the right path of action. The methodology described in this book has proved essential when living through several unusual situations including:

- Surviving a military coup d'état that overthrew a government.
- Evacuating a country following credible threats of Americans being kidnapped.
- Doing business in the middle of a guerrilla path in rural areas of a developing country.
- Receiving personal threats from strong local competitors in a tightly held industry.
- Being surrounded by people rocking my car in rural areas of an emerging country.

It's time for you to get started with the beta-testing of "You 2.0." After reading this book, you will be able to start practicing new techniques and be increasingly at ease in your interactions with the rest of the world, personally and professionally.

You will feel comfortable dealing with people of all backgrounds in society, business, and government and will turn traveling and working in other countries into the extraordinary and rewarding experience that it should be.

Are you ready?

— Zlática I. Kraljevic, PhD
Washington DC, 2014

Acknowledgments

There is no doubt that writing a book takes dedication and persistence, but it can also be an enjoyable and rewarding experience. What made this book enjoyable to me were the memories that writing it brought back, from my early childhood to the present. At all times, I have been surrounded by extraordinary people within my immediate and extended family and in my business and travels. They have all contributed to teaching me about the world and its people. Without each one of them, this book would not exist. While it's impossible to mention them all, I shall mention a few.

I want to thank clients and colleagues who in so many ways contributed to my professional growth over the years: Manuel T, Sue P, Juan M, David L, Rob W, Marti S, Alan V, Frank S, Lane S, Issa A, Scott B, and David H.

My thanks also to those who dedicated time to reading the manuscript and advising me on how to improve it. Special thanks to Lynda McDaniel and Virginia McCullough of The Book Catalysts for their constant encouragement and primary editing, and to Werner Hahn for finding the time to comment on the book from beginning to end. I know how difficult it was to find those extra hours after long days at work.

Finally my thanks to my exceptional family, who taught me about the good things in life. From my husband I learned kindness and generosity; from my son, courage and logic. From my father, persistence; from my mother, compassion. From teachers, endurance; from friends, companionship. From colleagues, competitiveness; from clients, camaraderie. From the very rich, vision; from the very poor, joy in the simplicity of life.

About the Author

Dr. Zlática Kraljevic is widely recognized as a leading expert in emerging markets as well as a successful business strategist, tactician, educator, and public speaker. Specializing in risk management related to global operations and strategic expansion, she has worked for over 25 years with senior leaders in Fortune 500 companies and high-ranking officials in foreign governments and academia while covering over 30 countries across six continents.

As an international executive, public speaker, writer, and associate professor, Zlática has inspired thousands of individuals around the world. She has the distinction of being the first female dean at a private university in Saudi Arabia, and the first woman to earn a doctorate degree in chemical engineering from the University of Arizona. She is a fellow at the George Mason University School of Law.

An active member of the international community, Zlática received the "2006 World Oil Best Outreach Program Award" for co-creating a volunteer organization of 27 energy companies, professional associations, and educators bringing energy education to K-12 students in the Greater Houston area. She serves on several boards of directors of nonprofit organizations, including the Library of Congress Asian Division Friends Society. She is a founding member of the Financial Risk Institute and a past director of the Global Energy Management Institute.

For more information about Zlática Kraljevic, visit her websites at www. andersfrontiergroup.com and www.zkraljevic.com.

Write to Zlática at zkraljevic@gmail.com.

PART I
AWARENESS

Awareness: The Ability to Notice Things[*]

---

[*] Merriam-Webster Dictionary

Chapter One

Lost but Not Alone

*Success does not consist in never making mistakes but in
never making the same mistake a second time.*

— George Bernard Shaw[*]

*Imagine one day you wake up and discover that you are not in your own home.
You're in another, utterly unfamiliar place. You get up, go outside, and start wandering around, trying to understand your situation. You recognize you're in a city,
seemingly normal like any other one, until you realize that all signs are in a foreign
language, in which symbols have replaced the common alphabet. People have hard
facial features, seldom smiling; they dress differently, some in costumes you have
never seen before.*

*You hear them talking amongst themselves, but they speak in tongues you don't
understand. You try to ask questions and they ignore you, or worse, look at you with
suspicion. Some make demands that you cannot begin to interpret. They act according to no pattern you can identify, and there are so many of them—millions and
millions of them—each different from the other. You are paralyzed with fear.*

Is this a scene in a horror or a sci-fi movie? It's actually a description of how
many executives were feeling during the first decade of the 21st century. And it
only got worse . . .

---

[*] George Bernard Shaw Quotes. BrainyQuote.com, Xplore Inc, 2018. https://www.
brainyquote.com/quotes/george_bernard_shaw_121841, accessed February 10, 2018.

In your dream, occasionally you encounter a few others who look familiar, and you feel overjoyed with hope. But it is a fleeting moment that evaporates as soon as you grasp that they are as confused and helpless as you are. You feel crowded, claustrophobic; alone in a sea of people. There is nowhere to turn and nobody to help. No way to go back to normal life as you knew it. Exhausted, you hope you are in a bad dream and yearn to wake up.

The sudden arrival of new and surprisingly business-savvy emerging marketers has caused the rules of the international game to change overnight. The world as we knew it has ceased to exist. *Wham!*

Of course, the above dramatization is exaggerated, but it serves to illustrate how much the world changed with the turn of the century. Until the 1990s, we thought we knew the world we lived in. We knew how to do business abroad and felt reasonably good about traveling to other countries for business or pleasure. In other words, we were comfortable and at the top of our personal and professional game.

That sentiment is now seemingly lost forever. Safety has become a big concern for those accepting relocation to foreign countries or those planning a simple vacation abroad. Widespread sociopolitical unrest has forced us to re-evaluate our views of the world, and social networks have transformed the way we interact with family, friends, co-workers, and strangers. As in the example above, we are exhausted, hoping we are in a bad dream and yearning to wake up.

Corporations are also struggling to understand the new kinds of needs and demands of their local customers. They face an urgent need to go through a drastic change in their corporate and leadership culture. To stay competitive, they need to become more agile and innovative and develop new business strategies.

As is often the case, the world's transformation seems so sudden—but indicators of what was to come were manifesting in the late 1990s and multiplied rapidly in the early 2000s.

The next section illustrates some of the disastrous experiences that multinational corporations went through for more than a decade, because these signs from emerging markets fell on deaf ears.

Sophia Loren and the Company That Missed the Point

In October 1993, Sophia Loren helped promote the opening of a mega project in Chile called the Alto Las Condes Mall, Santiago's most luxurious and exclusive mall at that time. It was history in the making, not only because glamorous Loren was present but because Chile was the "in" place to be.

Latin America was going through a phenomenal transformation, from a region mostly known for its political and economic upheavals to one of booming economies.

A majority of democratically elected governments were enthusiastically embracing open-market strategies. It seemed that Latin America was getting on board with progressive and more transparent economic policies that were attracting significant foreign direct investment.

Old and dilapidated government-controlled industries were being sold to the private sector; fresh capital and modern know-how helped renovate them and make them more efficient. Western companies actively engaged in being part of the new Latin economy were attracting young Chilean professionals exhilarated by the prospect of new jobs and entrepreneurship opportunities. It was indeed a riveting, captivating, and magic moment. And Sophia Loren made it glamorous.

At the time, I was a trusted business adviser to American CEOs in Fortune 500 companies and often traveled throughout the region for business. Regardless of how well I may know a country, I always set time aside to mingle with the local population. My secret to effective business closing is a simple golden rule that I follow time after time, regardless of how full my business schedule may be.

Always make time to walk the streets to
keep a finger on the local pulse.

Keeping a finger on the pulse of the local environment is crucial to succeeding in business. There is no real science behind this golden rule. All you do is invest a few hours on every trip in following the local crowd to popular places, observing individual behavior, and looking for clues about people's mood, their views on the economy, the political environment, and consumer confidence and preferences.

That's why on a sunny day I found myself visiting the Alto Las Condes Mall. Sophia was no longer there, but she still managed to display her megawatt smile at me from the nostalgia-evoking banners hanging outside the mall entrance.

On the day of my visit, the mall was packed and the atmosphere festive as entire families came out to explore. The local department store that sponsored Loren was buzzing with business. Not far from there, however, another store told a different story: The buzz seemed to slow down, the air grew colder, the crowd thinner, and the lights dimmer, making this store look oddly out of place.

I was instantly curious, mainly because I recognized it as a well-known American chain department store. It didn't make sense to me that it was clearly being bypassed by mall enthusiasts who usually welcome foreign goods. Going inside, I understood why. I was dismayed by a display of men's clothes consisting of solid and plaid green and dark red jackets and pants.

These were the colors and patterns reminiscent of happy and fun summers and major golf tournaments in the United States. And they were good quality clothes. There was nothing intrinsically wrong with them except that they were far from the mute and somber colors that Chileans tend to prefer.

Anyone visiting Chile for the first time will be quick to observe that Chileans dress extremely conservatively. This was particularly true before the social media revolution. They generally favor gray suits, white shirts, and dark ties—a uniform for everyone from bank tellers to top executives. Most Chileans are of European descent (due to a huge migration wave in the early 1900s), and the European influence is noticeable in Chile's social customs and protocol, architecture, education system, and military training.

Chileans are sharp and direct, and in the privacy of their homes they tend to be very witty. But in public and in business, they are rather phlegmatic and no-nonsense to a fault. Not surprisingly, Chileans have been called the "Englishmen" of Latin America. They even observe high tea at four o'clock every afternoon. No joke.

On closer inspection, I realized that color choices were not the only error the store had made. Sizes were typical U.S. sizes, made for the average American, who is easily six inches taller than the average Chilean. How could this company have missed its target audience so blatantly?

Clearly, whoever picked the clothing for this U.S. store in Chile was either blind or had never been to the country before. Bemused and bewildered, I left the store, visualizing the financial loss and predictable final demise of a foreign operation that had so grossly failed to understand its target customers.

The lesson they will soon be learning at a high cost to their stockholders reads like this:

Success in a highly competitive local market is not about the company: It's all about the local consumer.

The company was J.C. Penney, which at the time was the largest department store in the United States. J.C. Penney operated in Chile from 1995 to 1999 and was in the red every year. It finally sold its operations to a local group, predictably at a loss, its exit from what was then the newest and most prestigious mall in Santiago never to be forgotten.

During its brief and costly incursion in Chile, J.C. Penney maintained a 100-percent American management team that was clearly unfamiliar with the needs and inclinations of local consumers and therefore unable to secure a local partner or establish good relationships with local providers.[1]

The High Cost of Naïveté

For most of the 2000s, the American retail industry was plagued with failure. Stories of closed operations abroad made the news almost daily. The following is a recap:

Walmart®

Walmart opened in Germany in 1998, only to close at a loss in 2006. The problem was a familiar one: misunderstanding and thus failing to address the needs and preferences of local consumers. Walmart also failed in Mexico (1991), Brazil (1995), South Korea (1998), and Japan (2002) for basically the same reasons: trying to sell their American business model to other cultures without bothering to adjust to local customs, desires, and requirements.

Among other oversights, Walmart insisted on locating its stores on the outskirts of a city without taking into account that in countries outside of the U.S., access to private transportation is limited. Without personal transport, their stores were hard to reach.

Walmart also promoted an "all-in-one, stockpile" concept that required ample home storage space generally unavailable in other countries—particularly in Europe and Asia, where real estate is expensive. It also promoted packaged food without realizing that local customers preferred to buy fresh food as needed, on a daily basis.

Walmart also kept traditions that are better understood in the U.S. but seem out of place in other cultures. Germans, for example, felt uncomfortable with Walmart's tradition of smiling employees (interpreting it as flirting) and never understood why the staff would sing every morning.

One Walmart executive said it all[2].

> "Germany was a good example of (our) naïveté.
> We literally bought two chains and said,
> 'Hey, we're in Germany, isn't this great?'"

The Home Depot®

The case of Home Depot in China was slightly different but had similar results. Home Depot started developing operations in Beijing in 2004 and finally opened officially in 2006.

They believed they had taken the time to read the market, focusing on the new wave of middle-class Chinese who were increasingly buying new homes or homes in need of remodeling. According to the numbers, it was conceivable that Home Depot's do-it-yourself approach would be well received.

But Home Depot fell short of understanding the Chinese culture on a deeper level. While Chinese couples are more affluent today than in the past, they are not used to grabbing a hammer and start fixing things, nor are they inclined to. They haven't grown up with modern tools around the house, and they would rather hire low-skilled help or small local construction shops to do the job.

Such small local construction and repair shops either don't have the means or are unwilling to acquire expensive and sophisticated tools as are their counterparts in the U.S.; they continued to do business as usual. The company closed its Beijing stores in 2012.

A statement by Frank Blake, Home Depot's CEO, said: "We've learned a great deal over the past six years in China."[3]

What they had learned was that the Chinese have a "do-it-for-me" rather than a "do-it-yourself" culture. One must wonder if the expense of "going to school" in China to make this discovery can be justified, considering the loss of millions of dollars and stockholder value over six years.

Best Buy

Best Buy endured another financial fiasco. Just one month after Home Depot announced its departure from China, Best Buy was announcing its own demise.[4] It closed five of its nine stores in China after five years of failing to attract sufficient Chinese buyers to justify the initiative.

Whereas Walmart's failure in Germany was in part the result of limited access to private transportation, Best Buy suffered from traffic congestion caused by too many private cars on the streets of Beijing. Traffic patterns are not that hard to observe and assess even standing on a busy street corner!

Couldn't this problem have been anticipated at a much lower cost than by deploying a full multi-store operation in a foreign country?

Best Buy was also criticized for being too expensive and selling undifferentiated products that could be more conveniently bought elsewhere. By contrast, local competitors understand traffic jams and prefer to operate in small neighborhood stores that are easily accessible to their customers.

According to the World Bank, China received 20 percent of all foreign direct investment to developing countries in the last ten years—and over $100 billion in 2008 alone.[5] Even as the political friction between the Chinese and U.S.

governments is likely to rise, U.S. companies continue to increase their investment in China, reaching $49 billion in 2009 (an increase of 66% from the previous year) in the middle of the global financial crisis.[6]

This does not mean they are comfortable doing business in China, only that they are not giving up on a potentially huge market.

Like Ships that Pass in the Night

In the 1980s and 1990s, while multinationals were busy growing their businesses in the West and exporting their business models elsewhere, less industrialized countries as different as China, Chile, and Brazil were making significant strides toward becoming progressive emerging economies and attractive points of destination for future business growth.

Like ships that pass in the night, their transformation remained largely unnoticed by Western companies and governments until the late 1990s and early 2000s.

Back in the 20th century, non-industrialized countries had been plagued with poverty, corruption, political suppression, or unrest. International companies had thus focused primarily on expanding business within wealthy and stable Western markets.

While it's true that multinationals had been exporting to developing countries for decades, overseas expansion was generally considered an alternative—a cushion to help offset normal economic and business cycles. The expectation was that if revenues in the West hit a low economic cycle, then a diversified portfolio of operations in developing countries could generate enough revenue to offset low cycles at home.

By the turn of the century, however, Western markets were getting older and smaller, while countries around the world gained larger and younger populations with increasingly higher purchasing power.

Western companies had no option but to steer their strategies toward emerging economies and the frontier economies coming right behind, making them their primary focus of expansion and growth.

This was a daunting proposition. It required finding among "the rest of the world" a large consumer base that was also affluent enough to consume at Western-style levels. Brazil, Russia, India, and China (the BRIC countries) were first identified as fitting this profile, and Western multinationals were anxious to plant their flag on these new territories. They rushed to capture and consolidate large shares of these new markets ahead of other multinationals that had been their traditional competitors.

As it happened, emerging markets were both a blessing and a curse for Western economies. They were a blessing because they represented fresh and large consumer bases at a time when corporations in industrialized countries needed them most. They were a curse because these new markets were keenly aware of and ready to leverage the advantages they had over the West: a larger and younger consumer base with Western-style tastes and money to spend.

The West, still entrenched in the 20th century business mindset, was intent on exporting what they had rather than what these countries needed, and that was exactly where the surprises began. Basically, the level of sophistication and business shrewdness exhibited by emerging economies was incongruent with the West's past business experiences.

Emerging economies went from being passive recipients of financial assistance and know-how to taking leadership roles and demanding that Western powerhouses meet them at least halfway at the negotiation table.

A savvy middle class could make informed decisions about their preferences, instead of just accepting anything from the West as categorically better than what they could find at home. They became just as fickle as consumers in domestic markets.

Not surprisingly, local businesses were unwilling to accept Western practices as the norm and were intent on establishing their own, and local consumers showed a preference for local products over Western products. Thus Western companies found themselves utterly unprepared to succeed in emerging markets bearing no resemblance to those that existed in the past.

This lack of preparation, combined with the pressure to rush into markets and secure market share, virtually guaranteed the kind of costly failures endured by Walmart, Best Buy, Home Depot, and J.C. Penney.

To some extent this lack of preparation on the part of Western companies was understandable. Since before the 1980s, developing countries had been willingly following the lead of mature Western businesses, and the U.S. financial boom of the 1980s and 1990s created the illusion that this interdependence would survive the passage of time.

But again, like ships passing in the night, developing countries had not been idle while receiving foreign assistance, but were instead avid and quick learners of the way that the West conducted business. Foreign nationals acquired new skills and self-confidence through the Western-style work experience gained during the wave of East-bound outsourcing that manufacturing and services industries initiated in the 1980s.

The behavior of countries reflects the behavior of its citizens, and we know that individuals develop in stages. Young children follow their parents' advice during the first years of life, until they reach young adulthood. As teenagers, they feel empowered to think and act independently. Rebelling from their parents' tutelage, they're eager to take risks and willing to learn from mistakes before reaching maturity.

Societies and countries, being a conglomerate of individuals, behave similarly. After following the lead of mature Western markets, emerging markets are now experimenting, putting in practice their newfound capabilities, knowledge, and skills as they search for the role they want to play in the world.

Growing Pains

Life cycles for individuals as well as corporations go like this:

- Birth / startup
- Adolescence / accelerated growth
- Maturity / stable growth
- Decline / stagnation
- Death / closing

As members of a new generation, emerging countries are and will continue to exhibit similar patterns. Every day it seems that new, promising economies are born, while others at the adolescent stage become aware of their potential and struggle to define their identity. They scramble and experiment with new rules of the game, still unsure of their role in the new world.

But they know one thing: They no longer favor the traditional rules of the last century, largely set in place by well-established Western multinationals. They fear that these corporate giants might invade their space and quickly impose their way of doing business, quashing new ideas and smashing dreams before this younger generation of companies in new markets has a chance to succeed.

The emergence as a new economic power brings lots of responsibilities to a country. Its young, growing middle class aspires to have access to gourmet food, higher education, well-paid jobs, and financial success. Local governments must address these needs to maintain a stable sociopolitical environment.

China is a well-known example. It has added barriers to Western expansion within its borders, changed the rules of engagement at whim to give local competitors a chance to grow and strengthen, and helped create a new middle class with increasing discretionary income.

Not surprisingly, a number of other new economies have also reacted with protectionism—not unlike the attitude teenagers have when posting a huge sign on their bedroom door that reads "Keep Out!" The Chinese, for example, have used the term "step-motherly" in referring to the perceived U.S. attitude to hinder their progress.

Protectionism is cause for concern among investors. Reporting on global greenfield investment trends, the *Financial Times* assessed a more than 16 percent decrease in foreign direct investment projects in 2012: "All global regions experienced a decline in FDI. The main exceptions were: Chile, Spain, Indonesia, Poland and Oman, all of which experienced strong growth in inward FDI."[7]

Several factors affect these results, including economic downturns, unfavorable exchange rates of a country's currency, excessive debt, political instabilities, corporate taxes, labor constraints, and unclear or ineffective policies to deal with these challenges.

Strong new economies such as China, Russia, and India also seek to expand their influence in new territories in the U.S., Africa, the Middle East, and Latin America. China's investment in U.S. assets, for example, could reach $100 to $400 billion by 2020. Russia's foreign direct investment (particularly in oil, gas, and metals) has expanded rapidly since the turn of the century, starting with neighboring countries and more recently expanding into Africa. Indian companies also seek to invest abroad as they grow faster than the internal market.[8]

China continues to promote the global adoption of its currency, the renminbi or RMB (better known as "yuan"), as the preferred global trade currency in their bid to replace the current system based on the U.S. dollar, the euro, and the Japanese yen.[9]

All these reactions have given Western companies pause. The developing countries of the last century have now grown up, demanding to be recognized for the added value they bring to the new global economy. There is now a generational gap between the mature economies of the West and the younger economies popping up around the world. The former don't understand the latter, and the latter don't seem to care.

It gets worse when some younger economies seem to be more technologically driven than their elders. Such is the case with countries that exhibit well-honed entrepreneurial skills and ingenuity, such as India and China.

Ingenuity is born out of limited resources, when people are forced to make do with what they have at hand. It gives local companies an edge when coming up with good products at lower manufacturing costs. Ingenuity allows them to compete head to head with more complex and less agile multinational companies that are accustomed to manufacturing sophisticated products for consumers with high standards of living. With lower costs and affordable consumer prices, local competitors have quickly gained market share, sending Western companies scrambling to find ways of reinventing themselves.

Amid this dysfunctional family of old and new economies, there is a glimmer of hope as the smartest and more flexible Western companies have taken the wiser "if you can't beat them, join them" approach. They are adapting to the new reality both by taking immediate steps to learn from their local strategic partners and by paying more attention to the value that these local partners bring to the table because they better understand the mentality and preferences of local consumers.

For an older generation to willingly learn from the younger is a remarkable and rare attitude, particularly because it involves learning from those who, until now, were perceived as less sophisticated partners. The majority of Western companies and their employees find this difficult to accept. They are naturally proud of their sophisticated know-how and past successes and resist admitting that there may be more effective ways to do business.

Many Western companies, particularly those with aggressive corporate cultures, are still stubbornly trying to win the old-fashioned way, rushing to plant the flag where opportunities emerge without considering the cost and consequences of stepping on the hidden landmines they are bound to encounter along the way.

We have discussed some notorious examples of the difficulties companies face when they are ill-prepared to anticipate and adapt to new market conditions as well as a new and demanding set of customers. The next chapter describes the significant changes taking place around the world that surprised and changed the name of the game in the international field.

Chapter Two

The West Is
Hyperventilating—
Bring Out the Brown Bag!

---

*The more the centre of economic gravity shifts towards emerging markets,
the more businesspeople need to recognize that the emerging world
is a horribly complicated place.*

—*The Economist**

A World of Trouble

On January 12th, 2013, an article in the business section of *The Economist* dubbed today's emerging markets a "World of Trouble."[1]

These are eye-catching words that accurately reflect the sentiment of a good number of Western citizens, as well as business professionals and corporate executives working on projects with international reach. However, I rather disagree with *The Economist's* view.

The world has never been and will never be perfect or even peaceful, but to dub it a horribly complicated place doesn't help us understand it. On the contrary, it clutters the mind with thoughts of global havoc that provoke a surge

---

* *The Economist.* https://www.economist.com/news/business/21569361-which-risks-loom-largest-businesses-2013-world-trouble

of anxiety and negative energy at a time when what most people need is clarity and perspective. It's never emphasized, for example, that the views expressed in *The Economist* represent a primarily Western perspective of the world, which is to say they echo the opinion of roughly one billion people. This is a big number by itself but a very small number when compared to a total world population of over seven billion who live in non-Western and non-industrialized countries.

For six out of seven people on the planet, the world is either just as bad as it has always been, or in many respects, getting substantially better.

Non-industrialized countries have been making more positive advances in the last couple of decades than have ever been seen before: better education, better health care, better sanitary conditions, more gender equality, more job opportunities, more focused social entrepreneurship, and easier access to financial assistance for small business owners.

All of these changes are helping to fight poverty and resulting in higher standards of living. Although accurate data is still difficult to come by, according to the World Bank, poverty around the world has already decreased by roughly 50 percent in the last two decades, surpassing the expectations set for 2015 by the United Nations Millennium Development Goals.[2]

Education is a significant contributor to improved health, higher wages, and increased political stability. Uganda, for example, has added more transparency to its education reform, increasing girls' enrollment in schools from 30 to 50 percent.

More notably, according to the Center for Global Development, "several very poor countries—such as Burkina Faso, Madagascar, and Nicaragua as well as Mali, Guinea, and Mauritania—are increasing their primary school enrollment rates faster than today's rich countries did during their 19th century development."[3]

A new global middle class, defined as those with low probability of falling into poverty, is emerging rapidly in developing and emerging countries and will continue to strengthen. The World Bank estimates that the middle class in low- and middle-income countries (e.g., in Africa and Asia) will rise from 5 percent in 2005 to 25 percent in 2030.[4]

Among other advantages, this means that foreign students attending Western universities now have the opportunity to return to their home countries and find employment commensurate with their education and skills while enjoying the added benefit of rejoining family and friends. As education reforms fall into place, emerging countries will be able to provide quality education and retain the best students at home, thus continuing to strengthen local economies and contributing to the global economy and a more stable political landscape.

This is not to say that the world is perfect, but for the majority of the world's people, it's becoming a better place. So why are we Westerners so pessimistic about our future?

The Need for a New Market

The reason the world appears to be a horribly complicated place to us is that we are not prepared to understand the changes that globalization has brought. Our understanding is hampered by overreliance on our West-centered, ethnocentric attitude, which served us well and provided good results in the 20th century but is now out of date.

Back then, we were the unquestionable leaders of the business world, helping less industrialized societies advance innovation and develop best business practices. For half of the past century, we played an important role in leading the world forward. In the process, we created younger generations at home that, influenced by their environment, had a strong West-centered attitude of superiority.

In retrospect, the 20th century offered us the advantage of dealing with a two-dimensional world simplistically divided into two opposites: West and East, industrialized and developing countries, rich and poor societies, and so on.

> The 2D view of the world is no longer valid.
> We now need multi-dimensional glasses to
> see the world as it really is.

Today, however, globalization has decentralized the sociopolitical and economic environment. The world is multi-dimensional, with centers of power being disputed and redefined. The problem we face today is that nothing in our education has prepared us to deal with this new reality.

Our upbringing and obsolete education system have not helped us develop the skills necessary to understand and manage a new world that is changing right before our eyes in giant leaps and bounds.

It's not that the world is more complicated today than it was yesterday: It's just that we can no longer rely on a false dichotomy of East versus West to explain people's actions and predict behavior.

The perceived notion of world complexity is based on the fact that, as countries become more industrialized, individuals in those countries have more resources and opportunities; they are learning to depend more on their own talents and skills than on the support of the collective group. As societies become more individualistic, personal behavior and preferences matter more than country of origin.

> We want to lead people who are already ahead of us.

The solution to this conundrum is to update the way we acquire knowledge and how we interpret and act on new information. Today's success demands that we increase our exposure to the world and build familiarity with the multi-cultural nature of the modern global market.

Making Sense of the New World

This is not a difficult task. It can be accomplished with curiosity, persistence, determination, and, most of all, a fresh mindset. Much like socializing when you were young taught you to interact with different personalities, socializing with people in other countries will help you better understand the different business cultures around the world. Take every opportunity to do so, and try to learn from the experience instead of assuming it's too difficult or creating an isolationist barrier to the outside.

Familiarity with today's global market requires that we get rid of preconceived notions and seek the best way to connect and become more integrated with multiple cultures. It requires a mindset that is open to embracing new experiences and points of view in a wide range of environments and circumstances. It requires that we actively seek interaction with diverse groups of people around the world so we can learn about the ways they relate to each other and how they conduct business, make decisions, and come up with their own successful business practices.

Practicing awareness allows you to collect and build the practical kind of knowledge that acts as an antidote to the high level of anxiety that may have a paralyzing effect on your decision-making capacity.

The right mindset and the willingness to gain exposure to other cultures provide opportunities to meet extraordinary people who may have a positive impact on your life.

We grow up conditioned to focus on personal
differences rather than similarities.

By focusing on similarities among people of all backgrounds, we can establish meaningful personal and business relationships and create the basis for collaboration.

Telling the Good from the Bad

Collaboration with others and working through others allows us to achieve our goals faster and generate results that would otherwise be difficult or impossible to achieve on our own. Look back at your life and career success and you are likely to conclude that:

The right people help you succeed.
The wrong people let you fail.

Right people are those individuals who feel good to be around because they care for your wellbeing. They want you to succeed and are willing to collaborate with you to help you reach your goals.

Good people are individuals with whom you feel comfortable communicating and exchanging ideas; you come out of conversations enriched with new perspectives and knowledge. They're the kind of people with whom you want to be connected and engage in business with.

These are people whom you are aware of, understand, and respect. In turn, these people are aware of you, understand you, and respect you back. These individuals bring out the best in you every time you meet them. If a disagreement or misunderstanding arises, they are willing to open a dialogue to discuss different points of view with an open mind.

Our family and close friends usually fall into the category of good people. They are our support system; we know we can count on them, and they can count on us. In the office environment, it's harder to achieve this kind of trust. That's not because people are not good, but because the work environment is competitive, and oftentimes people choose to set aside their goodness to achieve the next promotion and reach the top echelons in their companies.

Another level of difficulty is added when we deal with people outside of our society. This might include nationalized foreign citizens living in our neighborhood or working in our office and foreign citizens we meet while traveling abroad.

Similarly, we refer to bad people as those who make us feel uncomfortable, diminished, and insecure. They are the kind of people who try to take advantage of us, seek success at the expense of others, and are prone to engage in fraud or other criminal activities in order to succeed.

They believe that the end justifies the means. They are also the kind of people we avoid because of their negativity toward us and the world. Like black holes, they suck our positive energy away and leave us drained and empty.

Good and bad people are part of the human fabric, and they live all over the world. Unfortunately, we wrongly assume that the difficulty in connecting with good people in other cultures arises from the fact that they are foreigners. We believe that those who have been raised in a different society and subjected to different environments cannot possibly have the same set of values that distinguishes good people from bad people.

Our obsolete 20th century mindset inhibits interaction and prevents us from making meaningful contact as we subconsciously classify foreigners as aliens.

Five Steps to Overcoming Misconceptions

The real difficulty arises from our own misconceptions. We meet so many people that we take mental shortcuts when determining another's goodness. We assume, too often incorrectly, that the more people appear to be like us, the more likely they are to be good. A common mistake is to jump to the conclusion that a foreigner who speaks good English and acts with self-confidence is a better business partner that the less flashy person with broken English. The reality may be just the opposite.

We assign meaning to the way other people look, dress, or speak. We allow external appearances to dictate the opinion we choose to have of those who look different from us. But remember that while speaking, dressing, and behaving in a different way may create barriers to spontaneous communication, these external manifestations don't mirror the person. It's only when we are able to go beyond external barriers that we can identify the intrinsic value of the people we meet. Only then can we identify the good or "right" people with whom we would like to surround ourselves wherever we go.

Perhaps learning to distinguish between right and wrong among perfect strangers and foreign nationals seems a daunting proposition to you. Don't worry; the good news is that these skills can be learned.

All it takes is these five steps:

1. **Awareness.** Take note of others as individuals with interests and needs likely to be very similar to your own.
2. **Understanding.** Capture the essence of the realities, interests, and needs of those you meet for the first time.
3. **Knowledge.** Use reasoning to take away truths, facts, information, and principles about others.
4. **Internalization.** Incorporate new learning into your conscious or subconscious database and take ownership of your new mindset.
5. **Practice.** Apply your new way of thinking as often as possible until it becomes second nature.

Once you are able to assess who is the right or wrong person for you among strangers, I guarantee that you will find more than enough good people to work with and relate to anywhere around the world in business and social settings.

Investing time in acquiring and fine-tuning these skills is easily justified when you pause to consider that the most effective path to success is working with and through the right people.

In today's globalized world, it works to your advantage to increase your familiarity with strangers in faraway countries. Remember that regular individuals in any country, just like you and me, have a tremendous capacity to accomplish and deliver results under the most difficult circumstances. Make them your ally!

In this book, I describe the five-step methodology I have developed and tested over decades. But before beginning on this path, let's start with a preview of our current world reality.

Welcome to Your Global Backyard

In today's global environment, individuals like you and me are constantly exposed to news on events and changes around the world that have a significant emotional impact on our daily lives. Social media is utterly intrusive and unavoidable, forcing us to accept that, like it or not, we are an integral part of a global society we barely know. Corporations are scratching their heads trying to figure out how to deal with new social markets and a new breed of consumers.

The sentiment is that the entire world has landed in our backyard. The volume of information that plagues our modern life is staggering. We live in a complex environment with unprecedented access to a virtual world that permeates all boundaries. Everyone is multitasking: talking, emailing, texting, twittering, blogging, and vlogging nonstop. Our brains are bombarded with more information than we can consciously register, let alone digest.

There are hundreds of social platforms to choose from to communicate with others, and the number of active users is increasing exponentially. In the 2012–2013 period, the most popular ones were:

- Facebook (1.11 billion active users)[5]
- Twitter (280 million active users)[6]
- LinkedIn (200 million individual members and over 2 million companies)[7]
- Google (359 million active users per month)[8]
- YouTube (1 billion unique visitors every month); over 6 billion hours of videos were watched each month, equivalent to one hour per every person on earth (50 percent more than a year before), and 100 hours of video were uploaded to YouTube every minute.[9]

The internet is indeed a powerful enabler that acts as an extension of our collective minds. Everyone demands our attention at once, and we yearn for the attention of everyone. We sleep with smartphones under the pillow to stay connected with the outside world and are disappointed if nobody out there misses us. We live so fast that we have no time to express our emotions with words. We have replaced laughter with a quick "lol." Even the conveniently short "Okay," already shortened to "OK," has now been replaced with just "k."

At the office, we are expected to stay on top of news related to our work. Clients expect us to provide on-the-spot analysis of what's happening around the globe and how it may affect their businesses. We are required to read and absorb every piece of news out on the wire.

We hear that the best job opportunities are abroad, away from family and friends. International corporations are pressing employees to accept relocation abroad as part of career-advancement planning. Those who agree to relocate are overwhelmed by the responsibility of exposing their spouses and children to harsher, less safe environments and the added stress of dealing with foreign cultures, languages, and schools. Thus the need to globalize our mindset is real.

It's tempting to believe that because of social media we are automatically "plugged in" to the rest of the world. We don't realize that subconsciously we still cling to our old comfort zones. When looking at the news, for example, we may prefer to quote a well-known Western newspaper instead of an unfamiliar one in Asia or the Middle East. We still operate with an obsolete "us versus them" mentality. We are still far away from accepting, let alone inviting, the world into our backyard. And that is precisely why writers and readers of *The Economist* believe that the world is a horrible place to live in.

Like the proverbial monster under the bed, we dread the unknown, the unfamiliar, and the mysterious; we associate it with darkness and danger. It doesn't help that our schools dedicate little time to teaching us about foreign individuals and cultures. As innovative as we are, our curiosity to discover the outer world has been repressed. Our interaction with other cultures is limited and distant, driven by comfortable indifference.

The problem with our complacency regarding other cultures is that the world has evolved rapidly in the last few decades, and not exactly in the way we might have anticipated. This evolution doesn't necessarily equate with progress.

If anything, the world seems to be moving backward and forward at the same time; a perpetual rocking motion that has everyone dizzy. This rocking motion is cyclic and typical during transition times, when we reject obsolete business, social, and political models while scrambling to find new ones. This evolution has brought more confusion than sophistication.

Take for example the backlash caused by the worst financial crisis since the Great Depression, which unraveled in 2008. The market liberalization that the world had enjoyed from the late 1980s through the early 2000s had almost vanished by 2010.

The open-market movement that made "globalization" a household word was slowed by an increasing preference for isolation and protectionism. Although less severe than the isolation era of the Great Depression, governments are again raising barriers to trade as they pick and choose whom they want to do business with and how they want to work together. In October 2013, *The Economist* used the term "Gated Globe" to describe a world that has become less open than in past decades.[10]

Information saturation is the
ailment of the 21st century.

In the middle of this transition period, we are bombarded with information 24/365. Usually access to information is good, but information saturation, the ailment of the 21st century, does not lead to more knowledge and better understanding. On the contrary, too much information builds a high level of white noise, that annoying static that interferes with communications and makes it difficult to separate relevant from irrelevant news.

Instead of adding clarity, information white noise leaves us with more questions than answers, with more uncertainties and concerns, with more fear and apprehensions about the future. The end result is confusion and mental paralysis. At times it seems that technology has finally caught up with our brain's ability to think and sort problems through. There is an overwhelming sense of helplessness, and in an attempt to manage the unmanageable, we end up with a propensity to jump to conclusions and make poor decisions.

What can we do?

We can update and adjust our mindset to better match current realities. Let's see how.

Geography Died on January 1, 2000

Agreed, geography has never really been alive, but it served a purpose at a time when life was more easily defined. The predominant mindset of the 20th century was that the world was divided between West and East. In politics it was the USA and the USSR. In business, it was the mighty Western companies and poor developing countries. In society, it was "us" versus "them." The world was conveniently compartmentalized and so was our mindset. We could deal with the "West," with "us," and with being "Americans."

At school, we learned to divide the Earth into continents, then continents into regions and regions into countries. We colored them in pretty colors and drew neat magic lines called borders. We learned to treat these borders as some kind of sealed containers and added labels to their citizens: Africans, Asians, Australians, Arabs, Europeans, and North and South Americans. We went on dividing people into smaller containers: Chinese, Indian, Brazilians, Kenyans,

Dutch, and so on, and we learned to treat them as separate entities with no resemblance or similarities to us. They are there and we are here. They do things that we don't.

This conveniently compartmentalized idea of the world died with the arrival of the 21ˢᵗ century and the solidification of the Internet-based virtual global world. Today, geographic borders are meaningless, and geography-based distinctions among populations are obsolete. Western Europeans, for example, find themselves surrounded by Arabs, Africans, and Asians. In the Middle East, Arabs are surrounded by Pakistanis, Filipinos, Sri-Lankans, Africans, and Malaysians.

Notably, America is an exception in that geography, for the most part, died here many decades ago. Even after 9/11 led to an increased awareness of the presence of Americans of Asian, Latin, and Arab descent, the United States continues to be a model of cultural integration relative to the rest of the world.

Major American cities may reflect different levels of income but rarely reflect forced segregation based on ethnic origins. While the United States is not a perfect union yet, and many civil rights issues need to be addressed, this land of opportunity is still strongly characterized by an inclusion of different customs and beliefs, and its citizens live in significantly more freedom and peace than most countries. The reason is that immigrants by and large identify with America, and America identifies with its immigrant past and population. There is little pressure for immigrants to adjust to the "protestant way of life" today, and this cultural and ethnic openness is what has made America an exceptional country.

Ethnic tolerance usually goes hand in hand with economic cycles. The more prosperous a country, the more tolerant its society is to immigrants. During low economic cycles, people struggle to find jobs to stay above water.

Competition for fewer jobs highlights the notion that immigrants are "stealing" jobs and ethnic tensions tend to increase. Terrorism has become another source of concern and, together with current economic uncertainties and sociopolitical unrest, it has increased the level of anxiety we feel about immigrants in particular and foreigners in general.

Aside from ethnic considerations, we tend to form opinions and draw conclusions about people in other countries based on their local economies. Without thinking, we may believe, for example, that people in poor countries are lazy and don't work hard enough to improve their living conditions. Jumping to conclusions, we may ignore the fact that some countries have limited or no natural resources to trade.

Take Africa for example: Some of the poorest African countries are those geographically located in the interior of the continent, with no access to oceans or rivers suitable for navigation, an essential factor for the development of commerce and trade that bring hard currency to a country's pool of resources.

Building highways to access ports is not only expensive but requires a level of multinational collaboration with neighboring countries that is practically impossible to achieve. If their natural resources happen to be abysmal, these countries depend on others for the provision of food and nourishment. It's then not surprising that many of these societies languish and lag behind the most fortunate ones.

In the past, when communications were limited and we saw the world from the distance, it may have been easier to assume that poor people in poor countries lacked the drive to change their living conditions. With infrequent news and reporting, perhaps we rarely stopped to think that poverty breeds dictatorships and the kind of repression that is hard to break away from.

We rarely stopped to think that citizens in these countries were mothers and fathers and children that dreamed of living in better conditions, going to school, and becoming active contributors to the global economy if only provided with the right opportunity.

Today, however, we're better equipped to act with a broader sense of universality, as globalization and demographics have made us increasingly aware of the need to provide opportunities to all. A good example of this paradigm shift is the significant transformation of the traditional charitable notion of "giving." Charity has been replaced by philanthropic "empowerment" as a more effective way to improve living conditions in developing countries, and private and public institutions along with a younger generation of professionals are actively engaging in social entrepreneurship.[11,12]

But while we are making significant strides in understanding the needs of poor countries and taking more effective measures to help solve poverty and improve sanitary conditions, we continue to lag behind in our understanding of those societies and still struggle to become a more integral part of the global world.

I am reminded of a classmate and tennis partner I had in my college years. She was extremely bright and popular but had a hard time all through college trying to be the perfect student. She suffered from what I call a "too bright syndrome." School and college kids who are too bright tend to ask fewer questions because they think they are expected to know everything and are afraid of showing weakness.

Accordingly, they grow up with pockets of ignorance as they miss out on the opportunity to learn from others, expand their knowledge, and gain a broader perspective. In the work environment, they pretend to know the lay of the land the moment they show up at their new job.

They fail to ask silly questions because they think they are expected to be knowledgeable from day one. When they finally realize that they have no clue about the simple things that "everyone knows," it's too late. By that time, silly questions really sound silly.

This is what happened during the last century when the West was actively doing business abroad. We forgot to ask simple questions.

We missed out on the opportunity to learn how other people conduct business, gather and process information, and make decisions. Connecting personally with the rest of the world used to be a choice. Today, to succeed and maintain our leadership position in the world, we *must* learn about the global market and its citizens as much, if not more, than they know about us.

We can achieve this goal by being proactive in creating opportunities to increase our understanding of others. Without losing our identity, we can start building a global network of "right" or "good" people by reaching out, interacting and incorporating into our circles those that live in or are from far away countries, particularly countries we are likely to do business with. I expand on how to build a support network abroad in *Part II—Understanding*.

Without interaction, there is no learning. You've heard some version of the saying: "Give a man a fish and he will eat for one day; teach a man to fish and he will eat for a lifetime." *That's interaction.* You learn by doing, by interacting with someone or something. Once you make a commitment to interacting with others, the rest falls into place.

To facilitate interaction, start by setting aside obsolete, pre-conceived ideas and wrong assumptions about peoples from non-industrialized societies. Open your mind to realize and accept the fact that, regardless of location and standard of living, the majority of human beings on this planet aspire to satisfy their basic needs just like you do. Incorporate into your vocabulary universal concepts that help predict human behavior.

Half a century ago a man born in Brooklyn, New York, developed a needs-based theory to explain human motivation. His theory became a classic, and I borrow from it here to help you connect with the realities that the rest of the world faces right now:

In 1943, psychologist Abraham Maslow published *A Theory of Human Motivation*.[13] In this paper, Maslow states: "There are at least five sets of goals, which we may call basic needs. These are briefly physiological, safety, love, esteem, and self-actualization." He went on to say: "In addition, we are motivated by the desire to achieve or maintain the various conditions upon which these basic satisfactions rest and by certain more intellectual desires."

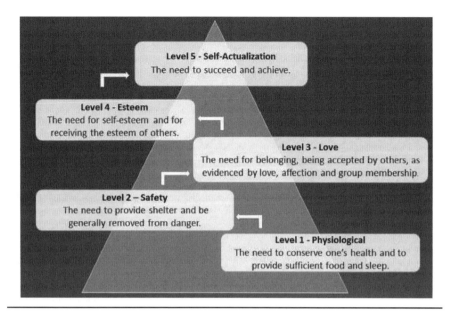

Figure 2.1 Maslow's Hierarchy of Needs.

Maslow's Hierarchy of Needs is often depicted by a pyramid (Figure 2.1) with five levels within, progressively moving up from satisfying physiological needs (Level 1) to achieving self-actualization (Level 5).

Citizens in industrialized countries usually enjoy a high standard of living that satisfies all their basic needs. They have been able to provide food, shelter, and safety for themselves and their loved ones. They have the means and education to become respected members of society who are recognized for their achievements. Finally, they have achieved success and are comfortably enjoying Level 5 of Maslow's Hierarchy of Needs.

But those in emerging markets, and particularly those in developing or frontier economies, are still struggling at the bottom or the middle of the pyramid.

Citizens in non-industrialized countries are just as good and honorable people as everyone else, but economic development in their countries is still lacking and the means to allow them to move up in the hierarchy of needs is still elusive. Progress is becoming more evident in urban areas of emerging economies such as China and Brazil, where a new middle class is coming along rapidly and strong, but progress is still lacking in rural areas.

Learning to connect with the world on a personal level is easier than most people believe.

To get started, we need to first understand where people are in their socioeconomic development cycle. Just like the video I mentioned in the Preface to this book, professionals tend to see the world through the eyes of a Level 3, 4, or 5.

They have a job, a home, a car, possibly a family. They likely have satisfied their need for belonging and self-esteem, and chances are they are on their way to self-actualization. From this perspective, they find it difficult to relate to people around them who may come across as different and annoying.

It's only when they stop to consider that the old cashier and the mother of the cranky kid in the video may be in Levels 1, 2, or 3 that their view of the situation changes.

Awareness of the different levels of needs leads to understanding, cooperation, and, ultimately, compassion. More important, it leads to learning how to connect with strangers beyond external signs, reaching into the inner persona of individuals they hardly know so they can find that intrinsic value that each one of them brings to life.

Connecting with strangers requires a willingness to make a mindset adjustment, shifting from the one we learned in the past century to one that reflects the realities of the present.

In summary, connecting to and becoming part of the rest of the world requires the adoption of universal tools and new techniques that allow you to not only survive but enjoy the new world you live in. Updating your mindset will allow you to see the world from a different angle that enables you to gather new data, interpret information in a fresh way, acquire new knowledge, and develop skills better suited to managing the world today.

Let's review how you can get started on the path of a universal mindset transformation.

A Rude Awakening—The Perils of Overconfidence

When the reality of the world in the 2000s started to sink in, American companies became painfully aware that they were encountering a kind of market resistance never seen before. It wasn't just one emerging country. Customers all over the world seemed to have developed, almost overnight, minds of their own. They had increased their purchasing power and were exhibiting a higher level of sophistication, choosing and often preferring qualified local providers over foreign companies.

It was a rude awakening for Western companies when they started to realize that they were too big, too expensive, too sophisticated, and too complex to adapt to a sudden shift in market behavior. For the first time they were behind the curve, unable to compete effectively with and losing big chunks of market share to local competitors.

As is often the case, market changes had been in the making for at least two decades, but nobody in the West had taken notice.

Here is why:

Up until the 2000s, the Western world had lived through a century of unprecedented growth. This seemingly unlimited growth started with the industrial revolution of the 1800s and the technological revolution of the 1900s. Both catapulted the economies of Western Europe and the United States way ahead of other countries. After the 1950s, the disparity between the economy of the United States and that of the rest of the world was significant. Americans were enjoying an unparalleled standard of living, and America was the most admired country in the world.

Governments in non-industrialized countries were eager to attract foreign and particularly American investment and know-how. Local consumers were hungry for high-quality American manufactured goods and considered them highly appreciated "status" symbols.

While playing a leadership role in the internationalization of business and trade, America chose to follow an ethnocentric approach: that is, one based on the premise that the American business model was superior to any other.

This strong sense of superiority also meant that Americans and American institutions doing business abroad were not particularly in need of nor interested in understanding, let alone integrating with, the cultures with which they were doing business. America focused on exporting the American way and did so successfully for half a century.

The Japanese had a different approach: In 1982, when Bridgestone, the largest tire manufacturing and auto supply company in Japan, entered the American market, it bought the newest operating Firestone plant (1,000 American workers) in Nashville to learn the American way to market.

The purchase is said to have inspired the script for a 1986 Paramount Pictures movie directly by Ron Howard, *Gung Ho,* with Michael Keaton and Gedde Watanabe, which parodies Americans and Japanese working together in a car plant in America.

Parody or not, in 1988 Bridgestone shocked the market when it bought a 75 percent controlling stake in Firestone Tire & Rubber for a whopping $2.6 billion, almost $1 billion over the French-Italian coalition bid made by Michelin and Pirelli.[14]

Then in the mid-1980s, American corporations adopted a "bottom line" approach to business, cutting costs wherever they could and focusing on generating ever more dazzling quarterly financial reports.

Among the cost-cutting strategies: the reduction of professional development programs, the virtual elimination of research and development (R&D) divisions, the outsourcing of manufacturing and service activities that could be performed by lower-wages workers in developing countries like China and India, among others.

The drastic reduction in R&D had a significant and immediate impact on the American highly skilled workforce. Out of a job and with limited opportunities, it was not rare to find a physicist driving a taxi cab to make a living. It was the beginning of the U.S. decline in technical innovation and technical education, as many of the children of R&D professionals, learning from their parents' experience and sensing the way the future was going, decided to avoid cyclical and comparatively low-paying technical careers and instead join the strongly emerging financial and service sectors.

Some of you may remember that there had never been more applications to enroll in MBA programs than in the late 1980s and 1990s. The quarterly "bottom line" approach to business elevated financial and legal services to the top of influence in the corporate world, and by the late 1990s, Wall Street was at the heart of corporate success.

With few exceptions, Wall Street saw a bull market from the early 1980s to the year 2000, and the Dow Jones Industrial Average saw a spectacular rise of over 1,500 percent, rising from less than 800 points to surpass the "magic" 10,000 mark, ending the first year of the new millennium inching close to an unbelievable, at the time, 12,000 points.

The belief that the U.S. economy was at the top of the world was stronger than ever, and the spirit of America was flying high. It was a decade of Western exuberance that promised everlasting success well into the new century.

Dark Clouds Loom

In March 12, 2013, U.S. National Intelligence Director Gen. James R. Clapper presented the U.S. Intelligence Community Worldwide Threat Assessment Statement to the Senate Select Committee on Intelligence in Washington, D.C., on current and projected national security threats:

"This environment is demanding reevaluations of the way we do business, expanding our analytic envelope, and altering the vocabulary of intelligence. Threats are more diverse, interconnected, and viral than at any time in history. Attacks, which might involve cyber and financial weapons, can be deniable and attributable. Destruction can be invisible, latent, and progressive. We now monitor shifts in human geography, climate, disease, and competition for natural resources because they fuel tensions and conflicts. Local events that might seem irrelevant are more likely to affect U.S. national security in accelerated time frames."[16]

CNN MONEY SPECIAL REPORT:
A CENTURY OF WEALTH[15]

In the 1990s, the Dow Jones industrial average posted its biggest gains of any decade in its history.

CNN Money, Dec 31, 1999: "Wall Street finished the 1900s at an all-time peak Friday—capping a century of unprecedented growth punctuated by two market crashes, the longest-running stock rally in history, and the emergence of technology companies as leaders for the 21st century.

"In fact, so many market records were set in 1999 that it's almost mind-boggling: The Nasdaq composite rose 85.6 percent, the biggest annual gain for a major market index in U.S. history.

"The Dow industrials gained 25.2 percent in 1999, a record fifth year in a row that the blue-chip index posted a double-digit percentage gain.

"The S&P 500 rose 19.5 percent, a record fifth straight year the index posted a double-digit gain.

"A record 203.9 billion shares were traded on the New York Stock Exchange and a record 265.6 billion shares changed hands on the Nasdaq."

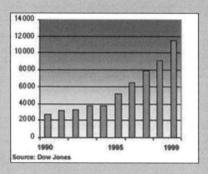

Although Director Clapper was referring to national security, the sentiment is also applicable to individuals and corporations. Threats are growing more interconnected, and events that at first seem local and irrelevant could quickly set off transnational disruptions affecting U.S. national interests. Cyber attacks that infringe on large banks can potentially impact and bring down not only the corporation and its employees, but also its customers. That means you and me and our families and friends.

This picture leaves no doubt that the world is complex, and the way we deal with complexity is by learning new skills and gathering new knowledge.

> Decision paralysis is not an option.
> The solution is a new mindset that provides
> the right information to act upon.

It's also not an option to continue to ignore the fact that we are part of a global environment and no longer contained within a country with well-defined borders to protect us. We no longer survive by staying on our own turf and in our comfort zone.

As in sports, we need to have a deep understanding of how the other team plays: its past performance, its known strategies and tactics, its strengths and weaknesses. We use this information to develop our own strategies and tactics for defense and attack, and then we prepare and practice intensely to strengthen our skills and to be in good shape when meeting our opponents. We assign specific roles to team members so that when they are on the field, they are prepared and know how to deal with their counterparts.

Nobody can do this alone, and that's why in addition to the head coach, football teams have individual coaches who work with players day after day and year after year, helping them develop the skills they need to play a good game and win. No football, basketball, or baseball team gets out in the field without a strategy and alternative scenarios to play depending on how the field reacts to their moves. On top of strategy, players are provided intensive training, preparation, and coaching, without which they could not possibly perform well.

Imagine what would happen to a sports team that assumes their opponents play just like they do, think just like they do, and behave just like they do. Imagine the results of the game if each team assumes that the other will buy into their strategies and tactics and would agree to play their game the way they envision it. We know it wouldn't work.

Yet, that is exactly what we do when we interact with the outside world. As a result, we end up facing the world utterly unprepared, without realizing that we bring defeat to ourselves because the other team, sensing and taking advantage of our lack of preparation, will confidently run ahead of us and score big.

We admire and enjoy watching our favorite sports warriors week after week; we cheer them as they play their best against all odds. Still, when it comes to us facing the challenges of the world today, we disregard strategy, training, and coaching. Even if we consider strategy and preparation, we do it based on a last-century mindset.

We have not consciously and systematically tried to update our way of thinking to the realities of the 21st century.

To succeed in today's world, we have to go out and play our best game. Sadly, many corporations still choose to try to compete in emerging markets with insufficient preparation, training, strategy, and alternative moves to adjust to drastically different market conditions.

As individuals, we go to work hoping that we will never have to relocate to foreign countries, instead of embracing change and preparing ourselves to understand how the world works and build a circle of people whom we can trust to care about our success as well as theirs.

More needs to be done to help companies understand and find new ways to address current market conditions. Part II highlights new data to help us understand the drastic changes that came about at the turn of the century.

PART II
UNDERSTANDING

*Understanding: The Power of Comprehending; the Capacity to Apprehend General Relations of Particulars**

---

* Merriam-Webster Dictionary

Chapter Three

They Did What?

Never doubt that a small group of thoughtful, committed citizens can change the world. Indeed, it's the only thing that ever has.

— Margaret Mead[*]

After two decades of observations and data collection, away from the public eye and behind the walls of the World Bank, a team of economists was reaching a conclusion that would forever change the way Western companies did business.

The World Bank had regularly been reporting on migration patterns, taking note of the fact that workers living and working in foreign (host) countries had consistently been remitting their personal savings back to their (home) countries of origin. Their report on migration and remittance patterns, released in 2002–2003, was one of the most significant pieces of information affecting today's global business.

Fresh Capital and Discretionary Money

The early 2000's data made a stunning revelation: The value of remittance to developing countries had more than doubled, from about $25 billion in 1988 to $50 billion in 1995, and then doubled again to $100 billion by 2002. This kind of jump is difficult to ignore, and since then it has become even more striking. It doubled again by 2005, and tripled by 2008.

---

[*] https://www.brainyquote.com/quotes/margaret_mead_100502

Officially recorded remittance to developing countries reached $410 billion in 2013, and global remittance—including those to high-income countries—reached $550 billion in the same year. Growing annually at 9 percent, global remittance is forecast to reach a record $707 billion by 2016.[1]

This unofficial secondary economy, which represents the personal savings of low-wage workers in host countries, was contributing to the annual national income or gross domestic product (GDP) of countries such as:

- India ($71 billion)
- China ($60 billion)
- The Philippines ($26 billion)
- Mexico ($22 billion)
- Nigeria ($21 billion)
- Egypt ($20 billion)

Countries with slightly lower GDP amounts included Pakistan, Bangladesh, Vietnam, and Ukraine.[2]

Remittance to India in 2013 was nearly three times the foreign direct investment the country received in 2012.

Nobody could have anticipated that a migrant workforce made up primarily of low-wage (not necessarily low-skilled) workers, moving from country to country in search of higher incomes and a better life for their families, could generate a combined second economy that would shift the way we look at the world.

In my travels and while working abroad, I've come across many of these migrant workers in their quest for a better life for them and their dependents. Here is the story of one of them:

Life of Ashok

I first met Ashok on a hot desert night in Saudi Arabia as my husband and I went outside for a short walk around the neighborhood. We were both working for Saudi companies and had moved into a gated, high-security community, as is customary for Western expatriates. As we left the house, we noticed a middle-aged man coming out of the house next door.

The man saw us and immediately came over to introduce himself: "Good evening. My name is Ashok," he said in perfect English, and proceeded to welcome us to the neighborhood. Sporting dark pants and a light shirt, he was cordial, friendly, well-mannered, and clearly delighted to welcome us and share some stories, such as the origin of the 18-hole, all-grass golf course located right behind our backyard (grass is a true luxury in the Arabian desert!).

His smiling face and enthusiasm were contagious, and we were pleased to have such a friendly and well-educated neighbor.

After the normal pleasantries, Ashok offered to help us with everything we might need. Of course, we assumed he was talking generalities, being polite and supportive, and we thanked him for his kindness. Sensing our assumption, however, the always-smiling Ashok took extra time to clarify that he was employed by our neighbors to clean and take care of their home on a daily basis. Overcoming our initial surprise and realizing that we too needed help, we jumped at the opportunity and asked him to come back the next day to discuss details.

Ashok turned out to be the most respectful and accomplished housekeeper we had ever had. A native of South Asia, he works in Saudi Arabia to provide for his wife, four children, and aging parents. As a young adult, he dreamed of being a chef and running his own restaurant. He enrolled in a well-known Western university to follow this dream, but as fate would have it, his father became ill, and he was forced to return home to take care of his extended family.

His family was reasonably well-to-do but has suffered hardship due to the country's political and economic downturns. The situation finally forced Ashok to seek alternative sources of income. He applied for a work visa in Saudi Arabia to work as a housekeeper for Western expats, and what a great housekeeper he was!

Reliable, attentive, courteous and professional, Ashok was always looking for more work to do. Every time we returned from a trip abroad, we would find prepared food in the refrigerator or the oven, ready to serve (a blessing after long and tiring trips!), yet he refused any payment for his off-duty attentions.

Over the years of working in Saudi Arabia, Ashok was able to accumulate enough savings to buy a larger house for his close and extended family, cover their medical expenses, send his wife and children to school, and earn enough discretionary money to travel often to see his family.

After he retired, Ashok returned to his native country and used his savings to start his own business, applying and sharing with others the new skills and knowledge he acquired while working abroad, proud to contribute to elevating the standard of living of people in his village.

Ashok was just one of nine million foreign workers or expatriates living in Saudi Arabia, about one-third of the total population. It's estimated that only 200,000 of all expatriates working in Saudi Arabia are Westerners (mostly Americans, British, Canadians, and Australians).

The rest are primarily from India, Egypt, Pakistan, and the Philippines (more than one million each) followed by smaller numbers from Jordan, Syria, Lebanon, Sri Lanka, and Africa.

Just as India and China are at the top of the list of countries receiving remittances from their nationals working abroad, the United States and Saudi Arabia are the #1 and #2 countries hiring the workers who send those savings back home. Saudi Arabia alone contributes more than $25 billion each year to developing countries that receive workers' remittances.

As one might expect, world-wide remittance of savings to the tune of $400 billion to $550 billion exerts enormous impact on the world economy. In the late 2000s, remittances became the second largest contribution to the GDP of developing countries,[2] after Foreign Direct Investment (FDI), and significantly larger than Official Development Assistance (ODA) (see Figure 3.1).

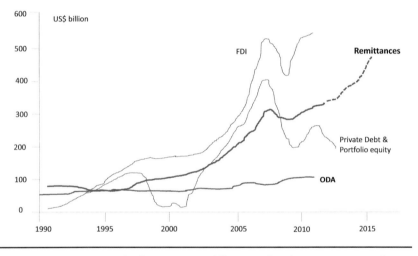

Figure 3.1 Remittance and other sources of flows to developing countries.[3]

As a percentage of GDP, the World Bank reports that the top receiving countries in 2013 were Tajikistan (48%), Kyrgyz Republic (31%), Lesotho and Nepal (25% each), and Moldova (24%).

> The dollar value of remittances today is more than four times higher than official development aid (ODA) sent to developing countries. Those remitting savings are also more consistent contributors to GDP than foreign direct investment (FDI), which diminishes significantly during low economic cycles.

Here is how the cycle works

1. **Standard of Living.** Migrant workers help elevate the standard of living of families left behind in their home countries by providing extra income to pay for better homes, better education, and better coverage of health expenses for their immediate and extended family.
2. **Better Education.** Better-educated people can access higher-salaried positions and help create new jobs through family businesses and individual entrepreneurship. Migrant workers continue to contribute when they return home, usually turning to entrepreneurship, sharing and putting to work the experience and new skills they acquired abroad, including language skills.
3. **More Experience.** Higher numbers of experienced and more educated workers allow the home country to attract foreign manufacturing and service companies to establish local operations, thus adding hard currency to the government coffers.
4. **Higher Resources.** Governments are able to collect more income through taxes, services, and trade. With the additional help of foreign investment, they start building new infrastructure and modernizing old infrastructure, making it easier for goods to be transferred into, out of, and throughout the country, which allows businesses to reach new consumers and suppliers.
5. **More Stability.** A more prosperous country is likely to be more politically stable. As they enter into a positive economic cycle, governments are more inclined to institutionalize transactions, which adds transparency to internal systems and helps curb corruption. This, in turn, attracts more foreign direct investment, and the local standard of living continues to increase, education and healthcare are improved, and family and corporate businesses prosper.

In the past century, multinational companies (MNCs) used to compete with other MNCs. Today they are learning to compete with new and strong local national competitors (LNCs).

Stronger economies abroad have allowed LNCs to grow, modernize, and reach an unprecedented new level of financial might and business sophistication. Thanks in part to the experience gained through outsourcing, goods designed and manufactured abroad today are nearly as good as those manufactured in the U.S.; in many cases they are better-designed and more affordably priced to appeal to local preferences and accommodate lower purchasing power. LNCs have the additional advantage of having a deep understanding of the culture and being fluent in the local language.

We go into this topic in more detail in *Chapter 7: Simplicity, a New Way of Life* and *Chapter 8: Expect the Unexpected, a New Kind of Leadership.*

Amazing Demographics

Just as migrant workers were quietly building a multibillion-dollar secondary economy, the world population outside the industrialized world was growing at a fast pace. The transformational change in demographics at the turn of the century was yet another rude awakening for Western companies.

> When population grows at an extraordinarily fast pace, the pressure to satisfy people's needs sparks creativity, innovation, and progress. The connection between the revolutionary inventions of the 1800s and 1900s and high population density becomes clear when we devote some attention to the evolution of demographics in modern times.

This is what happened between 1800 and 2000, and what is expected by 2050[4]:

1800–1900

- The European population doubled from 203 million to 408 million.
- The population of the U.S. and Canada grew by a factor of 12, from 7 million to 82 million.
- By contrast, the Asian population grew only 33 percent, from 635 million to 947 million.
- India's population remained basically constant, around 260 million.

1900–1950

- The population of U.S. and Canada almost quadrupled from 82 million to 316 million.
- The Latin American population more than doubled from 74 million to 167 million.
- The European population increased from 408 million to 547 million.
- Asia's population increased from 947 million to 1.4 billion.
- Africa's population increased slowly from 133 million to 221 million.

1950–2000

- Population growth rates in North America and Europe slowed down and in some cases were negative, hinting at a future of smaller and aging populations.
- The population of the Middle East and North Africa (MENA) quadrupled from 104 million to 432 million.

- Asia almost tripled its population, from 1.4 billion to 3.7 billion.
- China's population more than doubled, from 560 million to 1.2 billion.
- India's population tripled, from 350 million to 1.18 billion.
- Latin America's population tripled, from 167 million to 511 million.

2000–2050

- The population of MENA countries is expected to reach 700 million by 2050.[5]
- Asia's population will reach 5.2 billion.
- Africa's population is expected to grow to 1.7 billion.
- The population of Latin America and the Caribbean is expected to grow to 800 million.
- North America's population will grow slowly to 392 million.
- Europe's population will also grow slowly to 628 million.
- Approximately 37% of the European population will be over 60 years old.
- Only 10% of the African population will be over 60 years old.
- Roughly 45% of the population of MENA countries is under 18 years old.
- According to the United Nations, the total world population will surpass 9 billion by 2050.

Large populations in healthy economies translate into an attractive customer base. This has been the motivation for commercializing innovative ideas for centuries.

Inspiration, Innovation, and Consumerism

A potentially large consumer base has been the inspiration behind the commercialization of all scientific and technological inventions in the past. Here are just a few examples:

In 1806–1807, Humphrey Davy invented the first arc lamp that turned out to be "too good" for commercial consumption: It generated a light so bright that it was blinding if used in small spaces such as offices and households, and so it was relegated to be used at lighthouses.[6]

But the prospect of putting a light bulb in every household and office in the world kept 19th century inventors working hard to modify Davy's invention. It wasn't until 1879 that Thomas Edison's research team finally succeeded, and the Edison-Swan United Company became one of the world's largest manufacturers of the "practical" light bulb.

In a similar case from 1901, a fast-growing market motivated Ramson E. Olds, owner of a car factory in Detroit, to invent the assembly line that quadrupled the speed of manufacturing of his Oldsmobile, then a hot item demanded by an increasing number of customers.

Twelve years later, in 1913, Henry Ford would apply Olds's idea to large-scale manufacturing, announcing his goal of creating a motor car "for the great multitudes."

It is not surprising that Western companies first turned their attention (if not yet their wisdom) to the most populated emerging economies: Brazil, Russia, India, and China (BRIC), with a secondary tier of prospects that included Mexico, Colombia, Turkey, and Indonesia.

But lists of countries in this context are meaningless, because the selection of most promising target countries is different for companies that are involved in business-to-business (B2B) or business-to-consumer (B2C) sales. It also depends on the kind of offerings (products or services), differences within offerings (luxury or generic products), and the corporate culture (market leader or follower).

Moreover, an important factor widely overlooked by Western companies when selecting new markets is the mismatch that may exist between the company's current capabilities and those required to operate profitably in the target market—a topic covered later in the book (Chapter 8).

Let's now turn our attention to the new threats that resulted from changes in demographics and migration patterns: Threats that are forcing Western companies to hurry up and revisit their traditional business models, hopefully with change in mind.

Chapter Four

Up, Down, and Sideways

If you don't like something, change it.
If you cannot change it, change your attitude.

— Maya Angelou*

The end of the Cold War in 1989 and the buoyant financial activities of the last decade of the 20th century opened the door for an accelerated expansion of global commerce and solidified attention on potentially billions of new consumer markets primarily in Asia and Africa.

Wall Street's optimism, however, was dampened in the early 2000s by the scandalous collapse of multibillion-dollar companies such as Enron and WorldCom, and the uncertainties associated with post-9/11 market conditions. Fortune 500 companies went into a wait-and-see period, freezing expansion projects and consolidating operations—a policy designed to build cash reserves in anticipation of uncertainties and emergencies.

As market volatility continued, the accumulation of cash among multinationals in the first decade of the century was unprecedented. Market instability also resulted in record high crude oil prices, surpassing the $100-per-barrel mark, which quickly became the new norm.

High crude oil prices further enriched the coffers of oil-exporting countries, particularly the Gulf region of the Middle East. Among these countries, a progressive United Arab Emirates attracted a large number of Western companies, and Dubai became the most celebrated icon of modern and vibrant Middle Eastern economies.

---

* Maya Angelou Quotes. BrainyQuote.com, Xplore Inc, 2018. https://www. brainyquote.com/quotes/maya_angelou_101310, accessed February 10, 2018.

The upcoming new, large, and young consumer bases abroad were excellent news to Western companies. Realizing that demographics could not sustain continuous growth in industrialized economies, Western multinational corporations (MNCs) quickly turned their attention to emerging markets.

The bad news for the West was that the governments of these new economies had become highly aware of the value their large consumer base represented to foreign investors and multinational players.

The Evolving Role of Government

Unlike in the 20th century, emerging economies today have easier access to hard currency, manpower, and know-how, which makes them more independent from Western foreign aid. We discussed earlier how workers' migration and savings repatriation are effectively increasing GDP in their home countries. Fresh capital is giving these countries the opportunity to acquire capabilities that resemble or surpass those of industrialized countries.

Empowered by higher revenues and global market accessibility, local governments have been quick to alter their traditionally passive roles when it comes to Western expansion. They are becoming increasingly more protective of their internal markets by demanding stricter terms and conditions from foreign companies that want to operate in their land.

China, for example, has become notorious for changing the rules of engagement, without notice, in favor of local companies. This has created havoc among Western multinationals accustomed to operating under more transparent institutionalized rules.

Western companies are also being subjected to strict environmental laws and are expected to invest more in the development and environmental safety of the local communities in which they operate. Budget cuts for international aid also add pressure on the private sector to help build the physical and institutional infrastructure needed in markets of interest.

Governments of emerging economies are also showing new muscle by extending their sphere of influence abroad, competing directly with traditional Western interests. For example, by the end of 2012, China had invested more than $50 billion in African countries, out-pacing the U.S. in the region and, in the process, drawing criticism for its unsustainable exploitation practices.[1]

Access to natural resources to ensure future grow has also accelerated Chinese investment in Australia, Latin America, and the Middle East.

In the past, China has not been particularly inclined to engage in geopolitical expansionism. Instead, it has been intent on avoiding conflict with its neighbors while at the same time promoting conflict among them as a distraction. This philosophy, however, may have died when the old leadership of the Communist Party of China gave way to a younger generation of leaders who have not experienced the rigors of the Mao era and the cultural revolution.[2]

China today may be more tempted to use newly strengthened military and navy power to annex neighboring regions, particularly those that have large off-shore oil reserves.[3] And it doesn't hurt China's plans that, in the process of acquiring natural resources and increasing trade throughout the world, the government is gradually advancing the adoption of the yuan as the primary global trade currency.

South–South Trade

But perhaps the most ominous news for Western enterprises is the increasing trade and commerce among emerging markets, or "South–South" trade, which has intensified in the last decade. Countries in Latin America, the Middle East, and Asia are increasingly doing business among themselves, thus changing the traditional North–South and West–East flow of commerce.

According to the United Nations Conference for Trade and Development (UNCTAD), in 2010, South–South exports were worth $3.5 billion, accounting for 23 percent of world trade. Between 2000 and 2010, South–South exports grew at an average of 19 percent per year compared to 12 percent per year of world total exports. After the global financial crisis of 2008, South–South exports recovered faster than overall world exports, growing 30 percent from 2009 to 2010.[4]

Trade among emerging economies today is dominated by the exportation of natural resources, manufactured goods, equipment, and miscellaneous articles. But as interaction among Asia (primarily China), Africa, the Middle East, and Latin America continues to strengthen, commerce on a global scale will be expanded and significantly transformed.

According to *Bloomberg Businessweek*,[5] trade between Africa and Asia is expected to reach $1.5 trillion by 2020, prompting companies in the freight industry, such as Danish AP Moeller-Maersk A/S and German Deutsche Post AG, to expand shipping links between the two continents.

Statistics from the World Trade Organization indicate that in 2011, 53 percent of Middle East exports went to Asia, 53 percent of Asian products went to other Asian countries, 27 percent of Latin American products went to other Latin countries, and 22 percent of products from Central America and the Caribbean went to Asia.[6]

On the other hand, Gulf Arab investors have been eyeing China, India, and Pakistan as the preferred repositories of their wealth by making multibillion dollar investments in real estate, power generation, and natural gas projects.

The United Arab Emirates (UAE) has become India's largest trading partner, with UAE–India bilateral trade rising from only $180 million in the 1970s to a massive $43 billion per year in 2009–2010.[7] Etihad Airways, an Abu Dhabi–based airline, has been adding flights to Indian cities to meet growing demand.[8]

Another example: The $11.7 billion investment agreement to promote regional investment and trade signed in Bangkok in August, 2009, between China and the Association of South East Asian Nations (ASEAN), which includes the countries of Brunei, Indonesia, Malaysia, the Philippines, Singapore, Thailand, Vietnam, Myanmar, Laos, and Cambodia.[9]

Another factor that is just as significant is that, in 2008, the Arab countries of the Gulf Cooperation Council (GCC)—Bahrain, Kuwait, Oman, Qatar, UAE, and Saudi Arabia—suspended negotiations of a trade agreement with the European Union that had been 20 years in the making.[10]

Instead, they turned their attention to trade agreements with Southeast Asia, starting with Singapore.[11] While informal conversations with the European Union continued, the message was clear: The GCC was exercising options and starting to engage in South–South trade.

Trust—Our Achilles Heel

In January 2013, General Electric (GE) released its annual Global Innovation Barometer,[12] which specifically examined what factors business executives believe to be drivers and deterrents of innovation. It analyzed approaches and policies that enable innovation and drive growth.

GE surveyed 3,100 senior executives (28 percent of them C-level) in 25 markets with an average company size of 1,200 employees. Here are the responses to three of the questions:

1. "Executives reporting their company has already developed a new product, improved a product, or created a new business model through collaboration with another company." Percentage of executives that strongly agree:
   - Germany (50%)
   - China (46%)
   - Brazil (44%)
   - Sweden (44%)
   - U.S. (35%)
2. "What are the main reasons why your company would seek to collaborate with entrepreneurs or other companies?" Responses from executives surveyed:
   - Access to new technologies (79%)
   - Access to new markets (79%)
   - Improve existing product or service (75%)
   - Speed up time to market (72%)

3. "Still on collaboration, what are the main reasons why your company would be reluctant to collaborate with entrepreneurs or other companies?" Percent of respondents who selected the item as a barrier:
   - Lack of intellectual property (IP) protection (64%)
   - Lack of trust in the partner company (47%)
   - Talent knowledge poaching (45%)
   - Lack of test collaboration process and collaboration tools (39%)
   - Fears about unequal revenue split (36%)
   - We don't know how to attract potential partners (31%)
   - We don't have time to allocate to managing the partnership (28%)
   - I don't know if my company is ready or able to be working in partnership (28%)
   - We don't have time to allocate to meeting possible partners (22%)
   - The company is bigger than ours (22%)
   - Our culture is too closed (18%)
   - The company is foreign (16%)

The GE results indicate that the U.S. is lagging behind other countries in its interactions with other companies when it comes to developing new products or improving business models through collaboration (question 1). Results also show that although collaboration among partnerships is highly desirable (question 2), lack of trust (question 3) is a significant barrier to collaboration taking place.

The rest of the mistrust-related issues should be well within a company's capability to address—with two exceptions: (a) lack of intellectual property, which is a matter for government and public policy, and (b) talent knowledge poaching, which is labor-market driven.

The GE study highlights the pressing need to develop the skills necessary to establish the kind of trust that results in long-lasting relationships. As we increasingly deal with collectivistic societies, in which personal relationships are the key to success, the need to achieve a deeper understanding of different cultures and establish borderless trust has become more relevant than ever.

The so called "soft" side of business is now at the heart of 21st century financial success.

Outside industrialized societies, personal relations tend to precede business relations.

Overconfidence ignores cultural sensitivities and infringes on local people's own comfort level, raising imperceptible barriers that kill trust and relationships that otherwise may have been fruitful. People on both sides walk away frustrated and disappointed, and the opportunity to connect with others and bring home good memories and good business is, at least for the time being, lost.

Whereas individualistic societies tend to think in terms of contract signing, collectivistic societies (most of the world) believe in doing business with those they know and feel comfortable with. For them, signing a contract is important but secondary to understanding what kind of person you are as an individual. This is what they want to know:

- What are your personal values?
- Can they trust your integrity as an individual?
- Are you truly representing the values of your organization?
- Do you have decision-making power or influence?
- Do they like you as a person?
- Would they enjoy doing business with you in the long run?

Contracts are more easily broken than
personal relationships.

To get answers to these questions, they invite you to participate in social gatherings, at which they expect you to relax and be yourself. This socializing may include invitations to a restaurant for food or drinks, if local customs allow it, or in many cases, the honor of an invitation to a private residence.

Whatever the venue, their intent is to observe how you react and behave outside the office, in a more personal environment. From their viewpoint, although contracts are a necessity, they are not sufficient to establish good and long-lasting business relationships.

Unfortunately, socializing is not usually on the agenda of Western executives who, missing the business intention behind the social invitation, consider these invitations rather awkward and a waste of time.

Too often during discussions on the need for relationship building on a personal and business level, these executives roll their eyes and sigh. They consider it a superfluous activity, a dreaded task to be avoided at all cost. Executives who think this way are proud of being transaction- and contract-driven, and emphasize bottom-line hard facts as opposed to accepting the value of interpersonal relationships.

That mindset worked in the 20th century but not anymore.

Ironically, these same executives are ready to admit that they prefer to do business with those they trust and feel comfortable with. Just like their foreign counterparts, they enjoy relating to people they can understand, establish rapport with easily, disagree with freely and amicably, negotiate with, and achieve mutual understanding with.

That's why when they meet new people at private parties or the office, they immediately want to know where others live and what they do for a living.

These hard-nosed executives also try to learn about others' education and social background, political interest, religious orientation, and so forth.

But when it comes to repeating this process with foreign nationals, they tend to reject the idea and dismiss it as irrelevant. This reaction is rooted in their lack of familiarity, misperceptions, and preconceived ideas when it comes to multicultural environments.

They compound the problem when opting to practice abroad what they do at home and end up pushing too hard when trying to get to know others. Asking personal questions on a first encounter, for example, may be acceptable in the United States, but it's considered impertinent in many countries. There is a certain pace and protocol to follow to do it right.

Because every country is different and globalization is changing traditional patterns, there is an increasing need to learn how to do it right and be sensitive to custom rather than exporting personal interpretations of what may be acceptable.

Successful executives today understand and embrace the opportunity to interact with their prospective partners in a social environment. They enjoy the moment while maintaining their professionalism and keeping the business purpose of the social event well within sight. They know that to "pass the test" their behavior has to be genuine, because phony stances are spotted quickly. They also know that multimillion-dollar deals often depend on simple things like eating or declining to eat a local delicacy.

Learning to deal with others is an art, not a science, and the more you practice, the better you become at it. To acquire and sharpen this skill abroad, think of it as a tennis match: They throw the ball at you, and you respond. You continue to play the game with the intent of learning your opponent's strategy and moves, which allows you to become a better opponent.

21st Century Smarts

If you live in an industrialized country, you are likely to be ahead of others in terms of education, economic means, and political stability. Granted, the tragic wave of terrorism and the global financial crisis of the 2000s, coupled with increased world political unrest in the 2010s, have shaken your sense of safety and the level of acceptance of your nation by the rest of the world. It's not inconceivable that you may have gone down a notch in your position within Maslow's pyramid of needs.

But your upbringing and ideals help you move forward in pursuing personal, professional, and entrepreneurial success. Over time, you have learned your way around and have learned to make use of the orderly systems your nation has in place. You also know that the more people you know socially, in your neighborhood or at work, the better off you are in achieving your goals. Interaction with others provides you with information that you then use to make decisions.

A good part of this information relates to people: their personalities, human traits, intentions, values, and beliefs. Through interaction with others you build a database of human behavior that helps you detect if people are being honest or deceptive. Thanks to this database stored subconsciously in your brain, you reach a point at which, just by hearing people talk and how they express themselves, you can decide on the spot if you like or dislike a particular individual.

This subconscious analysis is your gut feel. It helps you sort through the diverse kinds of people around you and separate friends from foes. In other words, thanks to a high level of interaction with others, you accumulate the valuable information you need to make experience-based decisions.

You can do the same with total strangers in or from foreign countries.

> The more interaction you have with individuals of any nationality and ethnic background, the larger your database of global human behavior.
>
> This global database will lead you to develop the same instinct or gut feel you exercise now, without even thinking about it. Although you have the capability of developing that instinct, chances are your education and business practices are still stuck in the 20th century.
>
> Your brain is busy collecting signals the old-fashioned way, with pre-conceived ideas that lead to apprehension instead of curiosity, to anxiety instead of excitement, to isolation instead of integration.

To develop a global instinct, all you need to do is repeat the learning process you used when growing up—only this time focus on the world that is inhabited by seven billion people you have yet to meet. It's like learning to walk again, and you know you can do it.

You can develop the knowledge and skills that will allow you to trust your gut in foreign countries. Not because you are arrogant and believe you can read people abroad just as easily as you do it at home, but because you recognize that you don't know them yet, and you've made the conscious and professional decision to adopt a new mindset and learn new skills to foster your global instinct.

It's no secret that everything looks complicated until we understand how it works. Take the case of smartphones and social media: They are still horribly complicated to older parents and grandparents who didn't grow up surrounded by intelligent machines. But these devices are not at all complicated to children, teenagers, and young professionals who have embraced them enthusiastically; they can learn to use them in no time.

This is not because the younger generation is smarter, or even more inherently in tune with how machines work. Today's grandparents have had computers in the home for 30 years, and smartphones are not drastically different in terms of operation than those computers. It's simply that smartphones function differently. Gone is the mouse and keyboard, replaced by touch screens and Swype keyboards.

Not unlike learning a language, young persons are uninhibited about trying new things. They accept the fact that they don't know how to make the phone do what they want and set out to quickly learn the processes necessary to make the phone function. They are unimpeded by thoughts of "this should work" (*why doesn't it?!*) or "this used to be like this" (*why did they change it?!*).

Older people accustomed to particular processes balk at the idea that those processes are constantly redesigned. This makes it difficult to learn how smartphones work, because previous experiences get in the way of learning new processes.

The same applies to the world around us. It's not more complicated or dangerous than it's always been. Our grandparents also went through a life they thought was crazy and dangerous: automobiles, air travel, space travel, fax machines, and wireless phones. They also lived through difficult and dangerous periods in history: wars, violence, plagues, human rights violations, insurgencies, and more. Many of our ancestors worried that the industrial and technological revolutions were a clear sign that the world was coming to an end.

We have seen it all before, so why are we whining?

We whine because we have not yet consciously embraced globalization and all the opportunities it brings to our future success.

Is Emotional Intelligence Teachable?

Yes, it is. But companies need to make a 180-degree mental turn to make this possible.

I never worry about action, but only inaction.

— Winston Churchill*

Let's go back to the results of the GE Global Innovation Barometer discussed in the previous section. In that study, more than 70 percent of executives indicated a strong desire to collaborate with foreign partners to access new technology and new markets and improve products and services.

* Winston Churchill Quotes. BrainyQuote.com, Xplore Inc, 2018. https://www.brainyquote.com/quotes/winston_churchill_156874, accessed February 10, 2018.

The same study showed, however, that the primary barrier for achieving meaningful and productive collaboration was lack of trust. Many of these relationships started with optimism and high expectations. What caused them to fail?

The majority of the reasons listed on page 49 can be addressed more successfully if companies care enough to incorporate multi-ethnic and multicultural human interaction into their corporate strategies and professional development programs.

Stubbornly, some companies continue to focus on the bottom-line business approach to the exclusion of the human impact on business transactions.

Thus, they fail to realize the need to train managers and employees throughout the organization how to manage and relate to people from a wide range of cultural backgrounds.

Lack of commitment to the so-called "soft" side of business is still wasting valuable time, costing money and keeping companies from being truly competitive.

Typically, when faced with an extra cost, some companies opt for a shortcut and outsource the problem to others. Rather than training their employees and developing a true global culture, they hire local managers who don't understand their employer's culture; they use a Band-Aid to create the illusion of a long-term solution.

The real long-term solution is to hire abroad while also educating Western professionals and managers on how to operate in foreign markets. Whereas foreign nationals continue to benefit from access to Western know-how, Western professionals are losing their competitive edge due to lack of training about global skills.

Two decades into the future, companies will regret having lost their ability to lead the world and will wonder what happened.

Collaboration between employees of different companies fails because, even if the top echelons of partnering companies understand the benefits of collaboration, those charged with execution have not been involved in the decision-making process.

They lack first-hand information, have never met their counterparts, and most likely are concerned about losing their job or have misgivings about the outcome—all factors that allow mistrust to set in. Because mistrust feeds on itself, the situation deteriorates rapidly, and nobody has the responsibility, time, knowledge, or experience to fix the problem.

In typical fashion, we have coined a new term—*emotional intelligence*[13] (EI)—to refer to (but not necessarily teach) the skill set we wish our professionals would have. EI refers to the ability to combine the soft, emotional side of the business equation with the ability to make and exercise hard business decisions.

Unfortunately, our ability to deal with emotions in individualistic societies has been suppressed by the predominance of numbers-driven decision making and contract-driven business relations to the exclusion of emotions. It's generally accepted that the emotional side of individuals has no place in the work environment; only the analytical side is considered important to success.

But it turns out that less industrialized cultures still operate based on emotions as well as analytical input, and this difference is at the heart of the Western confusion regarding how to deal with, understand, and make meaningful connections with the rest of the world.

Also in typical fashion, the training and development of this skill is not considered to be a management problem or an educational responsibility. We don't see corporations actively engaged in developing these skills, and schools and colleges are not teaching emotional intelligence either.

The expectation seems to be that younger leaders will conveniently find ways to develop those skills on their own. Or, better yet, that future generations will be born with them, and perhaps they will if we succeed in changing the way we think and start teaching our children the importance of becoming an integral part of our global society.

In the meantime, our next discussion, *Part III – Knowledge*, fills the vacuum left by traditional education by proposing a novel concept and an empirical model that I have developed and tested with excellent results over years of international business activities.

Most revealing in this novel approach is the parallelism that exists between this empirical model and modern concepts discovered in the realms of applied mathematics, which have been found to have a wide range of applications from science and medicine, to movies, graphic design, telecommunications, and a number of other fields.

The premise of *Part III* is that these mathematical concepts also apply to human behavior. Let's open the door and step into a new world.

PART III
KNOWLEDGE

Knowledge: The Circumstance or Condition of Apprehending Truth or Fact through Reasoning; the Body of Truth, Information, and Principles Acquired by Humankind

---

* Merriam-Webster Dictionary

Chapter Five

In Search of the Human Fractal

*The most incomprehensible thing about the world
is that it is comprehensible.*

— Albert Einstein[*]

Economists today believe that the traditional clustering of countries into continents and the delivery of general information on Africa, Asia, Australia, Europe, the Middle East, and the Americas are no longer enough to describe the economic evolution of the world. International organizations that monitor economic development are currently using subsets of clusters to help take into account more subtle differences among countries within a continent.

Statistics about Africa, for example, are broken down into Eastern, Middle, Northern, Southern, and Western Africa. Likewise, Asia is divided into subregions: Central Asia (from Russia to Tajikistan), South Asia (from Afghanistan to India), and East and Southeast Asia (from China to Papua New Guinea).[1]

Close but No Cigar

Such sub-classification is still insufficient. Everyone knows or can imagine that India is very different from Afghanistan in almost everything: culture,

---

[*] http://www.gurteen.com/gurteen/gurteen.nsf/id/X00025E0A/

technology, business opportunities, and type of government, to name a few factors. Yet institutionalized research still groups them together under one label—"Central Asia"—leaving decision makers with more questions than answers when they turn to macroeconomic data to prioritize and define their growth strategies.

Aware of these shortcomings, international organizations (e.g., the World Bank, the World Economic Forum, the International Monetary Fund, and the CIA) attempt to add clarity by dividing the world according to multiple factors: market capitalization, market liquidity, gross domestic product, institutional structure (political, legal, financial, and academic), physical infrastructure, and political risk.

Unfortunately, classifications used by different institutions are not standardized and cannot be readily compared with one another. Classification criteria are also continuously revised and modified. In the past, for instance, the World Bank published data based on gross national product (GNP); today, this term is referred to as gross national income (GNI) per capita,[2] and countries are grouped by:

- low income ($1,035 or less per year)
- lower middle income ($1,036–$4,085)
- upper middle income ($4,086–$12,615)
- high income ($12,616 or more)

This is one of a large number of criteria used to shed some light on what a given country represents in terms of investment, business opportunities, and risks. Countries aspire to be ranked higher in economic terms to attract and maintain investors' confidence. Thus, sensitivities about classifications run high, and there are those who complain bitterly if they don't agree with another's point of view. I once wrote something less than charming about a particular African country, and my office immediately got calls accusing me of slowing down the progress of the entire continent.

Compounding the problem is the fact that economic change occurs very rapidly nowadays, and it's difficult to keep track of and forecast accurately based on a country's level of development. The World Bank adds this disclaimer in a footnote: "Income classifications are set each year on July 1. These official analytical classifications are fixed during the World Bank's fiscal year (ending on June 30), thus countries remain in the categories in which they are classified irrespective of any revisions to their per capita income data."[2]

Back in the first decade of the 2000s, the general consensus was that the most attractive emerging countries were Brazil, Russia, India, and China, but at the start of the second decade of the century, the consensus of leading countries was less clear. Lists of "top emerging markets" proliferated and included countries such as Mexico, Indonesia, Turkey, and Colombia, as well as South Africa, South Korea, and the Philippines.

Opinions about which countries represent the best opportunities vary widely and change frequently. Those stating that emerging markets are losing their luster tend to reflect a reaction to current events and often lack convincing explanations to back such statements.

You get the picture: Information about emerging markets is far from user-friendly. It's voluminous, highly fragmented, and confusing.

Geography and macroeconomic analyses don't help your family understand foreign neighbors or how to make friends and trust parents and children when your family travels to foreign countries.

Worse yet, information is not knowledge, and it doesn't tell you what you most need to know: How to attract loyal customers, trustworthy partners, reliable vendors and suppliers, and collaborative government officials; or how to deal with breaks in local infrastructure, sociopolitical unrest, and other operational risks.

Traditional learning doesn't help your family become integrated into the local community and live an anxiety-free life abroad. The same goes for foreign citizens living in your neighborhood. They may attend your church, and their children may participate in the same sports events that your kids attend, but more often than not, they are not invited to social gatherings in private homes.

The key to understanding the world is to shift from focusing on generalized, impersonal data to learning how humans affect our lives, from people in urban communities to those living in remote areas in every corner of the planet.

The Elephant in the Room

What if you could identify a set of human behavioral characteristics that is repeatable and predictable and unifies the seven billion individuals on the planet, regardless of background and location? And what if you could create a mechanism or a tool that reduces the complexity of understanding the people of the world to a manageable number of rules?

You've probably heard the expression, "The elephant in the room," and the joke, "How do you eat an elephant? One bit at a time." The need to understand and relate to other people is similar. Nobody wants to talk about this.

Corporations still regard the human factor in business as "soft," and individuals tend to avoid the subject because it is perceived as too hard to grasp.

Few realize that it can be done, one step at a time.

The key resides in having a process that helps companies and individuals tackle the seemingly impossible task of comprehending what we have been raised to believe is incomprehensible. We need a blueprint that shows us how to go about this and helps accelerate the process. This chapter provides such a blueprint.

After years of observation, I have developed a methodology to guide the process of analyzing individual behavior to build trust and rapport across cultures. I have tested and fine-tuned this methodology over years of travel and close, meaningful interaction with foreign nationals from more than forty countries.

In this chapter I invite you to embark on a journey that will show you how to break the world down into manageable pieces of information. You will discover sets of human characteristics that hold the key to connecting with all kinds of individuals around the globe. You will be able to more easily identify those you want to befriend and do business with, as well as those you may want to avoid, just as you do almost subconsciously at home on a daily basis.

This fascinating approach will allow you to dissect human behavior, going from large to increasingly smaller scales so you can then go back to dealing with the global market armed with new personal and business smarts.

In the process, you will get rid of obsolete thinking and adopt a new, fresh mindset that lets you see the world from a totally different perspective—one that adds clarity to the staggering and absurd amount of static or white noise that interferes with human communications and makes it difficult to separate relevant from irrelevant information.

On this journey, you will also be exposed to the parallelism that exists between this methodology and the concept of self-similarity advanced by a modern applied mathematical theory. This theory has revolutionized the way scientists, researchers, movie moguls, artists, and medical doctors, among many others, are seeing and interpreting the world around them. Self-similarity refers to the property of splitting complex structures into pieces—called *fractals*—that are approximate copies of the whole shape, allowing us to advance the understanding of nature to levels never before anticipated.

Let's start by taking a look at what others are doing to simplify and better understand the complexities of the world.

Fractals Defined

An online search for the definition of fractals comes back with nearly eight million answers, including:

/'fraktəl/:a fractal is a rough geometric structure or body that can be split into pieces that are approximate copies of the whole shape, a property called self-similarity.

/'fraktəl/:a curve or geometric figure, each part of which has the same statistical character as the whole. Fractals are useful in modeling structures (such as eroded coastlines or snowflakes) in which similar patterns recur at progressively smaller scales, and in describing partly random or chaotic phenomena such as crystal growth, fluid turbulence, and galaxy formation.

A basic set of rules (fractals) that repeat multiple times (self-similarity) to form a complex body or structure is a phenomenon found to occur widely in nature, not only on our planet but also in the formation of galaxies.

The fractal geometry theory was first proposed by Benoit B. Mandelbrot in his 1982 book *The Fractal Geometry of Nature,*[3] and it has mesmerized mathematicians and scientists ever since because of its capacity to explain the complexities seen in nature.

Fractals are around you all the time. Take a close look at the picture of a cactus that, oddly enough, I took while visiting the National Orchid Garden in Singapore (Figure 5.1).

At first glance the cactus looks like a very complex geometry. Look closer and you will see that the cactus is actually composed of one single unit—the branch fractal—that repeats itself over and over to form the complex cactus system you see in the picture. At the fractal level, the system is incredibly simple.

Figure 5.1   Fractals in nature. (*Source:* © Z. Kraljevic.)

Our mind is trained to focus on the complexity of the
system rather than on the simplicity that resulted
in the complex system.

I encourage you to do a Google Images search for "fractals in nature." It will come back with a wide range of pictures of fractals that occur in forests, oceans, mountains, the universe, and the lightning that fills the sky during thunderstorms. Use them to train your eye and your mind to "see" the world á la Mandelbrot—that is, through endless single units with self-similarity.

In the next section we examine how researchers and business people in a variety of industries have opened their minds to "see" what has been there all along, but that they have never seen before. We'll explore how this new approach is helping them make sense of complex systems in nature that until now nobody could understand.

By the end of the chapter, you will see how this approach applies to our quest to advance and accelerate our understanding of human behavior, and how we can retrain our brains to see the world from a different perspective, adding clarity to an otherwise chaotic and complex environment.

Learning from the Trees

On August 24, 2011, PBS aired a *NOVA* documentary[4] entitled *Hunting the Hidden Dimension.* Narrated by Neil Ross, the program begins with this impactful statement:

"You can find it in the rain forest, on the frontiers of medical research, in the movies, and it's all over the world of wireless communications. One of nature's biggest design secrets has finally been revealed . . .

"You may not know it, but fractals, like the air you breathe, are all around you. Their irregular, repeating shapes are found in cloud formations and tree limbs, in stalks of broccoli and craggy mountain ranges, even in the rhythm of the human heart . . .

"For centuries, fractal-like irregular shapes were considered beyond the boundaries of mathematical understanding. Now, mathematicians have finally begun mapping this uncharted territory.

"Their remarkable findings are deepening our understanding of nature and stimulating a new wave of scientific, medical, and artistic innovation stretching from the ecology of the rain forest to fashion design."

The *NOVA* program explains the mathematical concepts used by Benoit Mandelbrot until he died on October 14, 2010. If you haven't seen it yet, I can guarantee that watching this video will forever change the way you see the world.

Without going into the world of applied mathematics and chaos theory, let's concentrate on one of the many practical applications described in a *NOVA* interview with Brian Enquist, a professor of ecology and evolutionary biology at the University of Arizona.

Enquist and his team are studying fractals found in trees as a potential way to model the behavior of rainforests around the world. With the high levels of carbon dioxide being released into the atmosphere, rainforests play an important role in regulating the Earth's climate. Scientists are using fractal geometry to infer the behavior of complex forest systems on Earth from the behavior of a single tree.

If you look carefully at a tree, you will see that the pattern of branches is very similar throughout the tree, with the younger and smaller branches at the top being an almost exact replica of the older and larger branches at the bottom. Look, for example, at the pictures of Japanese Cherry trees taken while walking along the Potomac River in Washington D.C., USA (Figure 5.2 on next page).

The picture on the left (Figure 5.2A) is a full-grown cherry tree with a complex system of branches, leaves, and flowers. The picture on the right (Figure 5.2B) is a detail of a growing branch in the same kind of tree.

The detail shows how each branch is composed of a small "unit" branch, a fractal that repeats and multiplies along each branch with self-similarity; a trunk shooting off into branches that, in turn, have smaller branches shooting off into even smaller branches. Eventually this repetition will generate the complex system pictured in Figure 5.2A.

The line of fully grown cherry trees in Figure 5.2A also helps illustrate the similarity that exists amongst a group of trees. They all look alike because self-similarity not only occurs in a single tree but also in groups of trees, implying that from the study of a single tree one can draw conclusions about an entire forest.

In another *NOVA* interview, James Brown, an ecologist at the University of New Mexico, explains it this way:

"The beautiful thing is that the distribution of sizes of individual trees in the forest appears to exactly match the distribution of the size of individual branches within a single tree.

"This allows ecologists to extrapolate, for example, how much carbon dioxide can be absorbed by a forest anywhere in the world based on what they know about a single tree." It's further explained that:

"Even though the forest may seem random and chaotic, the team believes it actually has a structure, one that amazingly, is almost identical to the tree they are studying." In other words, "the relative number of big and small trees matches the relative number of big and small branches . . .

". . . For generations, scientists believed that the wilderness of nature could not be defined by mathematics. But fractal geometry is leading to a whole new understanding, revealing an underlying order governed by simple mathematical rules."   — James Brown

(A) COMPLEXITY OF A CHERRY TREE

(B) COUNTLESS REPITITION OF A BRANCH FRACTAL

Figure 5.2   Complex system as a result of self-similarity of a tree fractal. (*Source:* © Z. Kraljevic.)

The premise of this book is that the mathematical approach that helps explain the complexities observed in nature, including the physical aspects of the human body, also applies to emotions and human interaction. In other words:

> Even though there are no two groups of people on Earth that are the same, they are similar enough that they can be compared and in most situations be treated as the same.

Let's explore how Mandelbrot came up with a way to explain a seemingly complex environment in simple terms, just like we are trying to explain the complexity of the human population on Earth in simple terms.

It's About How You Measure It

In 1967 Benoit Mandelbrot published a paper entitled, *How long is the coast of Britain? Statistical self-similarity and fractional dimension.*[5] In his paper, Mandelbrot examined the "coastline paradox": the fact that the length of the coastal line depends on the scale of measurement.

A Wikipedia illustration of the paradox (Figure 5.3) shows that the longer the measuring device, the shorter the length of the coastal line becomes, and the shorter the measuring device, the longer the coastal line becomes.

In other words, measuring the coastal line with a yardstick will yield a smaller and less accurate measure of the coastal line than measuring it with a one-foot

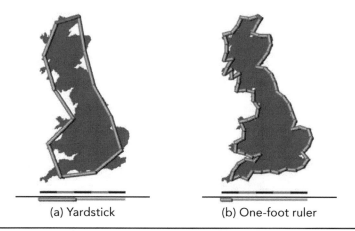

(a) Yardstick   (b) One-foot ruler

Figure 5.3 Measuring the rough line of England. (a) Unit = 200 km, length = 2400 km (approx.); (b) Unit = 50 km, length 3400 km (approx.) (*Source*: www.en.wikipedia.org.)

ruler. But this leads to a paradox. Why stop at a foot: Why not measure in inches? Why not millimeters? Eventually the coastline turns out to be infinitely long, and that measurement is clearly absurd.

So if measuring the coastline of Britain with a stick is absurd, how can we describe the complexity of the coastline in a more meaningful way? Why is it important that we find a better way to describe it at all? It's important because understanding the nature and complexity of any coastline allows scientists to model soil erosion, just as understanding the complexity of a forest allows scientists to model the impact of trees on the formation of carbon dioxide in the atmosphere.

For movie fans, having the proper way to model the complexity of mountains and valleys allows graphic designers at Lucasfilm, for example, to produce computer-generated landscapes for movies like *Star Wars*.

Mandelbrot's ability to see the world differently helped him realize that the complexity of nature's roughness is actually the sum of simple basic units that repeat themselves multiple times to form a complex system. His empirical observations illustrated the fact that the traditional way of "measuring" anything with a long yardstick is meaningless.

Traditional geometry is not a good representation of nature and leads to inaccurate conclusions because the smooth geometric shapes we learned in school—triangles, squares, and circles—are inadequate to represent the complex "roughness" of naturally occurring systems on Earth, from mountain ranges, coastlines, and river basins to blood vessels and lung systems and the formation of clouds and the clustering of galaxies.

To gain a more practical understanding of complex systems, Mandelbrot looked beyond simple metrics to identify better ways of describing the world. Today, you can read about Mandelbrot's unconventional but realistic views of the world in an IBM report on fractal geometry. An excerpt reads like this:

"Geometry: Its principles are taught to young students across the world . . . This classical, or Euclidean, geometry is perfectly suited for the world that humans have created. But if one considers the structures that are present in nature, those which are beyond the realm of smooth human construction, many of these rules disappear.

"Clouds are not perfect spheres, mountains are not symmetrical cones, and lightning does not travel in straight lines. Nature is rough, and until very recently this roughness was impossible to measure. The discovery of fractal geometry has made it possible to mathematically explore the kinds of rough irregularities that exist in nature."[6]

Just as Mandelbrot rejected traditional geometry as a useful but oversimplified way to represent the "roughness" of natural systems, I reject the notion that the world's population can be understood through useful but oversimplified economic indexes and geographic boundaries.

My hypothesis is that humans, not being man-made, develop according to rules of nature. It's now well accepted that fractals are found throughout the human body: in the blood vessel system, the structure of the lungs, and the rhythm of the heartbeat. This is not surprising if we consider that we are a product of nature. It's my contention that Mandelbrot's fractals can also be found in human behavior.

These fractals exist among groups of people just as they occur in groups of trees in a forest. Once we look for fractals in human behavior, we can use them to better understand the "roughness" of human behavior and model its complexity.

If you look at the surface, you see complexity . . . but do not look at what you see but at what it took to produce what you see.

— Benoit Mandelbrot*

Companies operating in emerging markets already know that they can't address local markets with a yardstick mentality that fits all sizes. As local consumers grow more sophisticated and demand locally relevant products, executives are scratching their heads about how to understand and address the needs and interests of specific groups of consumers, almost to the individual level. Globalization has made it necessary to find new ways to understand and better model the complexities of human nature and human behavior.

> The business equivalent of Mandelbrot's approach is that the complexity of the human race can be better understood and managed by identifying human fractals that repeat themselves over and over again, generating the complex global population that our brain is used to seeing.

Fractals in Human Nature

Although I am not a mathematician and am not about to propose a mathematical theory around a "human fractal," I do believe one could be made and argued brilliantly. What I do have is a doctorate degree in engineering and extensive business experience in international markets, and I am trained and naturally inclined to put new knowledge to work fast. For that reason, I'm using this parallelism with Mandelbrot's fractal geometry to suggest that by considering

---

* *Rational Thinking Styles and Natural Intelligence,* Phyllis Chiason, ed., 2002.

this new paradigm, human interaction—both personal and business—becomes much clearer and more manageable.

Once we understand how to make good use of our self-similarities as individuals, we can consistently accomplish success working with and through diverse groups of people.

For the skeptical reader, if humans are part of nature, why would nature create humans differently from the way it creates mountains, rivers, and trees? And why would nature use fractals to build the complexity of the human body but skip the brain, emotions, and personalities?

Like a tree that starts from a seed and grows from small to larger branches until it reaches maturity, so do human beings start from a seed and grow to become a replica of their original "branch." All trees are born the same way, with similar characteristics, which include growing in the direction of light used for nutrition and survival. But trees' ultimate health and growth depend on their surroundings. Their life cycle is affected by natural events (such as storms and fire) as well as by their interaction with other trees, plants, and animals. A tree that has limited access to light may not develop to its fullest, and one that is infested by plague may not survive long.

Similarly, humans' life cycles are dictated by their interaction with society, other species, and the forces of nature. We are all born the same way and programmed to search for food and shelter to survive. Our ultimate health and growth depend on our surroundings. While the environment shapes the way we handle emotions and develop our personalities, we are all born into groups with the same toolbox of emotional capabilities, talents, and personality types.

On the surface, we are very complex individuals, but if, as Mandelbrot proposes, we look not at what we see on the surface but to what originally took place to create that complex human personality in front of us, we can actually see the human fractal at the core of a person. That is, we can identify individuals for what they are, regardless of the complexities added by circumstances and the environment in which they were raised and educated.

It is not uncommon that we hear people say that the eyes are the windows to the soul or that they can reach into the hearts of people. Intuitively we believe that there is something in each human being that helps us uncover the real person behind the façade. That something is a human fractal. We need to bring to our consciousness what we intuitively already know.

We then need to systematize it in a way that helps us relate to the myriad strangers around us so we can achieve personal satisfaction and business success. Just as scientists focus on understanding a single tree to extrapolate and understand the complexity of a forest, we can extrapolate to better understand the complexity of the world population by focusing on individuals and identifying a set of personality and character traits (human fractals) that repeats itself among people.

Practical Applications

Try this exercise to get your mind started in this direction:

Imagine you are cooking something special that requires a variety of fruits, all within the citrus family: lemons, limes, oranges, grapefruits, and tangerines. They all look different from the outside: Some are yellow, some are green, and some are orange, and they come in different sizes. Quick! Thirty seconds on the clock! How many similarities can you identify among the fruits?

These are the similarities that I observe when cutting them in half around the circumference:

1. All have a soft, porous skin
2. All have seeds
3. All are juicy
4. All show ten separate sections
5. All have an outer layer or rind

There you go: five similarities among fruits of different size and color. The next time you come across an unfamiliar fruit, after you look inside and discover that it has these same characteristics, you can safely say that it belongs to the citrus family, regardless of how different it may look on the outside.

The same exercise applies to people. Just as you can do with citrus fruits, instead of classifying people based on external image, you will start classifying people by their inner characteristics. For example:

1. Honesty	6. Responsibility
2. Integrity	7. Control
3. Generosity	8. Friendliness
4. Insecurity	9. Aloofness
5. Envy	10. Courage

This set of characteristics is a human fractal that repeats with self-similarity around the world. If we can find honest and courageous people at home, we can also find them abroad. This way of classifying people, regardless of where they live or how they look, is a powerful tool for identifying people with whom you may want to establish a relationship. It also helps you steer away from those who don't satisfy your values and standards and can bring you more trouble than benefits.

Thanks to our similarities we can:

- Communicate effectively
- Close win–win deals

- Select trustworthy partners
- Select reliable suppliers
- Preserve strategic alliances
- Understand and motivate a multi-ethnic global workforce

Make a list of the personality traits you see in those you like and love, and then set out to find them among people you barely know. You will find them in people working in every company and in every city you happen to live and work in. You already know how to handle them, and I can guarantee that it's no different when you travel and work overseas.

Regardless of the degree of development and industrialization of a country, people are just people, just like trees are trees.

From the Passing of Time to the Essence of Things

My methodology for understanding and connecting with people from any culture is based on the ability to identify fractals and self-similarities occurring in humans. This skill can be learned and developed. All it takes is direct observation and practice.

The following story provides ideas for you to try anywhere you happen to be:

Every day of the week, rain or shine, hot or cold, the young girl rode a bus to school. It was not a school bus. In her time, in her country, the concept of school buses didn't exist, and owning a car was still a novelty even for families of means. In a city with several million, public buses were always overcrowded with people of diverse age and social background going to school or work. The city was spread out, making the ride to school long and boring. But this was never a problem for a young girl with a curious and inquisitive mind, fond of inventing games inside her head to keep her occupied.

Because of her small size, one of her favorite mind games was to observe the hands of those sitting or standing near her on the bus. At first, the challenge was to imagine something about people just from watching their hands—not faces, or clothing or gender, just their hands. It didn't matter if her guesses were right or wrong. It was just a game to pass time. The more hands she observed, the more she learned to differentiate features, and soon she was classifying hands under simple labels: artistic hands, working hands, romantic hands, aggressive hands, submissive hands.

To make the game more entertaining, she decided to form an opinion of perfect strangers based first on their hands and then try to match the hands to facial features and expressions. Did artistic hands go together with an artistic face? Did an aggressive looking person also have "aggressive" hands? With time, her game expanded to guessing professions and emotions: Could she infer just by analyzing hands if someone was a secretary, a dentist, or an accountant? Could she infer if they were happy or unhappy?

She knew that her conclusions were totally subjective, because she couldn't possibly confirm her observations by going around asking people about their professions or emotions. But that was not the point of the game. The point was to make the long trip to school seem shorter by keeping herself mentally entertained.

What the young girl didn't know at the time was that her brain was accumulating a large database of valuable information about external human characteristics.

As she grew older, the game of observing people became second nature, and the mental database of human characteristics continued to grow, and her ability to confirm her predictions through trial and error evolved. The ability to "read" people eventually became a professional attribute.

From a young age, I had always been fascinated by people. What started as a game to pass idle time on a bus became a habit deeply ingrained in my daily routine, an unconscious exercise that kicked in every time I met new co-workers, new clients, or strangers living in urban and rural areas of the world.

As my practical human-behavior database increased, I continued to fine tune my ability to read people. My natural curiosity didn't diminish with age and has been a definitive factor in steering and developing a successful career in international business.

Curiosity and well-trained observation skills also helped expand the scope of my research from analyzing people to analyzing situations at home and in foreign countries. When working with Fortune 500 companies, for example, I became skilled at quickly identifying internal inefficiencies across functions based on how people behaved and interacted.

Breaks and redundancies in communication and workflows within divisions or work teams would jump out at me almost instantly. When I started doing business in foreign countries, I was able to expand and develop patterns of human characteristics and people-driven operational efficiencies (or lack thereof) across cultures.

The methodology I initially developed consisted of focusing on three levels of human expression:

1. **Physical expressions.** Eye stare (warm or calculating), voice inflexion (passionate or detached), hand gestures (calm or nervous), mouth setting

(pleasant or sour), and touch (body language open and confident or guarded and suspicious). As an aside, there are 43 facial muscles that can combine to produce 10,000 expressions. Fortunately, you just need to study a few to get excellent results. Typical clues: a smile without eye wrinkles is not a smile, a sagging mouth indicates deception, a hand going to the back of the neck or scratching skin may expose manipulation, a fist indicates anger, a smirk indicates disgust, and a twitching mouth indicates contempt or impatience.

2. **Basic attitudes (and opposites).** Straightforward (dishonest), trustworthy (corrupt), capable (inept), confident (insecure), frank (evasive), witty (dull), anxious (comfortable), sharp (slow), analytical (illogical), courageous (cowardly), creative (unimaginative), compassionate (unfeeling), shrewd (naïve), selfless (selfish), good-natured (vicious), and witty (boring).

3. **Character attributes.** Wisdom, intelligence, veracity, knowledge, integrity, aggressiveness, compassion, cruelty, and loyalty.

Traveling outside major cities in emerging markets created opportunities to interact with a wide range of local citizens in diverse social and work settings. Culture, economic conditions, and geographic location notwithstanding, what has consistently called my attention is not how different people seem to be but how similar they actually are.

The important thing to remember is that it doesn't take a lifetime to learn how to "read" people. The process outlined here gives you a jump-start and gets results in just a few weeks.

The range of different situations in which I have had the opportunity to verify my hypothesis on self-similarity is wide. As mentioned earlier in the book, these are the kind of situations I have experienced in the course of my business travel:

- Leading meetings in the middle of a guerrilla path in Central America while conducting business with more than fifty farmers in remote rural areas.
- Conducting negotiations with senior board members in sophisticated business environments in progressive emerging countries.
- Leaving a country in a hurry on corporate orders because of credible threats of possible kidnapping of American citizens.
- Receiving personal threats from strong competitors when successfully launching a new international venture.
- Discouraging robbery attempts on busy streets in foreign countries.
- Handling threatening mob situations in rural areas in Central Asia.

On each one of these occasions, I have made use of my understanding of human nature and also gathered valuable information, not in the way a scientist might do it but through the eyes and savvy of a pragmatic business traveler.

This extensive research has corroborated my premise that no matter where we are, we can find the right people to bring into our personal and business circles, as long as we have the open mindset that transcends ethnicity, language, religion, political preferences, social strata, economic environment, customs, personal preferences, and other factors that affect human behavior in social or business settings.

You may have this skill right now but are not using or developing it. Sharpening this skill will enhance your ability to communicate effectively, choose partners wisely, understand the unspoken needs of both sides across a negotiation table, develop meaningful strategies and value propositions, and drive complex new businesses to a successful conclusion.

While systematically developing this skill, keep in mind what I call the "3ARE":

- **Acquired**—You can acquire and start developing this skill right now.
- **Accessible**—The conduit you need to collect new information is already at hand, ready to be used (see next section).
- **Applicable**—You can apply this skill to your benefit with everyone.
- **Repeatable**—You can make effective use of this skill anytime, anywhere.
- **Expandable**—You can build a database of actionable knowledge as large as you wish.

Coming to Our Senses—Literally

As mentioned, the conduit you need to collect new information—and develop the skills that allow you to connect with diverse groups of people—is already at hand and ready to be used. This conduit is your nervous system.

I am not talking about the traditional way we think about the nervous system, but rather about new scientific discoveries that are helping explain how the human brain collects and interprets information. We know the nervous system is composed of nerve cells, called *neurons,* which are present in our body in staggering numbers; there are more than 100 billion neurons in each person's brain.

Part of our nervous system is referred to as *voluntary,* in the sense that is activated with our knowledge—for example, when we get up and walk or move our arms to reach for a cup of coffee. Another part of the nervous system is called *involuntary* because it acts without our participation; it controls activities such as breathing, heart rhythm, and metabolism.[7]

The purpose of the nervous system is to help you interact with the outside world and make the right choices. It collects information that comes through your senses and through the spinal cord—eyes, ears, nose, mouth, skin, joints, and muscles. It processes this information and sends electrical signals to the brain. The brain uses this information to send instructions that help you react, think, remember, and make decisions based on the type of information and the way it is processed.

Because your brain reacts based on the information it receives, the more practical and diverse data you can collect and feed to your nervous system, the more information your brain has available to help you make better choices and better decisions.

Here is a simple example of how the brain works based on the information we choose to feed it.

When my son was fifteen years old, he and I teamed up to help him learn how to drive a car. We started in deserted areas with no traffic or pedestrians, and as his confidence grew, we ventured into more populated areas. Eventually, he was comfortable driving on busy streets.

That's when I started to entice him to think outside the mechanics of driving and traffic regulations. As he drove, I would ask "What could happen right now that requires you to make a quick decision?"

Some of the options we came up with were: (1) a kid could suddenly run from behind a parked car and cross our path; (2) a car could suddenly turn into the lane we were using; (3) a person exiting a public bus could cross in front of the bus, unseen by oncoming traffic, and cross our lane; and (4) the car in front of us could face a similar experience and brake unexpectedly.

He learned then to expect the unexpected, and to read "car body language," focusing on the slight change of direction of other cars' tires to anticipate where the driver was going before it became obvious. He learned to search for shadows under the front wheels of a bus at a bus stop to detect if children or adults were crossing in front of the bus and might suddenly appear in front of his car.

Today, he often comments on how well this training has helped him anticipate maneuvers and make the right decision in a split second.

This process is something that many of us have to learn through real life experiences, but by bringing up different scenarios for him to consider, my son was able to simulate experiences and learn from them. It took a little longer than just learning the basics, but he was more effective in anticipating challenges, and he used these pre-defined scenarios to react more rapidly to unexpected situations.

Feeding our brains with a diverse range of information is like putting information into your computer or doing an

Internet search. The information will be there when you need it, almost instantly.

Better yet, if you have already visualized a possible outcome, then when that situation presents itself, your brain already knows the solution, and you can make the right decision faster.

Retraining the way our nervous system collects and processes information is a simple and fun exercise that can generate immediate results. All you need to do is "sense" the world in a different way.

Research suggests that what our senses register is closely linked to our memories. If we grew up with certain preconceived ideas, either our own or those instilled by society, we are likely to react to external stimuli in the fashion in which we have been "trained" to react. But instead of remaining stuck with old ideas, we can choose to build a new set of information that better reflects the realities of the world today.

In his paper entitled *Decision Theory: What "Should" the Nervous System Do?*[8] Konrad Körding, Associate Professor in Physical Medicine and Rehabilitation Physiology at Northwestern University, wrote:

The nervous system constantly integrates information over time, and a range of new studies analyzed how it does so.[9] In many such experiments, one of two stimuli is given, for example either a stimulus that moves to the right or a stimulus that moves to the left.

If the stimulus is sufficiently noisy, the nervous system needs to integrate information over an extended period of time to make a good decision. Neurons were found that exhibit activities that correlate with the predicted process of optimal information integration over time. The nervous system takes into account probabilistic knowledge of potential rewards when integrating evidence for decision making.[10] The resulting models are particularly useful because they have a normative component (optimal integration of evidence) while having a straightforward descriptive component (neurons can integrate inputs over time).

Another intriguing set of studies recently conducted first by neurologists at the University of Parma and then by UCLA and the University of London researchers, among others, indicate that neurons are better at multitasking than originally thought. Routine laboratory studies measuring the activity of neurons in monkeys showed that when a monkey reaches out to grab a peanut, a neuron consistently lights up. This motion-specific neuron is called a *motor neuron.*

But scientists at the University of Parma accidentally discovered that some neurons lit up not only when a monkey grabbed a peanut, but also when the monkey saw someone else grab a peanut. In other words, some neurons allow the monkey to see and also "experience" what the monkey is seeing.

These neurons are called *mirror neurons,* and until a few years ago, they had never before been observed at the cellular level.

Mirror neurons also exist in humans, and research has increased our understanding of how they operate. Researchers are concluding that mirror neurons help explain why some people "suffer" when they see other people suffer. In sports, for example, we see fans making all kinds of facial expressions while yelling, jumping, pulling their hair, crying, cheering, and generally exhibiting emotions that seem utterly out of control.

What is happening is that some fans get so immersed in the game that they experience the same frustrations, stress, and joy as those playing the game; they are not only seeing or watching but also experiencing the intensity of the game. Other spectators consider these to be exaggerated reactions to a simple game. That's because not everyone has the same number of mirror neurons and hence not everyone reacts in the same way.

According to Daniel Glaser, a researcher at the University of London[11]:

"What we've found is the mechanism that underlies something which is absolutely fundamental to the way that we see other people in the world."   — Daniel Glaser

---

Mirror neurons help us "connect" with others at a different level. They may be the reason why yawning and laughing are contagious; they allow us to both see and experience what others are doing.

They may also be behind the fact that we empathize with people who act like us, which may explain why job seekers are advised to mimic their interviewers' body language to increase "bonding" and likeness.

Although everyone has mirror neurons, their number varies from person to person. Studies involving entire families indicate that they may be hereditary. Also, autistic individuals have been found to have fewer than average mirror neurons, which helps explain why they learn considerably less than non-autistic people from socializing.

Furthermore, studies are confirming these observations and finding a distinct correlation between the existence of mirror neurons and empathy—the feeling that you understand and share other people's experiences and emotions; the ability to share someone else's feelings.

Mirror neurons are behind our display of empathy toward others. Using the story of my son learning to drive, and having experienced the benefit of scenario playing, I believe that we can train our brains to see more than we are seeing today. It may be that by doing so we let the mirror neurons do their job without our blocking the information that our brain could receive.

In sum, to understand human behavior we need to literally come to our senses and open our mind to new stimuli. Just as Mandelbrot saw nature from a different angle and was able to break down nature's complexity into simple, repetitive fractals, so can you start seeing the world and its inhabitants from a fresh perspective. You will break down the complexity of human behavior and understand what at first glance seems incomprehensible.

Start today. Let your mirror neurons gather and process information without the interference of pre-conceived ideas. This way your brain will receive objective information and help you make the right decisions. It's amazing how many clues people are continuously sending out about themselves, only to have them ignored or misread by the average observer. Next we will examine a few of these commonly ignored clues to give you ideas on how to sharpen your observation skills.

Chapter Six

First Impressions— Skewed and Backwards

> *The greatest actors aren't what you would call beautiful sex symbols.*
>
> — Brad Pitt[*]

Job seekers know everything about the importance of good first impressions. During an interview, you want to look your best and be on your best behavior to make a positive impression on your interviewer. Professional coaches might tell you to mimic the interviewer's gestures and body language to connect at a deeper personal level. If the interviewer leans forward, you lean forward; if he or she smiles, you smile; and so forth.

For the most part, this game works because it's easier to judge a book by its cover, so we like people who, on the outside, appear to be like us; they seem confident and appear to fit within our normal circle of influence. We are convinced that each person's exterior is a reflection of their personality and value system. Undoubtedly, if we like what we see at first glance, we are more inclined to listen to what they have to say.

The opposite happens when we dislike the external appearance of the person in front of us. If it doesn't conform to our expectations, or if we have a preconceived notion of a particular type of person, we close our mind and reject the idea of uncovering who this person really is.

---

[*] Brad Pitt Quotes. BrainyQuote.com, Xplore Inc, 2018. https://www.brainyquote.com/quotes/brad_pitt_463943, accessed February 27, 2018.

Appearances Are Deceptive, Character Is Not

Using first impressions as the yardstick to appraise a person can easily backfire when you are dealing with foreign nationals who look different from what you consider as the norm. When interacting with other cultures, most people focus almost entirely on external factors:

- Appearance
- Clothing
- Language
- Food
- Habits and mannerisms

Because first impressions are based on past experience and pre-conceived notions, many Westerners are uncomfortable with and likely to be disinclined to interact with people who look and dress differently. This would be an unfortunate decision, because those judging by external appearances would miss out on the opportunity to meet some of the smartest, fairest, and progressive individuals I have ever met.

Focusing on uncovering and understanding the individual behind the outer appearance is the key to identifying the kind of person you want to befriend or work with.

Consider this:

Even when the behavior of societies, as groups of people, may differ significantly from each other (the topic of the next section), people within those societies exhibit remarkable similarities when it comes to personality traits (e.g., energetic, enthusiastic, and optimistic) and internal character traits (e.g., honest, trustworthy, and fair).

We know we cannot judge the character of a person based on external image alone. If we could, then job interviews would not be necessary; we would just hire the person whose external appearance we like the most. We can only imagine the disastrous consequences of such an approach, yet we are susceptible to doing it because it's the path of least resistance.

It follows that one of the most important shifts in mindset necessary to succeed in today's globalized environment is to retrain your brain to go beyond external appearances and superficial assumptions about personality traits. This will allow you to uncover the full potential that people different from your norm may bring to your personal and working life. You will be surprised at the results and will benefit from expanding the database of people you can trust.

Why Is this important?

It's well documented that one of the main barriers to business success today is the significant lack of trust that exists between international partners.

Lack of trust is not a reflection of intentional actions but is largely a subconscious reaction to a lack of familiarity with and understanding of others. When we deal with family members and close friends, we understand their behavior and can manage the relationship.

But when we deal with people of other cultures, that level of familiarity and understanding is absent, and we find it difficult to interact, let alone develop meaningful relationships and trust with strangers. It's about not being able to grab hold of the familiar patterns.

We lose perspective on the true indicators of a person's character because we conflate the superficial traits for the underlying truth. Without the superficial traits to lean on as a short-cut, we tend to be confused by people who are new to us.

Busy as we are, we find it much easier to jump to conclusions and avoid the unfamiliar than to change the way we collect information. We think this way solely because we have been conditioned to do so. Remember that young children don't discriminate against anyone when making friends. We learn to categorize people later, as we grow older and are more influenced by societal norms predominant in our environment.

In the process, we suppress the curiosity to learn and the intuitive openness toward others we are born with. In the past, no major consequences resulted from this societal practice because the world was well compartmentalized.

But in today's globalized and borderless world, when we are so exposed to people who appear to be so different from us, we need to realize that this mindset is outdated, démodé. In fact, it's so old-fashioned that it creates more trouble and anxiety for us than it's worth. It fails to help us deal with today's realities.

Let's figure out how to modify the way we gather information through observation.

Sometimes we come to amazing realizations in an indirect fashion. That happened to me years ago, when I had just started to travel for business with clients of different nationalities. In spite of their obvious external and cultural differences, I noticed that they all reacted enthusiastically to the natural beauty of the particular places we were visiting.

You may have experienced a situation yourself when you or other people visiting new cities or countries exclaim: *"Oh, look, what a beautiful view. It reminds me of (a place in their country); it looks just like this."* A person from Alaska, for instance, may feel "at home" on the glaciers of Patagonia, and a fruit grower or wine maker from California may feel at home in the central region of Chile, where the Pacific coast resembles California's Highway 1 right down to the yellow wildflowers and the sea lions sunbathing on the rocks.

The more you travel, the more you realize that there are a finite number of landscapes around the world: valleys and mountains, rivers and oceans, forests and deserts. Subconsciously, these geographic similarities help people feel at home in otherwise unfamiliar territory (thus the enthusiastic response to familiar places). The moment we see something we recognize as familiar, we relax and enjoy the moment.

Based on the reaction of a wide range of people to visual stimuli, I started to notice and make notes on the significant similarities in behavior that existed in people across cultures and backgrounds. After a while, I could often predict their reactions to different situations. The personal experience I accumulated over two decades of international travel led me to conclude that people across cultures are very similar to each other and share a common set of personality and character traits.

The realization that people from around the world share a common set of characteristics that is repetitive, comprehensible, and manageable has proven accurate time after time as I travel the world. You may have also experienced the fact that the moment you meet a stranger who reminds you of a friend or a relative you like, you relax, open your mind to the experience, and enjoy the interaction.

This means that instead of trying to understand people from other cultures, you just need to treat them as one of your own and assess their personality and character traits that are already familiar to you. The world is significantly simplified when you use these new metrics: a manageable set of human (personality and character) traits.

A common set of human traits repeats itself again and again throughout the world population.

I invite you to make this discovery on your own. Once you embrace this premise, the initiative of understanding, relating, and connecting to people in other countries becomes as attainable as building relationships with new coworkers in your office. No matter where you live and work, you can identify the human traits of those around you and manage them according to affinity, interests, and needs.

At work, for example, we are constantly pondering how to get along with those around us, and depending on the situation, we may decide to like someone, compromise, or get out of the way and move on. It's no different when we deal with people outside our own country.

Try this at work tomorrow:

Make a private list of the people you like and dislike. Then write down two or three dominant personality traits each of them exhibits that you find either enjoyable or annoying. You'll end up with a finite number of primary personalities, like those listed in Figure 6.1.

Those odious people who make your life difficult at work are everywhere, and so are the wonderful people who are always there to support you. All you need to do is adjust your mindset to "see" them for what they are, regardless of nationality, ethnicity, customs, and beliefs.

• Leaders—attract people like magnets.	• Protectors—care for those with real or imaginary needs.
• Doers—focus on getting the job done.	• Meddlers—plot to overthrow any kind of leadership.
• Procrastinators—leave everything for tomorrow.	• Machiavellians—play chess with human beings.
• Cheerleaders—organize social events.	• Destabilizers—dislike everything that works.
• Realists—pour water on any celebration.	• Victims—unhappy and miserable by definition.
• Idealists—dream of endless possibilities.	• Bullies—talk loud to hide insecurities.
• Control freaks—delegation is not in their vocabulary.	• Pretenders—all smoke and mirrors with no substance.
• Mediators—reconcile everything and everyone.	• Yes-sayers—agree, unquestionably, with authority.
• Bureaucrats—regulate your every move.	

Figure 6.1   Personalities found in every corner of the world.

As you expand this exercise to foreign nationals, you will discover that the list is no different. They exhibit the same personality traits as everyone else. I guarantee that once you realize and internalize this piece of information, you will find that no matter where you go in the world, the same personality traits show up among those around you.

The more you put this exercise into practice, the more you'll discover the accuracy of this simple statement. Bring this concept to your conscious level, and eventually you will make this practice an intuitive one. Aim at becoming a better "reader of personalities," and you will be more effective at connecting with total strangers, identifying those you want to relate with and those you want to avoid.

You should not be more concerned about relating to
people in other countries than you are about relating to
people you work with when joining a new company.

Does this sound too easy to be true on a global scale?

Yes and no.

As in sports, developing and fine-tuning new skills requires dedication, practice, and consistency. And there are always exceptions to the rule. Some cultures appear to be more inscrutable than others, but it has been my experience that this is more perception than reality. If you encounter people who are difficult to read, don't let that deter you. Just treat them as you would treat any other person, and you are likely to discover that they can be as approachable and friendly as most. In *Chapter 9: Real-Life Anecdotes from a Business Globetrotter,* I share a story about my interaction with a seemingly inscrutable Chinese man.

Depending on your own personality, disposition, and experiences, you may find it easy or difficult to embrace the notion that people around the world are "just like us." Both kinds of reactions—"too much trust" and "too little trust"—need to be managed.

People who are "too friendly" and "too trusting" toward strangers leave themselves open to unpleasant or even dangerous experiences. On the other hand, those who reject the notion that others are just like us may miss the opportunity to succeed through working with others by attempting to isolate themselves in a global world in which isolation is no longer possible.

Give yourself and others the opportunity
to uncover the inner self.

By ignoring the external image, you give yourself the gift of discovering excellent human beings among perfect strangers in every country. For the most part, strangers you come across while you travel are also mothers, fathers, brothers, sisters, and grandparents.

They may be wearing high heels and designer suits in America or brightly colored dresses, turbans, and sandals in Africa. But inside, they share similar values, behavior patterns, concerns, fears, and qualities such as pride, tenacity, courage, and the pursuit of happiness. They may be social or antisocial, friendly or unfriendly, optimists or pessimists, trustworthy or corrupt, and so on. The point is that behind their external appearances, these human beings are just as valuable, intelligent, funny, and wise as the people we meet back home.

A common mistake that I have observed Western executives make is that they often confuse personality with character traits. Thus foreigners who are impeccably dressed in Western-style clothes and communicate effectively in English may be attributed character traits they don't possess, such as honesty and trustworthiness. Only later it is discovered that they were shrewd con-men—and by then it is too late.

You are as likely to discover a gem dressed in
rags as a crook dressed in silk.

I have helped clients expose pretenders by asking the right questions and listening carefully for hollow but carefully formulated answers. By the same token, foreigners who appear to be clumsy and lack fluency in English shouldn't be dismissed as potential allies. What they lack in personality may be amply surpassed with knowledge, honesty, and loyalty.

This reminds me of a young man I met while traveling through the Saudi Arabian desert. My chauffeur (a necessity because, at that time, women still could not drive in Saudi Arabia) was driving me to my office, located outside the city where I lived, when we came upon a herd of camels crossing the road guided by a young shepherd. There was a desert sandstorm blowing in the area, and for protection, the shepherd was wearing a turban that covered most of his face. I asked my driver to stop the car so I could take a picture of the young man. Half expecting indifference on his part, I was willing to take the picture of his back as he kept walking away from us behind his camels.

To my sheer delight, however, the young shepherd stopped to look at the car and at me.

Realizing my intentions, he started to rearrange his turban to make sure it was properly in place. At that moment, he not only looked every inch the handsome boy he was but revealed his kind personality and sense of humor, which shone through his eyes as he waited for me to take the picture (Figure 6.2). What a memorable moment! This example shows that people define who they are by what they see inside themselves, not by what society tells them to see.

Figure 6.2   The shepherd in the desert. (*Source:* © Z. Kraljevic)

Connecting to total strangers on a one-on-one level is not as difficult as you may think because there is a core set of personality and character traits that is common to all people regardless of the society they live in.

The familiar process we use to befriend a person
at home is readily exportable abroad.

I encourage you to corroborate this statement on your own. This mindset modifier will allow you to "connect" on a personal level with strangers that at first sight couldn't be more different from you and those you know.

Don't Let Larger Patterns Fool You

Earlier, we discussed how macroeconomic data and traditional geographic borders are too broad to help us understand the behavior of regular citizens and individual consumers.

Economics and geography are not the only fields of study that produced large-scale data that were helpful in the past but are inadequate today. Sociology has also generated volumes of information after taking a generalized view of the world.

When studying the behavior of societies, sociologists have concluded that humanity can be divided into two major groups:

- **Individualistic societies** (also referred to as *individualistic behavior,* or *individualism*)
- **Collectivistic societies** (also referred to as *collectivistic behavior,* or *collectivism*)

There are volumes of in-depth studies of these two types of societies explaining how they behave.[1] Undoubtedly, such studies have value and shouldn't be discarded offhand. In fact, back in the 1980s, when there were about 160 countries in the world and the global population was approaching five billion, it was appealing to believe that individuals operating in groups could be categorized by two convenient classes.

I was among those tempted to think that this characterization was a practical first step in the process of understanding how and why people behaved in different ways. Moreover, when I discussed the principal characteristics of these two types of societies with my college students and executive clients, they easily identified with these characterizations.

But the nature of my international work kept me in regular and close contact with diverse groups of people in different regions and settings. This interaction made me keenly aware of the accelerated social transformation taking place in the 1980s and 1990s and particularly in the 2000s. I came to the conclusion that such classification no longer applies, not because it is intrinsically wrong, but because the world is not what it used to be.

Globalization has resulted in an increasingly interrelated society that makes the distinction between these two societal behaviors difficult. The concepts are helpful, but to use them without further analysis and conditional provisions would be highly inaccurate and misleading.

Let me explain by starting with a simple definition of these two types of societies. Note that I take a look at these societies solely from a practical business perspective, choosing intentionally not to engage in a deeper analysis as a sociologist, psychologist, or anthropologist might:

- *Collectivistic societies* have a community orientation and tend to favor the success of the group over that of the individual. Collectivists are often risk averse and seek safety in group consensus. They prefer a safe environment, both in business and on a personal level, and tend to count on their superiors or other authority figures to guide their actions. Their sense of community is manifested in a high level of respect for their elders and taking care of their extended families and neighbors.
- *Individualistic societies* favor the success of the individual over the group. Individualists prefer challenging environments in both their business and personal life. They enjoy empowerment, have a higher tolerance for risk taking, preferring to depend on their own capabilities to succeed. They tend to make decisions based first on individual gain and consider the impact on the community second. Empowered as individuals, they tend to disregard the wisdom of their elders and are less inclined to take care of extended families and neighbors the way collectivists might do.

As shown in Figure 6.3, studies further indicate that:

- Regions of the world that have generally been found to exhibit mainly individualistic orientation are those normally referred to as the "Western world" or "developed countries":
  o United States
  o Australia
  o Canada
  o Northern European countries

Note that Japan, an industrialized country, is excluded from this list. This is because its society, while in transition, is still considered to exhibit mostly collectivistic characteristics.

Regions of the world that have generally been found to exhibit mainly a collectivistic orientation are those usually designated as non-industrialized countries (Figure 6.3).

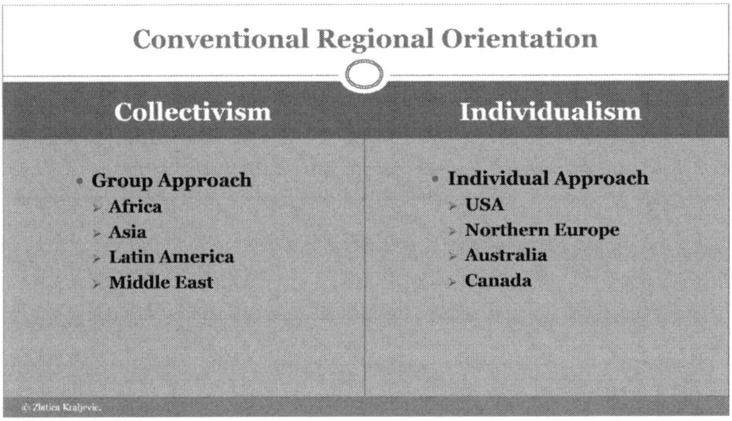

Conventional Regional Orientation

Collectivism	Individualism
• Group Approach	• Individual Approach
‣ Africa	‣ USA
‣ Asia	‣ Northern Europe
‣ Latin America	‣ Australia
‣ Middle East	‣ Canada

© Zlatica Kraljevic.

Figure 6.3 Conventional behavioral orientations.

Past convention dictates that individualistic societies are generally found in countries that have access to advanced technology and produce value-added products that attract high market prices and result in higher per capita income. Likewise, past convention dictates that collectivistic societies are generally found in countries that depend heavily on the trade of non-processed agricultural products or the extraction and exportation of natural resources, both activities requiring low-skilled labor and low-income jobs and resulting in low per capita income. Figure 6.4 illustrates how the world was divided using this now outdated approach.

Unfortunately, the world is not as simple as Figure 6.4 may suggest, because globalization has transformed it into a vibrant place in which traditional societal

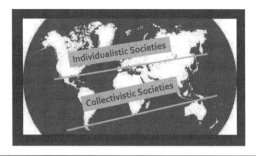

Figure 6.4   A generalized societal behavioral view of the world.

behavior is more and more integrated and where distinctions are becoming ever more blurred:

- First, migration patterns have altered the fabric of societies around the world. A good number of foreign nationals or naturalized individuals living abroad have been born, raised, and educated in host countries, exposed to both collectivistic and individualistic behavior at home, in school, and at work. They are likely to exhibit hybrid societal behavior. In turn, they and their families have increased their levels of awareness and influenced the views of the local society in which they live, thus contributing to a two-way transition toward a hybrid behavioral pattern.
- Second, the old definition of developing countries has been adjusted to include "developing, frontier, and emerging markets." Each of these categories indicates a different level of industrialization and income per capita. As poverty in these countries diminishes, a new middle class has started to emerge and strengthen. Local citizens have access to higher per capita income, which translates into improved sanitary living conditions and better education and development. Having satisfied their basic needs, they start moving higher in Maslow's pyramid of needs and begin transitioning into hybrid societal behavior.

A more accurate representation of the world's societies is pictured in Figure 6.5.

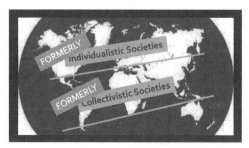

Figure 6.5   A global society in transition.

Why is this observation important? Because being unaware of it may easily lead you to wrong conclusions.

The coexistence of collectivism and individualism in a single person is neither good nor bad. Both types of behaviors offer advantages and generate good results. But it can be confusing if stereotyping gets in the way. Typecasting individuals or groups of individuals based on pre-conceived notions of how traditional societies behave is always risky. Generalizations preclude us from recognizing the root causes that are behind a particular human reaction.

While doing business in East Asia, I met a young woman who had just graduated with a degree in computer science. Her dream was to earn a doctorate degree in the same field. Her mother, however, was worried. Girls that are too smart, she believed, would find it difficult to marry because, in her words, "nobody likes a girl who is smarter than her husband." The mother was a product of a traditional collectivistic upbringing, and her expectation was that the daughter would marry and later care for her aging parents, a custom deeply ingrained in her society. An unmarried daughter, she feared, wouldn't have the financial means to care for her aging parents.

The young woman was torn between the old practice dictated by her collectivistic upbringing and her desire to pursue the education that she wanted and that was more in tune with the opportunities offered by the global market. She finally decided to pursue her dream and wait to see what the future might bring. Her rationale was that if she was as successful as she envisioned herself to be, not only would she be happier, but she would also have the means to care for her parents, with or without a husband.

In the struggle between collectivism and individualism, the latter allowed her to choose the means by which she would satisfy the obligations dictated by the former.

From a business perspective, conventional stereotyping involves higher risks than ever before. It would clearly be a mistake to classify this young woman as purely collectivistic based on her ethnic origin, unaware of the fact that she is transitioning from one type of society to another. Her strong determination to be highly successful to prove herself to her parents is likely to make her a formidable competitor for career advancement and financial success in the work environment.

Based on personal experience, I have selected some of the most contrasting differences that exist between individuals raised in collectivistic and individualistic societies. We often observe these differences in routine interaction, but they can be particularly noticeable and, if not well understood, rather aggravating in the work environment.

Conventional Behaviors to Watch Out For

Although you may have no control over the way others think and behave, it's within your power to modify your reaction to their environment. With practice you can:

- Read between the proverbial lines when interacting with foreign nationals.
- Anticipate barriers to achieving your objectives.
- Reposition your value propositions according to needs and interests.
- Identify the kind of people you want to be associated with.
- Develop more satisfactory relationships on a business and personal level.
- Become more aware of your surroundings.
- Anticipate potentially threatening situations.
- Adjust your business strategy and culture to meet local needs.

The intent here is not to take a position on issues but to highlight them as important characteristics of traditional cultures. By way of a disclaimer, it should also be noted that the primary differences described in this section are general and are advanced as a first step in breaking down the process of understanding people's behavior. As such, these differences apply mainly to individuals living in their own country, as opposed to those who have lived, studied, or worked in a foreign country, where close interaction with a different environment may have altered their behavior.

With the forewarning that societies are in transition, and therefore citizens of a particular country cannot be "assigned" a particular set of behavioral characteristics, it can be argued that some generalizations are useful as a first approximation. With that in mind, let's examine some "typical" behavior that is still observed in certain regions, to point out differences between these two societies.

Let's focus on only six of the most prominent behavioral differences I have found that affect the majority of business relations. Remember them, and you will start to understand why people make decisions the way they do, why they think the way they do, and why they behave the way they do (see Figure 6.6 on next page).

1. Planning versus execution

The Pareto Principle,[2] also known as the 80/20 rule, states that for many events observed in societal behavior, roughly 80 percent of the effects come from 20 percent of the causes. This doesn't mean that all societies follow this rule in the same fashion. This is what I have observed in the business environment:

- Collectivistic societies tend to collect information and examine a situation until they feel 80 percent sure they have considered all the possibilities. The root cause for this intense analysis is that being wrong in front of their peers or superiors is unbearable and can potentially be disgraceful for them and their families. They prefer to act with a high level of certainty in the results, in part to protect their reputation in case the solution fails to achieve the desired results.

One of my clients was a government agency located in a country with a predominantly collectivistic society. When we presented our proposal for a major project, they told us that they liked our proposal the most, but ours was not as well-known a company as a famous multinational firm that was competing for the same project.

Their dilemma was not that we couldn't do the job. They were concerned about what would happen if the results were different from what was expected. They were convinced that members of the board would immediately dismiss our results on the basis that our company didn't have the credibility to propose something out of the ordinary; those who had recommended us over the larger company would risk losing face and possibly their jobs. In the end we won the project, but only after gaining access to the board and convincing its members of our capabilities and benefits.

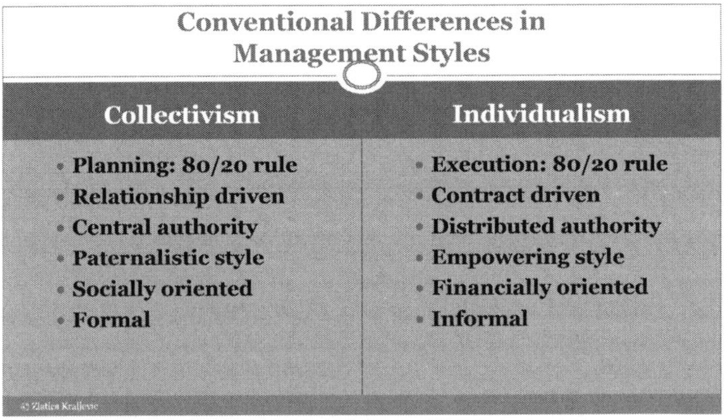

Conventional Differences in Management Styles	
Collectivism	**Individualism**
• Planning: 80/20 rule	• Execution: 80/20 rule
• Relationship driven	• Contract driven
• Central authority	• Distributed authority
• Paternalistic style	• Empowering style
• Socially oriented	• Financially oriented
• Formal	• Informal

45 Zlatica Kraljevic

Figure 6.6   Conventional differences in management styles.

- By contrast, individualistic societies tend to be action-driven even when only 20 percent of the information may be available. The expectation is that the other 80 percent will be duly acquired during execution. Individualism doesn't assign as much importance to mistakes as long as the end result is acceptable. Winston Churchill once said: "Americans always do the right thing . . . after having exhausted all other possibilities." In individualistic societies, action is considered more beneficial than the alternative, and worth the risks.

2. Paternalistic versus empowering styles

- **Conventional view.** Collectivistic societies have high regard and respect for senior leaders: the eldest of the tribe, the president of the company, the patriarch of the family. Older leaders have a paternalistic attitude toward their followers and dependents. They are protective and take care of things for others instead of preparing them to be self-sufficient. Teachers, for example, may reward memorization and obedience over debate and initiative.
- **Conventional view.** In contrast, individualistic societies tend to encourage children to exercise independent thinking, initiative, leadership, and team spirit, and to develop communication skills. As they reach college and join the workforce, they are ahead of their peers in collectivistic societies in terms of business performance.

Multinational companies may be surprised to find that the local workforce lacks the business skills that are common in the Western world. They may not realize that the reason is not related to intelligence or lack of initiative but to local traditions influencing social behavior and education.

On the other hand, those raised in collectivistic societies may be surprised to find out that Westerners don't tend to have extended families living all together or in the same neighborhood. They may not realize that individualism rewards independence, and thus family obligations are measured on a different scale.

---

3. Top-down decisions versus distributed decisions

- **Conventional view.** Collectivistic societies exhibit a central authority with a top-down decision pattern. While leaders may seek consensus among other leaders, they don't involve junior people in discussion and analysis or in their decision-making. Subordinates are afraid to make decisions, because the risk of "displeasing" the leader is just too big. In addition, those that exhibit independent thinking are shunned by their peers into conformity for fear of upsetting the status quo.
- **Conventional view.** With the exception of the military, individualistic societies favor a decentralized decision pattern in which the business decision-making process is distributed and shared with junior people at the lower echelons in the hierarchy. Junior personnel are encouraged and expected to use individual judgment in making decisions. The willingness to take risks is considered part of the job and is preferred over lack of initiative, as long as it doesn't break the company.

4. Relationship building versus contract signing

- **Conventional view.** Collectivistic societies make business decisions based on personal relations. They invest considerable time in getting to know you as a prospective business partner. They make use of business and social encounters to get a feel for what kind of person you really are and to determine if you can be trusted or not. The process emphasizes initial social, non-business exchanges and progresses gradually toward business discussions.

The executive team of a Fortune 500 company called on my services to help them salvage a relationship with a foreign agency that had gone very well for some time and had suddenly started to come apart for unexplained reasons. The project had significant strategic and financial value to my client.

For more than eighteen months, the executive team had been working diligently with their counterparts in preparation for a formal presentation to the head of the organization and the board of directors. As the day of the official meeting drew closer, however, the previously friendly relationship with foreign management became distant, and inquiries about when the big meeting might take place were met with evasive responses. The team realized that they were becoming increasingly isolated; the door was being closed.

My mission was to find out the reason for this change of heart and identify a solution to salvage the situation. I was to operate in complete anonymity in regard to the identity of my client and the nature of the project. Working indirectly with sources close to the situation, I gathered seemingly unrelated pieces of information until a pattern started to emerge. Finally, the root cause and solution to the problem became crystal clear.

The door had been closing because, unintentionally, the executive team had offended the leader of the foreign organization by consulting first with his underling instead of briefing him directly on the intended goal. The offense was compounded by the fact that the client was a major, well-known multinational, and the foreign leader felt humiliated by being ignored for so long. The solution was to provide an explanation of the well-intended approach and an apology from the client. The project and the relationship were salvaged, and I enjoyed repeat business from that client for many years afterward.

- **Conventional view.** Individualistic societies make decisions based on contract negotiations. They don't spend much time building relations and generally consider pre-contract social gatherings a waste of time. Accustomed to the transparency and consistency of the legal system at home, they rely on the signature at the bottom of the contract to engage in business. This explains why many international partnerships fail to generate expected results.

5. Formal versus informal interactions

- **Conventional view.** Collectivistic societies tend to be quite formal in their interactions among themselves and with outsiders. Because of their respect for authority, leaders are treated with extreme care. People don't address leaders unless leaders address them first and invite others to speak. Titles are important and never ignored; they may even be bestowed on elderly people in recognition of their wisdom. It is better to err by being too respectful than to risk offending with informalities.
- **Conventional view.** Individualistic societies tend to be informal, and they operate under the concept that everyone is equal. This is particularly so in the U.S., where business people address each other by first names, regardless of position. Titles and degrees are downplayed, in some cases to an extreme. Formality in social and business environments is seen more as a political maneuver than a genuine recognition for individual accomplishment.

It's worth noting that, except for academia, in American business circles formal titles are considered snobbish and are played down. Informality is encouraged in the interaction between younger professionals and supervisors. On the other hand, European countries tend to be more formal than in the U.S. For example, earning a doctorate degree significantly elevates a person among his or her peers, so in social and business circles they follow protocol and acknowledge higher education and titles (e.g., "Dr." or "Dra."). The same holds true in collectivistic societies.

---

6. Social versus financial decisions

- **Conventional view.** Collectivistic societies tend to make decisions based on the well-being of the group and the community as a whole. In business, the head of a company may decline to modernize the facilities if that would leave a good number of people without jobs. Given economic downturns, this practice is less common now than in the past, but it is still a higher priority in collectivistic societies than it is in individualistic societies. The tendency to protect the community is consistent with the belief that the authority or paternal figure is responsible for the well-being of the dependents. Thus the leader is expected to take care of those less fortunate. In turn, the leaders expect respect and devotion to the authority figure.

- **Conventional view.** Individualistic societies tend to make decisions that result in opportunities for the individual, not necessarily the community. This is not to say that the company may not adopt a community outreach program, but the moment the economy is in trouble, the survival of the business takes priority over the survival of the community. This is consistent with the belief that individuals are responsible for their own survival. Loyalty and dependence are neither expected nor offered.

Invariably, when I point out these six contrasting behaviors to a multicultural audience, people start nodding in agreement even before I finish. They recognize common practices in their own countries, and more importantly, they can now explain much of the behavior they have seen and experienced in other countries. Many of those listening to my lectures come to me saying:

"I wish I would have known this earlier. It explains so many things."

Hybrid Behavior

Globalization has intensified global interaction, which is quickly modifying our traditional way of thinking. As a result, we see hybrid behaviors in which seemingly contrasting elements of collectivism and individualism can be exhibited by the same person depending on the occasion.

Hybrid behavior that defies conventional thinking is becoming increasingly noticeable, particularly in urban areas, where people are more exposed to the effects of globalization. An example of hybrid behavior was illustrated in the earlier story of the Asian girl determined to earn a doctorate degree in computer science in spite of parental resistance and concerns.

To deal with this new blend of attitudes requires a higher degree of alertness. As you get more practice at reading human behavior and acquiring fresh knowledge about others, you will be able to sort through some hybrid behavior exhibited by those who have embraced globalization and/or have been exposed to a different type of society for a period of time.

Don't be surprised if you encounter individuals who have adopted the opposite behavior than you might have expected, based on conventional views. In other words, an individualist may choose to become a collectivist after living in or studying collectivistic societies; the reverse also holds true. This is to say that the person observing a group from the outside becomes part of the observed group.

While sharpening your people-reading skills, keep in mind that when in doubt, it's always preferable to err on the side of the conventional behavior already described.

While working at the offices of an international company, I was invited to join a virtual meeting held weekly between professionals in the U.S. and their counterparts in India.

Both teams were assembled in their respective conference rooms, which were equipped with video and audio. At the convened time, without preamble, the leader of the U.S. team got straight to the first point in the agenda. For about an hour, the meeting was dominated by the U.S. team. Unless asked specific questions, the Indian team remained silent. As decisions were clearly and quickly driven by the U.S. team, I was under the impression that the meeting was pro-forma and being used to communicate decisions rather than engage in bilateral dialogue.

Taking advantage of a break, I commented on my lack of familiarity with the Indian team and asked them to share their names and titles. The response was instantaneous. The screen was suddenly filled with smiling and animated faces eager to become part of the conversation. Clearly, they welcomed the opportunity to be addressed as real people rather than just virtual images on a screen. There had been no malice in the attitude of the U.S. team. This was clearly a difference in cultural behavior between an individualist and a collectivistic society.

When I became the leader of the U.S.–Indian team on a particular project, however, I made changes. I gave more responsibilities to the Indian team and more opportunities to present at meetings. The result was higher integration, motivation, collaboration, and promotions. When I later visited India, I received a warm welcome and was presented with token gifts of appreciation. It was the beginning of long-lasting personal relationships.

In another example of hybrid behavior, one day I invited an Asian colleague to lunch as a way to strengthen our business relationship. Sensitive to his traditional culture, I made it a point of discussing non-business issues for a while, only to be interrupted halfway through by my friend; he thanked me for the enjoyable conversation but also indicated that he was puzzled by the fact that I hadn't yet brought up a specific proposal for discussion! Did he really mean what he said or was he being sarcastic, mocking those who skip pleasantries and jump right into business? Still, being aware of the conventional views prevalent in each type of society, I knew that it was preferable to err on the side of politeness than to risk offending my friend by being insensitive to his national culture.

To recap, so far in this book we have discussed how an over-generalized geographic representation of the world is inaccurate and insufficient to describe today's globalized world. We have looked at new efforts by economists to further differentiate among geographic regions and concluded that these classifications still fall short of grouping like-countries, let alone like-people.

We have described a proven methodology to help unlock the mystery of complex human behavior by dissecting the world into smaller and smaller pieces until we can identify human fractals, a new metric that applies and helps uncover the striking similarities in character traits that exist among people all over the world.

We have also looked at the world from the traditional perspective of two dominant kinds of societies that appear to behave in very different ways and yet are currently evolving to exhibit hybrid behaviors that are becoming the norm rather than the exception.

Let's now turn our attention to how you can internalize these new concepts and adjust them to your own style. Eventually, they will even become second nature when you interact and connect with people you meet for the first time.

PART IV
INTERNALIZATION

*Internalize: To Incorporate (as Values or Patterns of Culture) Within the Self as Conscious or Subconscious Guiding Principles Through Learning or Socialization**

---

* Merriam-Webster Dictionary

Chapter Seven

Simplicity—A New Way of Life

To gain knowledge, add things every day.
To gain wisdom, subtract things every day.

— Lao-Tsé*

Whenever we face a complex situation, we consciously or subconsciously go through a process of awareness of the alternatives that can help us cope with the situation. This is followed by a process of understanding the value that each alternative represents and why it might make sense for us to act on specific options. To determine which option may best suit our needs, we make inquiries or do research to acquire the knowledge we need to make the right decision. But the process doesn't end there.

Internalization is the stage that occurs after we conclude that taking a particular action or adopting a new way of thinking makes sense and we learn how beneficial it is to us, at which point we embrace it, making it our own moving forward. Only after internalizing change can we act with confidence, armed with new and better tools that make our life easier, both at home and at work.

Earlier in this book, we discussed the difficulty of sorting through volumes of information about local and world events on a daily basis. Information overload has a paralyzing effect on the mind and deters action. We find ourselves knowing either too much or too little about everything. Too much knowledge makes

---

* https://www.goodreads.com/quotes/30297-to-attain-knowledge-add-things-every-day-to-attain-wisdom-remove

it hard to discern what's truly relevant; too little makes us aware of our limitations and creates self-doubt. We end up living on a rollercoaster of emotions that confuses the mind. Faced with fight-or-flight reactions, we would rather just go home and hide under the bed.

How do we regain control of our lives at home and at work?

We simplify: Examples throughout this chapter will help you get ideas on how to achieve simplicity at home and at work, regardless of location.

The key to preserving your sanity is to delegate as much as possible of the tactical and routine work you do at home and at the office. Smart delegating frees your mind to think strategically and systematically about your life, your family, your job, and your future. Granted, we cannot simplify everything, but we can and must simplify a few things. But first, let's explore what simplicity really means.

The Meaning of Simplicity

> Simplicity is not a beginning but a destination,
> the crowning reward of our development process.

We *achieve* simplicity rather than *start* with simplicity. Only those who are knowledgeable and wise achieve simplicity in life. Like building your financial portfolio, the sooner you start building your life based on simplicity, the sooner you will reap your rewards. Regardless of where you are in your personal and professional development, simplifying your life right now will not only be enjoyable but will bring immediate and long-lasting benefits. Less stress and anxiety will fill you with confidence and conviction.

Ultimately, you will gain the clarity of thought and clarity of purpose needed to get off the emotional rollercoaster and have the serenity and perspective you need to reach your ambitious personal and business goals.

Simplicity is the ultimate sophistication.

— Leonardo da Vinci[*]

*Simplicity is the final achievement. After one has played a
vast quantity of notes and more notes, it is simplicity
that emerges as the crowning reward of art.*

— Frederic Chopin[**]

---

[*] https://www.brainyquote.com/quotes/leonardo_da_vinci_107812
[**] https://www.brainyquote.com/quotes/frederic_chopin_212224

*The ability to simplify means to eliminate the
unnecessary so that the necessary may speak.*

— Hans Hofmann[*]

*Simplicity is the most difficult thing to secure in this world;
it is the last limit of experience and the last effort of genius.*

— George Sand[**]

As Simple as ABC

My golden rule for personal and business achievement in today's environment is as simple as ABC:

- Accept
- Build
- Capitalize

1. **Accept Complexity as a Constant in Life.** Life presents unavoidable roadblocks. We spend too much energy worrying about consequences that may or may not happen. Don't fight it, but rather accept it just as you have accepted the need to eat, sleep, talk, and walk. Positive energy will do the rest.
2. **Build New Support Systems.** Familiarity with your environment is essential to build self-confidence and clear your mind. To achieve familiarity, build support systems you can rely on. Your parents and school friends were your first support system. You added new ones in college and the work place. Why stop there? Continue to create support systems anywhere you go, because they add familiarity to new surroundings.
3. **Capitalize on A & B.** Accepting life's complexity and building familiarity with new surroundings gives you confidence; confidence provides clarity of thought and clarity of purpose, which help you stay in control and make better decisions. Clarity frees your mind to relax, go back to basics, and think creatively and strategically about essential rather than irrelevant things.

The first step—*Accept Complexity as a Constant in Life*—enables you to view the world through a different lens. Consider the world as an impartial observer would, without concerns about how the outcome might affect your life or work. This is much like trying on new prescription glasses and discovering details you hadn't noticed before. These details provide the clues that help you come up with fresh ideas to formulate solutions you haven't considered before.

---

[*] https://www.brainyquote.com/quotes/hans_hofmann_107805
[**] https://www.brainyquote.com/quotes/george_sand_390195

The second step—*Build New Support Systems*—is the key to increasing familiarity with your surroundings. Every time you face a new situation, think outside yourself about who you know that can help you deal with that situation. Chances are you tend to handle things by yourself. This may be because you believe you have all the necessary skills (overconfidence) or because you are change averse, and thus you fail to realize that no matter what you do, it's easier to do it along with someone else. The same is true when you live abroad. By building support systems wherever you are, you simplify your life considerably. Chapters 8 and 9 provide real-life stories that illustrate how I have learned to identify and surround myself with good people, those I can collaborate with to achieve mutually beneficial goals, regardless of geographic location and cultural background.

Finally, the third step—*Capitalize on A and B*—allows you to simplify your life and go back to basics. Once you try it, you will love it. My mother instilled this philosophy in me at a young age. She was an educator and, as you can imagine, rather picky when it came to written communication. Her favorite motto was: "When in doubt, erase." I heard her say this so many times that the concept stuck in my mind, and I have been applying it successfully ever since to control the chaos around my world. When a situation gets complicated, I take a step back, go back to basics and work at eliminating the superfluous, concentrating on the core business at hand.

> *I saw the angel in the marble and*
> *carved it until I set him free.*
>
> — Michelangelo*

The ABC of Business Smarts

There are two ways of doing business: the hard way and the smart way. Companies that do business the hard way are either too confident in their existing capabilities to justify change or are change averse. Unprepared to enter new markets, they end up fighting fires on the go and failing precipitously, as seen in the catastrophic results suffered by the Western multinationals discussed in Chapter 1.

Executives who resist change keep busy commiserating about how bad, inefficient, and intolerable the world is. By negating the complexities of emerging markets and sticking to obsolete practices, they fail to acquire the kind of knowledge that results in considering better options.

Fortunately, there are some signs that a new wave of executives may be emerging, one that uses the ABC process to achieve excellent results. One of these executives is Indra Nooyi, CEO of PepsiCo.

---

* https://www.brainyquote.com/quotes/michelangelo_161309

In 2009 Indra Nooyi made news not only because she was the first female CEO of this large multinational company, but also because she redefined the role of the CEO by taking a logical but seldom heard approach to connecting with the global market. Shortly after taking the reins as Pepsi's CEO, she took a trip to China, in itself not an unusual travel plan for a senior-most executive at any multinational corporation.

However, different from most top executives, Nooyi was determined to avoid the prospect of yet another trip abroad to conduct top-level meetings in lofty conference rooms that are physically and symbolically removed from the average consumer on the street. She claimed, rightly so, that the traditional way of visiting a country does not allow you to get a feel for the country, what the issues are and what makes people tick. With this in mind, she decided on an unprecedented two-week-long trip to China to visit not just the main cities, Beijing and Shanghai, but also cities such as Chongqing and Xian and going as far as rural Inner Mongolia to visit the company's potato farms.[1]

She was clever about exploring China and arranging meetings with scholars knowledgeable about China and its culture months before her planned trip. Once on the ground, she insisted that her executive team participate in experiential learning, joining her as she walked the narrow streets of old and poor neighborhoods and wandered inside shacks to meet their surprised inhabitants, old and young alike. Reportedly, a comfortable Nooyi and a few not-so-comfortable company executives dodged bicycles and hanging laundry to visit the cramped homes of Chinese families, asking them questions about the country's rapid economic development, their shopping habits, and preferences about Western brands.

Nooyi used the ABC of the new business smarts. Here is how she did it:

1. **Accepted China's Complexity.** She chose not to ignore or be intimidated by the complexities of doing business in China. She faced them fair and square by preparing ahead of time and planning a non-traditional trip that provided first-hand contact with the culture and maximized her personal and direct experience with the market.
2. **Built a New Support System.** Months before her scheduled first trip, she put together and met with a team of scholars, business leaders, and politicians well-versed in Chinese culture and business practices. She chose to educate herself as a way to increase her familiarity with common practices. Familiarity through knowledge and perspective boosted her confidence and resulted in a successful and rich experience.

3. **Capitalized on A and B.** Armed with the insight and confidence provided through steps A and B, Nooyi broke away from the tradition of many CEOs of paying a cursory visit to a foreign country and holding meetings in boardrooms in high-rise buildings, in a sophisticated environment that is far removed from the street-level reality of regular citizens. With clarity of mind and clarity of purpose, she went back to basics to gain a deeper understanding of her market. Instead of staying in the secluded comfort of the board room and reviewing complicated flowcharts, she chose to visit lesser-known cities and mingled, on foot, with regular people on the street.

Clearly, Mrs. Nooyi could teach a trick or two to executives who are still unfamiliar with, and thus intimidated by, foreign environments, resisting getting out of their ivory towers and putting their feet on the ground.

Born to Succeed

Before getting deeper into business, let's first discuss how we can condition ourselves on a personal level to achieve success. This requires that we are clear on the definition of success and our ability to achieve it.

Consider this:

> We experience success so many times in our daily life that we take it for granted. Even before we are born, we have been succeeding at life. Nature has given us tools and wits and has conditioned us to succeed even in adverse and alien surroundings.

In fact, no situation we face in life today is more complex and daunting than the one we faced at birth. We were literarily pushed into this world with our eyes closed, unable to walk or feed ourselves, and with no language to speak of. And yet we adjusted and learned how to deal with the situation. You may argue that as babies we had people around to help us with our adjustment to life. I would counter-argue that today we still have people around to help us with our adjustments to changes in life, and we also benefit from having access to a multitude of tools and knowledge to successfully face a wide range of situations.

The difference is that as kids we are fearless, and as adults we are fearful. Some time ago I wrote a series of articles related to living an anxiety-free life at home, at the office, and around the world. Here is an excerpt from one of these articles, entitled "Born to Succeed (or How We Graduated to Toddlers):"[2]

"During the nine months, give or take a few weeks, we spent inside the womb, we learned how to deal with a tough environment; one that allowed us no control over our fate. It was dark and uncomfortable, a space so small we couldn't even stretch or go for a walk. Our environment looked nothing like what we now associate with urban living on planet Earth. Yet we managed to stay alive.

"For almost two years after birth we still couldn't talk and had to cry to communicate our needs. We were forced to suffer through wet diapers and warm milk, and got bored looking at silly mobiles installed on top of our cribs. And we still couldn't even walk. Yet, in spite of our initial clumsiness and lack of knowledge, we managed to succeed at growing up, learning, acquiring knowledge, and practicing new skills."

We succeeded at making a successful transition from baby to toddler because we had:

- **Curiosity:** To learn new things.
- **Determination:** To practice new learning.
- **Confidence:** To learn at our own pace.
- **Ability to make friends easily:** Without judgment, for the sheer sake of communicating with others and learning new stuff.

Unfortunately, as we grow up, we lose the simple personality attributes that allowed us to achieve early successes. The good news is that the first two traits—curiosity and determination—involve an individual decision. You alone can decide to practice curiosity and act with determination, which will give you confidence derived from knowledge and the ability to make new friends.

We tend to believe that acquiring confidence is elusive and fragile because it involves interaction with the outside world. You may feel self-confident within the sanctuary of your home, but the moment you step out of the house, your self-confidence starts to crack and fail. Even the most self-confident person has inner fears that are kept hidden inside. Bullies, for example, are often people who cover their insecurities by being loud and obnoxious. It's a defense mechanism that blocks attack and rejection.

You will find an antidote to a lack of confidence in curiosity and determination, which in turn lead to knowledge and familiarity with a broader world. To increase awareness and acquire familiarity with the rest of the world you just need to follow seven simple steps:

Seven Simple Steps to Learn About the World

1. Build from strength. Concentrate on exploiting talents you already have: if you are a musician, travel the world as a musician; if you are a consultant, travel as a consultant.

2. Select a target country. Pick a country in which you feel the least threatened but that is outside your own continent. This is much like going to college in a city away from your parents' home—it forces you to be on your own.

3. Become a professional traveler. Take a genuine interest in getting a feel for places you visit and their people. (Later in this chapter I offer guidelines to becoming a professional traveler.)

4. Become a global speaker. Address a foreign audience and mingle with the local business environment. It will increase your confidence about interacting in that country and help you expand your network.

5. Practice cultural literacy. Divide and conquer to learn about the world in small bite-size pieces. Follow my golden rule of following the crowd to take a read on the local social, economic, and political environment. *[Warning: When visiting or working in other countries, stay far away from discussions about politics.]*

6. Uncover personalities and similarities. There are many more commonalities among citizens of the world than you may think. Practice what we discussed in *Part II—Understanding.*

7. Be persistent. Remember that the best results in life are not achieved overnight.

Success Redefined

Most people agree that pursuing success creates stress and makes us anxious. The reason? We are not in control of what success really means. Society has conditioned us to excessively focus on failure, which is why it's difficult to live a happy, anxiety-free (or at least, anxiety-controlled) life today.

Individualistic societies put significant emphasis on individual success and make it a quest to be #1 in everything. Encouraging everyone to be the best they can be is a good motivational technique. Unfortunately, it can also backfire and can easily be transformed into an effective weapon against individual success. Kids grow up being afraid of failure and cry when they don't make it onto the school's team. There is no fame for being #2. People carry that feeling, in different degrees of awareness, from school to college to the work environment and beyond.

Throughout life, the number of times we hear we are *wrong* far outnumbers the times we hear that we are *right*. In his essay, *The Relativity of Wrong,*[3] Isaac

Asimov wrote that we believe "right" and "wrong" to be absolutes, whereas in reality we are dealing with arbitrary rules and definitions.

The Relativity of Wrong—Excerpt

"Now where do we get the notion that 'right' and 'wrong' are absolutes? It seems to me that this arises in the early grades, when children who know very little are taught by teachers who know very little more. Young children learn spelling and arithmetic, for instance, and here we tumble into apparent absolutes. How do you spell 'sugar?' Answer: s-u-g-a-r. That is right. Anything else is wrong. How much is 2 + 2? The answer is 4. That is right. Anything else is wrong.

"Having exact answers, and having absolute rights and wrongs, minimizes the necessity of thinking, and that pleases both students and teachers. For that reason, students and teachers alike prefer short-answer tests to essay tests; multiple-choice over blank short-answer tests; and true–false tests over multiple-choice. But short-answer tests are, to my way of thinking, useless as a measure of the student's understanding of a subject. They are merely a test of the efficiency of his ability to memorize. You can see what I mean as soon as you admit that right and wrong are relative.

"How do you spell 'sugar?' Suppose Alice spells it p-q-z-z-f and Genevieve spells it s-h-u-g-e-r. Both are wrong, but is there any doubt that Alice is wronger than Genevieve? For that matter, I think it is possible to argue that Genevieve's spelling is superior to the 'right' one. Or suppose you spell 'sugar': s-u-c-r-o-s-e, or $C12H22O11$. Strictly speaking, you are wrong each time, but you're displaying certain knowledge of the subject beyond conventional spelling. Suppose then the test question was: how many different ways can you spell 'sugar?' Justify each. Naturally, the student would have to do a lot of thinking and, in the end, exhibit how much or how little he knows. The teacher would also have to do a lot of thinking in the attempt to evaluate how much or how little the student knows. Both, I imagine, would be outraged.

"If the teacher wants 4 for an answer and won't distinguish between the various wrongs, doesn't that set an unnecessary limit to understanding? Suppose the question is, how much is 9 + 5?, and you answer 2. Will you not be excoriated and held up to ridicule, and will you not be told that 9 + 5 = 14? If you were then told that 9 hours had passed since midnight and it was therefore 9 o'clock, and were asked what time it would be in 5 more hours, and you answered 14 o'clock on the grounds that 9 + 5 = 14, would you not be excoriated again, and told that it would be 2 o'clock? Apparently, in that case 9 + 5 = 2 after all."

This is why Asimov's *Theory of Wrong* is so refreshing. It tells us that there is more than one way to be smart and successful than those methods traditionally dictated by society. If we are not careful, we can become trapped in what others believe should be our definition of success, living constantly under stress to perform according to metrics that may not apply to us. Entrepreneurs are notorious for rebelling against society's definition of success and creating their own.

In his book *Get Rich Click!*, Marc Ostrofsky describes *The Minefield Game*[4] as follows:

The Minefield Game

Two teams are challenged to simply get across a path of 30 marked steps. Five of the 30 steps are "mines"—when stepped on, they light up. The player has to go back to the beginning and start over. The goal of the game is to see which team can cross the minefield the fastest.

Let's imagine how this game may look . . .

Both teams start out the same way, not knowing which steps are "mines." The first player from team #1 moves ever so slowly on the first step, then the second step, and so on until he hits one of the hidden "mines" under step #5. The next player from team #1 now crosses the first 4 steps, and then gently steps over the fifth one. This cautious approach continues until the player hits the next "mine" at step #12. Then the next team member begins, knowing to avoid the two previous mined steps.

It seems simple enough. But team #2 approaches the game very differently. The first person RUNS across the steps until hitting the mine on step #5. The next person then RUNS until hitting the mines under step #12. The next team member RUNS past the first four steps, jumps over #5 and #12, until they hit the next mine as soon as possible.

Needless to say, Team #2 won. The difference was that team #2 knew they had to "Fail Fast!" They knew that they would hit the mines, but if they learned from those mistakes fast enough, they would win the competition.

The Minefield Game helps illustrate how some of us, perhaps a majority of us, are trapped in the fear of making mistakes. At work, for example, we worry about saying the wrong thing to the CEO if we find ourselves together on the elevator, or we fear losing our train of thought at a client's presentation, or finding out that in spite of our best efforts we may get fired any day now.

We are plagued by negative thoughts, and while we worry about our worries, we never stop to consider those important moments in our daily life when we achieve one success after another.

Think about this: Have you ever noticed that, as stressed out as we may be, we seldom, if ever, entertain negative thoughts like: "What if I go to my closet today and don't find my brown shoes or my favorite jacket?" "What happens if I am running late and have to skip breakfast?"

Why don't we worry about these plausible and very real scenarios? Somehow we are confident that we can and will manage them successfully, time after time, without giving them much thought. Have you ever stopped to think why this is?

Two reasons:

1. We are in control of our daily routine and have designed it in a way that fits our needs, and
2. We have built enough alternatives in the clothing and food departments to help us out when we need it. Problem solved!

Taking the time to put back-up systems in place and familiarize ourselves with our surroundings allows us to have those daily successes, regardless of how busy we might be at work. Familiarity with our environment and reliable back-up systems are important reasons we yearn to get home and relax after a long day at the office. We have an established system that works.

Imagine how much more relaxed and confident we would be if we could achieve this same level of familiarity in our work environment and, even better, in our interaction with the global market. It's as simple as ABC.

ABCs at home

Let's use moving to a new house as an example of how to apply the ABC formula to make your life easier.

1. **Accept Complexity as a Constant in Life.** We all know how much work and stress is involved in moving from one home to another. Significant logistics are involved in making the transition, yet you accept the process as a fact of life and focus on getting organized, quickly building a new system and a new routine that supports your needs.
2. **Build a New Support System.** Once the movers are gone, you are surrounded by boxes to unpack. Almost mechanically, you assign a place for everything you own, making sure you have a place for all the essentials to support your lifestyle and business commitments. Using wardrobe as an example, you make sure you have more than one pair of shoes, as well as multiple sweaters, jackets, business suits, skirts, blouses, and casual pants and shirts, as the case may be. Why? Because you have anticipated that different situations require different solutions, just as unexpected situations require different viable alternatives.

3. **Capitalize on A and B.** Most people take advantage of moving to a new place to get rid of things they no longer need. Think for a moment of the steps you take while packing your things before the move: (1) you discard the superfluous; (2) you pack room by room, and (3) you label boxes according to final destination (kitchen, bathroom, bedroom, etc). Then, when unpacking, you make sure that kitchen utensils go to the kitchen and wardrobes go into closets. This simplicity gives you peace of mind and helps you relax. This kind of basic preparation and organization allows you to get up in the morning and rush through the house finding everything you need quickly and efficiently, without even thinking.

ABCs at the office

Let's use a similar approach to apply the ABC formula to the office environment.

1. **Accept Complexity as a Constant in Life.** Companies large or small are complex environments with their own particular sets of rules, hierarchies, and internal cultures. You automatically accept the complexities of the office environment when you accept a job offer. You are aware of the challenges but grateful to have landed the job, perhaps increasing your salary, too. Now you look forward to doing your best to succeed in the new environment. Make sure, however, that you also accept the fact that you need to build solid relationships with people at all levels in the company's hierarchy.

2. **Build a New Support System.** On your first day at the office, you are assigned a badge, desk, chair, telephone, computer, access to the network, and all the basic essentials you need to function. It's up to you to learn your way around the building and locate sources of food, drinks, technical support, parking information, and other "things" you may need. You do this diligently, because you know that to operate effectively you need a physical and virtual network in place. After the first week, however, the process stops, and that's when your problems start. You soon become involved in multiple projects and start running against deadlines. The build-up of stress and anxiety has begun and will never stop.

   Let's face it: If you are like most people, you seldom pay attention to putting in place the "people" network. You don't even consider stopping by the office of the president and other higher ups, assuming they have no interest in meeting you. That may be so. However, if you have something smart to say and manage to approach these individuals before the daily routine gets under way, you will stand out and they will remember you, if for no other reason than for your courage and initiative. Find out what time they get to the office and where they park and arrange for a casual encounter.

[Warning: If you live in a collectivistic society, this approach requires careful planning and more protocol, but the idea is that you seek opportunities to quietly demonstrate that you offer more than the average person.]

The head of Human Resources in a Fortune 200 company told me once: "I have never seen a new employee penetrate the organization as fast as you did. You wasted no time meeting with the president and all members of the executive team. You know everyone, and everyone knows and talks about you!"

One of the most unexpected and greatest compliments I received was from Frank, the president of a multibillion dollar company. We were both rushing to a meeting where I needed his presence to get quick buy-ins for a project, and he said: "I have to say that you really know how to delegate upwards!"

Don't forget that you accomplish much more when taking time to meet and work with other people, not only peers but those high up in the corporate leadership and experienced technical personnel. Anxiety in the work environment comes mostly from not knowing how to solve a problem. A diverse people network should be at hand to help you manage the complexities of your job. This includes people in your office as well as colleagues in other companies, clients, vendors, competitors, and members of professional societies that you belong to.

3. **Capitalize on A and B.** After taking care of steps A and B, you will not be alone tackling the responsibilities and complexities of the job. A carefully built support system that allows you access to technology and the know-how you need when you need it will free up time for you to think strategically about your projects and your future. The latter includes planning and building your professional profile so you are respected for your leadership and management skills and your ability to handle crises with confidence and seeming effortlessness. Be smart about how you manage people and projects, and aim at positioning yourself as an expert and a valuable resource to others.

Try this exercise tomorrow at the office:

Grab a piece of paper or your laptop and start jotting down how to build in your office the kind of familiarity and support system you enjoy at home. What do you need *more than one* of to help you cope with the demands of your office environment? Visualize surrounding yourself with people you can trust, both friends and professionals who can offer useful support services to busy people. Remember the way the CEO of PepsiCo planned her trip to China with enough time to assemble a team of experts. Maybe your team at the office will not include Henry Kissinger, but it can definitely include "the" expert that everyone admires and listens to.

ABCs in the world

The ABC formula works equally well as you travel the world and helps decrease the level of anxiety associated with international travel, particularly at times when sociopolitical instability is making the news.

1. **Accept Complexity as a Constant in Life.** Lack of familiarity with other countries and their people is a source of significant anxiety for professionals and their families when facing job-related relocation. Regardless of where you come from and where you relocate to, you will find that the local physical and technological infrastructure differs from what you are accustomed to; people also interact and connect with each other and with foreigners according to local customs.

    Instead of fighting this reality, accept the fact that things are different but not necessarily bad. In fact, you may discover that you can afford services you couldn't afford at home. Avoid making things more complicated than they are or worrying excessively about things that may or may not happen. Rather, spend quality time learning the lay of the land, preparing for eventualities, and getting to know the people you will be interacting with at work and at home.

2. **Build a New Support System.** Building good support systems in foreign countries requires more planning and attention than building those at home, but they are equally valuable in making your life easier.

    Remember that local citizens as well as expatriates that have been living in the country for some time depend on the local version of support systems. Stay objective, observe and listen carefully, and learn to use local systems as others do. Don't try to change what is already there just because you believe your system is better. You may end up with a system that is totally ineffective and doesn't work at all because it goes contrary to local customs and realities. Learning from others is your best bet.

3. **Capitalize on A and B.** After accepting the new environment as-is and learning how to use local support systems as others do, you will be able to make a smooth transition with the confidence, clarity of mind, and clarity of purpose needed to make better decisions. Put the methodology and

concepts described in this book to work by increasing your and your family's level of awareness, understanding, and knowledge about the place where you live. Then work at internalizing new learning so you can act with clarity of mind and clarity of purpose. The sooner you open your mind to learning new ways, the faster you will be on your way to having a rewarding and safe experience.

Balancing Personal Needs with Business Demands

Consider this typical situation: As we strive to balance the demands of work and family life, we may be missing good opportunities to simplify our lives. This happens because we are stuck with an obsolete mindset, an old way of thinking, and routines that we learned years ago when life seemed less complicated. We are not thinking creatively, and we remain unaware of new alternatives that may be waiting to be discovered if only we would change our mindset to positive thinking. Commiserating about our situation, we rarely think of asking for help that could help us better manage our time and eliminate undue anxiety.

This is how my good friend Jane simplified her life at home:

Jane is a successful executive at a major corporation. At times her travel schedule was such that she was spending a scant couple of days at home before getting on a plane again. One day she found herself in the absurd situation of having bought a new house but not being able to find the time to pack and move into it. The situation was becoming a big problem until an interior decorator she had known for years offered to move her things while she was traveling. The fee was reasonable, and her decision was immediate. Soon after, Jane left on another trip, and when she returned a few days later, she went from the airport directly to her new home. All her belongings were in place, and her friend was waiting for her with a glass of champagne in hand.

Jane had found a way to simplify her personal life to clear her mind and concentrate on her professional success by relying on her support system. Today, she relies on service professionals to take care of things she doesn't have time for. Her system is based on fixed service fees that she can budget for in advance.

By thinking outside the box and exploring options, Jane was able to delegate to a capable professional to simplify her life and achieve a good balance between personal and job demands.

How Jane used the ABC Approach

1. **Accept Complexity as a Constant in Life.** Jane understood that life was complex and fighting that reality would get her nowhere, so she decided to embrace it.

2. **Build a New Support System.** Jane shared her problems with her support system and discovered that her interior decorator was willing and capable of doubling his role as an ad hoc moving company. Problem solved.

3. **Capitalize on A and B.** Jane embraced simplicity when she decided to put her dilemma in the hands of her support system. That was the day she went on a trip and came back to a beautiful new home where everything was in place and she could immediately relax.

Sometimes we are too prone to take care of everything ourselves without asking for help. Or we rule out some good alternatives because we assume that they will be excessively expensive, and we end up exhausted and frustrated. In my case, my husband and son helped me understand that I was trying to do everything myself, only asking for help when I was already exhausted. It took me a while to realize that they didn't mind helping, but it didn't occur to them to offer. I now delegate at home just as I do at the office and it works well for everyone.

Try to avoid saying no to yourself. Instead, find out if you can add some simplicity to your life by budgeting for professional services that can help balance your personal and working life. It's the cost of doing business.

The story below illustrates the advantages of delegating to others tasks that you are capable of doing but are not the best use of your time.

A few years ago, I was leading an executive-level delegation of twenty companies interested in doing business in a particular foreign country. Organizing business meetings and visits to industrial sites was important, but it would consume valuable time that I wanted to dedicate to helping the participants strategize to take full advantage of the opportunities the trip was designed to offer.

The solution was to entrust part of the program to a third party who was well-established in the local market. From experience I knew that some local American Chambers of Commerce offer reliable and cost-effective services, and I arranged to work with Laura, an employee with extensive experience in handling foreign delegations. Using our respective business networks, Laura helped set meetings for all members of the delegation, including a one-day visit to a major annual industrial trade fair.

As it turned out, I fell sick on the day of the visit to the trade fair. This would have been a disastrous situation if I had decided to handle everything by myself. All I had to do, however, was ask Laura to fill in. She did an excellent job, and the members of the delegation were delighted with the experience. The entire trip was a resounding success.

Think Ahead

More and more professionals today realize that to succeed in the global market they need to develop a deeper understanding of foreign cultures and strengthen the skills necessary to establish better personal connections with foreign nationals. Undoubtedly, the best way to get experience and fine-tune existing or newly acquired skills is through real-life experiences. This means that instead of traveling with the mentality of the average tourist, professionals should travel with the intent of gathering specific information that is relevant to their business purposes.

Average tourists are those who travel outside their usual environment for leisure and recreation, typically on much-needed vacations. They seek to "disconnect" from the office the moment they get out of town. Depending on personal preferences, they may engage in physical activities or read a book while enjoying the peace of a beautiful beach or mountain lodge. Tourists also enjoy discovering the mysteries of a foreign country, learning about its history, visiting famous landmarks, trying out local food, and attending special events. Regardless, the goal is to clear the mind of business-related concerns.

On the other hand, as a professional seeking to expand your knowledge of the global market, you have a different agenda. You can still do what tourists do, but you will also look at the world from a business perspective. You will acquire business intelligence and cultural literacy through an agenda that includes a cultural orientation as well as business meetings with other professionals.

For example, even before you leave on a trip you can take any of these steps:

- **Build a database** of people from other cultures (e.g., foreign students, co-workers, and neighbors) who might be willing to share their experiences with you.
- **Join groups** that attract foreign nationals as participants and speakers.
- **Expand your network,** physical or virtual, contacting your company's offices abroad and establishing a dialogue or specific collaboration with local employees in those offices.
- **Ask for short assignments** that expose you to other markets. Travel abroad with a genuine interest in learning from others to build your own toolbox of skills and wisdom.

Once you are in a foreign country, your target list will include visits with:

- Local Chambers of Commerce.
- Local American Chamber of Commerce (AmCham).
- Commercial attachés at your embassies.
- Well-known university professors.
- Professional organizations, particular those you belong to in your home country.

If you are a member of an international professional organization, you can get information about colleagues or friends of colleagues that agree to meet you during the trip. These people can be great sources of valuable insight into how business is conducted in the host country.

For a more personal touch, ask a colleague to make a virtual introduction ahead of time. Then suggest that your colleagues' associate meet you for a cup of coffee, lunch, or dinner (at your expense) in a place of their choice. This allows you to gauge what's customary and get a feel for people and places in an informal setting. This also helps establish friendships outside of the more formal business environment. (Your travel budget should come from your professional development budget, and if planned correctly your trip may be tax deductible.)

Make sure to exercise precaution when traveling anywhere in the world. You need to know where it's safe to go and what neighborhoods or situations to avoid. It's always mystifying to see how many people think that they can ignore common sense when they are away from home. Somehow, they travel abroad under the false notion that, because nobody knows them, they are invisible and invincible and free to do and go as they please. Some are naïve enough to believe that because they are friendly, others will reciprocate in the same fashion. In that frame of mind, they may easily become involved in situations that put their lives at risk.

While walking down a popular boulevard filled with tourists in a major foreign city, my husband observed a Western woman and her daughter, a child of three or four years of age, walking ahead of him. Like everyone else, they were enjoying the festive atmosphere provided by boisterous street vendors and their colorful displays of produce, clothing and souvenirs.

The woman was suddenly approached by a local child, one of many street beggars that pester tourists for a few coins. Upon seeing the poor child, the women instantly stopped, opened her purse and started rummaging inside looking for her wallet. When she finally found it, she opened it wide revealing a chunk of bills, which she proceeded to examine in search for small denominations or lose coins. The purse was left hanging wide open from her arm.

All the while, her daughter had continued to walk ahead alone and was becoming lost in the crowd. The woman didn't notice that her child was no longer by her side, not even when the daughter, realizing that she was alone, turned around confused and started to walk back to rejoin her mother.

The woman never realized the danger she had created for herself and her daughter because she had been utterly unaware of her surroundings. In a split second, the situation could have turned into a tragedy. The daughter could have been snatched away, never to be seen again. The adult supervising the little beggar could have seized the opportunity to grab the woman's wallet and purse and then disappear with money, passports, and credit cards, leaving mother and daughter stranded in a strange city and without the means to even return to their hotel.

As a professional traveler, however, you are aware of your surroundings and stay alert to situations that are often created with the specific purpose of catching naïve tourists unawares. You know it's common for pickpockets to use children to distract their targets while they steal wallets, watches, or purses; in extreme cases, they may also kidnap people.

Awareness means that you consider ahead of time the possibility of danger in a situation like the one described above. Equipped with this information, your brain sends you a timely warning and you become instantly alert and act accordingly. You can still help the child beggar, but in a controlled environment. When thieves sense you are in control they go away in pursuit of easier targets.

Some people get into trouble because they try to save money by staying in a hotel on the wrong side of town. As a professional and business traveler you know better; as a general rule you stay in renowned hotel chains knowing that safety comes first and lodging is not where you want to save money. Choose the wrong establishment in the wrong neighborhood and your life could be at stake. The same applies to tourists visiting your home town and choosing to stay in a dilapidated hotel with poor security.

In addition to comfort, well-known hotel chains offer a number of advantages that justify the cost: they are located in safe areas, take an interest in your personal safety, and offer reliable taxi and tour services. They can send a taxi to pick you up at the airport, an invaluable service in most countries. The concierge can also advise you on the best places to visit, good restaurants, and local events.

Be sure to carry the hotel telephone number with you in case you are in trouble or just to request a safe taxi service to return to the hotel. When dining alone, beware of overly friendly people who end up offering a ride back to the hotel. Do not accept, and stay in the safety of a public place until you get a taxi service on your own.

When you travel to a country for the first time, it's highly advisable to arrange for a professional tour guide through the hotel or a trusted travel agency. (My travel agent covers the world and has a perfect record of recommending safe and high-quality services.) To get started, schedule a one-day guided tour of the main city to get a feel for the place and a basic orientation before you explore it on your own. Ask the tour guide as many questions as possible. Tour guides usually enjoy their jobs and like to talk; they are trained to know important and relevant information and will appreciate your interest in what they know. Again, hire the best you can find. In a later chapter, I elaborate on this topic and offer some tips about maintaining your safety when a country you are visiting is going through sociopolitical instability.

> Joining a group on a city tour is a good idea even if you are short of time. While in Hong Kong, I had only a few hours available for sightseeing and agreed to join a group tour for German tourists with a German-speaking Chinese guide. It turned out to be delightful. It provided the opportunity to practice the language and, as expected, the Chinese guide spoke fluent English and was happy to translate to English whenever necessary.

Ask the tour guide to meet you at the hotel, and let the concierge know which service you will be using. I have often engaged the help of the concierge to clarify unexpected charges that had not been stipulated ahead of time. If you happen to encounter a guide that does not speak acceptable English or doesn't seem to know much, consult with the hotel concierge and ask for another service. Remember that the guide's ignorance may put you at risk.

Spend some time reading about the country's history and the famous landmarks you should visit as a tourist. Get a general idea of the geography, demographics, type of government, current events, weather, favorite sports, political environment, social customs, and language. If you correlate reading material with sightseeing, you'll internalize facts faster and retain more meaningful information than if you only read about or see something for the first time. Just listening to different explanations of historical events generates valuable insight into how the local population thinks and behaves.

For security reasons, don't rely on a tour guide or a street taxi driver to suggest or even take you to a restaurant or shopping center you don't know. Frequently, tour guides are paid a commission for taking tourists to specific restaurants and shops, which may not be the best quality or located in the best areas of the city.

When it comes to suggesting restaurants, entertainment, or other evening events, it's better to rely on the hotel concierge. Their suggestions are bound to be more expensive but also more secure. Reputable hotels feel responsible for their guests and want to avoid the bad publicity that would result if anything bad were to happen to you. They can also provide safe transportation.

Using local transportation in any place involves risk. One that few people consider is the risk of meeting charming strangers at a restaurant or bar who offer you a friendly ride back to your hotel.

I was doing business in a famous cosmopolitan city known for its friendly people and feisty atmosphere.

Unfortunately, at that time the city was suffering from a wave of attacks on naïve tourists. Criminals would engage tourists at restaurants and bars and offer them a friendly ride back to the hotel, only to leave the unsuspected visitor stranded on a beach with no money, or worse.

Following my ABC formula, I accepted the limitations that this situation imposed on my plans to visit the city; then, I set out to build a local network I could trust. This network consisted of two people: the experienced concierge at the reputable hotel chain where I chose to stay, and the experienced chauffeur provided by the concierge whom I could call on from anywhere, at any time. The willingness to spend a bit extra for personal safety freed my mind of concerns and made it possible to enjoy the trip.

Because your goal is to build a reputation in the business environment, make it a point to visit places favored by professionals and business people, and observe their customs and behavior. Knowing about popular places that cater to the business community also gives you a conversation topic when you meet local colleagues or partners and makes you look and feel integrated.

Everyone likes visitors who take the time to be well-informed about local trends and preferences. It shows acceptance on your part and a desire to integrate into the local community. If you are traveling alone, avoid using room service. It wastes an opportunity to learn about local customs.

While in Shanghai, I stayed at a beautiful hotel with a magnificent restaurant. I had just arrived and didn't feel like going out, so I went down to the restaurant only to find out that the food, lavishly displayed in different "stations," was totally alien to me. I noticed that every dish was surrounded by a variety of sauces to choose from. Rather than risking disappointment by making the wrong choices, I approached the maître d' and explained my dilemma. He was delighted to personally escort me to every station, explaining the origin of the dishes and the wisdom of mixing the right sauces with the right food. He then ordered the waiter to take care of me according to his instructions on what dishes to bring, and I enjoyed a delightful evening being pampered and eating a most wonderful meal. It could have been awkward, but by following the ABC formula, I simplified my life and was able to turn the situation into a learning experience and expand my local support system.

What Companies Expect of You

Regardless of your idea of success, keep in mind that, in a globalized economy, corporations are looking for individuals who are mentally prepared to handle global businesses.

Companies Look for These Qualities:

Relocation. Willingness to work and live in foreign countries and experience traveling abroad.

Operations leadership. Ability to run complex operations in different geographic regions, developing a local talent pool and effectively dealing with the local community at every level.

Global competencies. Knowledgeable about world affairs, societal and cultural differences, and preferably the local language; confident when dealing with governments, corporations, and customers.

Team development. Skilled at building highly effective teams at all levels within the organization, both at home and abroad; skillful in dealing with a high degree of cultural diversity. Identifying, managing, and closing the competencies gap in a global workforce.

Adaptability. Able to deal with uncertainty and ambiguity, embracing diversity as a powerhouse for sustainable innovation and growth.

Geocentric skills. Capable of recognizing and respecting the knowledge and skills that local individuals and enterprises bring to the table, contributing to the achievement of company goals.

Awareness and assimilation. Adept at identifying and relating to external forces at play in the immediate and global surroundings, mastering the balancing the act of applying pressure or yielding as necessary to achieve business objectives on time.

Chapter Eight

Expect the Unexpected—
A New Kind of Leadership

To expect the unexpected shows a thoroughly modern intellect.

— Oscar Wilde[*]

With few exceptions, many emerging markets still suffer from significant lack of physical and institutional infrastructure, at least as seen from a Western perspective, and their regulatory systems are still fluid. Until these markets have time to build the kind of reliable systems we take for granted, the risk of operational disruptions in a local industry value chain is very high. Sometimes disruptions occur not because the local industry is ineffective, but rather because practices are different from, and at times better than, what we are used to. Whatever the cause, when local practices don't allow us to conduct business the way we want to, our plans are disrupted, and fixing things on the go is always costly.

Those Nasty Missing Links

Let's say that you are in the furniture industry. You manufacture and sell furniture, and you have a proven system in your country that allows you to cost efficiently move from acquiring raw materials to manufacturing to your end customer. Chances are your system doesn't exist in, and cannot be replicated in, another country. Unless you conduct a step-by-step "walk through" of the

---

[*] Oscar Wilde Quotes. BrainyQuote.com, Xplore Inc, 2018. https://www.brainyquote.com/quotes/oscar_wilde_130294, accessed February 10, 2018.

entire process using the resources available in the local market, you will not know what's missing relative to the system you are accustomed to. Worse yet, you'll not be able to budget ahead of time to handle system disruptions.

Here is a real-life example that illustrates how many companies operate when engaging in international business:

A young entrepreneur had identified an attractive business opportunity consisting of importing perishable food from developing countries into the U.S. using a route that significantly reduced the time usually needed to reach American consumers. He had spent two years searching for a $20 million investment for this new venture with zero results. He was finally referred to my office for help. His business plan was adequate but required strengthening to grab the attention of serious investors. After a few weeks, with a solid business plan at hand, I was able to secure $2 million in seed capital from private investors to assemble the first management team. According to the initial assessment, the project had significant merit and needed to be expanded to reach the critical mass that would ensure success. The team was charged with scaling up the project to a projected $60 million investment, and I became one of three team members charged with developing the project finance proposal.

Two of our senior team members were experts in the U.S. food industry and responsible for outlining the logistics of the entire process—from the moment the grower planted the seed in the ground to the day the food reached the consumer in a U.S. supermarket. Armed with a deeper understanding of the industry, we decided that the most attractive business structure was to act as an importer, while subcontracting services as needed along the value chain. With that decision made, we went to work on the proposal for project financing that would secure the funds necessary to launch and operate the new venture. It was an exciting time for everyone.

Little did we know at the time how wrong we were.   *(Continues below)*

Note that in this example, all the financial projections were based on the knowledge of the *U.S.* food industry. Time and time again, senior executives, confident of their own experience, fail to consider that their industry may operate in an entirely different fashion in other countries. Convinced that they know how things ought to work, they neglect to account for those nasty missing links that are likely to exist in almost any industry on the other side of the ocean.

Unfortunately, once those in charge make strategic and financial decisions, they then quickly deploy resources, and the business is launched, only to encounter one unexpected difficulty after another. By the time surprises start to appear, no approved budget exists to deal with necessary remedies, and the operation quickly pivots into emergency mode, usually missing target revenues and eventually collapsing altogether.

This is what happened to Walmart in Germany and Best Buy in China, where their stand-alone facilities built on the outskirts of major cities proved unreachable because the local infrastructure and customs didn't match those typically found in the U.S.

Expecting the unexpected should be a mantra for executives making decisions regarding emerging markets. Not surprisingly, the majority still stick to traditional thinking. With the right information at hand, companies can evaluate options before committing to new markets:

1. Come up with a more suitable business model;
2. Stick to the existing model but budget for additional activities (e.g., establishing convenient shuttle buses for customers to reach their faraway locations); or
3. Skipping the market altogether.

Expecting the unexpected allows business developers to uncover—at a much lower cost than closing operations—the barriers they need to address before getting in the game. Let's see how this approach changed the plans for the client's new food import venture:

As we started to work on the proposal for project finance, we engaged in playing with various scenarios and started to question the validity of our assumptions. On paper, the new venture was an importer dealing with well-established growers and exporters, plus land and ocean transportation services at the point of origin and point of entry. As soon as the produce was on a vessel heading our way, we could start selling it to U.S. supermarkets.

Questions that came to mind: What if the produce was delayed before it was loaded on the vessel? What could prevent the produce from reaching port on either side of the ocean? What if contract terms with suppliers were significantly different from ours? How competitive was this market? How were local competitors handling their operations?

We realized that to attract private and institutional investors and convince them to support the new venture we needed to provide hard data to answer these and other questions. As VP International, it fell upon me to come up with a fast and reliable way to learn about the status of the food industry in target countries in the shortest possible time. It was then that I developed a six-week, full "industry immersion" process that proved quite useful and successful. It basically consisted of talking to everyone along the local industry value chain to collect hard data, as well as putting together seemingly unrelated intelligence.

It quickly became clear that our original strategy was erroneous. The local competitive environment was tightly controlled and hostile to new players. This made conditions on the ground difficult, to the point at which we couldn't control any step along the local value chain unless we owned it.

Third-party services wouldn't be available or reliable enough without close supervision. Land and ocean transportation in target countries was poor, scarce, and nearly impossible to secure on a regular basis from a distance. Political ties were quite strong, and this demanded close interaction with local governments and government agencies.

Going back to the drawing board, we changed our entry strategy and allocated extra funds to support a different business structure that would provide the control we needed. With hard data at hand, we were able to raise considerably more than the initial estimated amount. The business launched with historical success and was later sold to a larger operator.

Investing a few weeks to add on-the-ground, first-hand perspective to your assumptions pays off in that you are better equipped to:

- Structure your business correctly
- Develop the right entry strategy
- Secure appropriate funding
- Understand the competitive landscape
- Develop personal connectivity with stakeholders

The benefits you will enjoy result from resisting the temptation to believe that you know what you need to know; this belief is the reason many companies jump into tactical mode too soon—and with half-baked strategies.

What about speed and accuracy? You may think that it takes too long to uncover everything you need to know about conditions on the ground, and the information you get may be misleading. This is true only if you don't know where to look or how to deal with foreign nationals.

An important factor in the success in this story involved the speed at which I was able to gather the right kind of information while interviewing people on the ground.

Using the same methodology described in this book, I interviewed and established quick rapport with diverse groups of local players in five countries representing different social strata and political views. The best information about the climate within the industry came from visits to rural areas, where I talked directly with growers who were at the bottom of the financial totem pole. We conducted meetings either outdoors or in small houses, intermixed with impromptu invitations to share a meal of local food and drinks.

On one occasion, when visiting poor growers outside the main city, I was invited to drink "mate" (MAH-teh), an herbal infusion commonly shared with friends in countries such as Argentina, Brazil, Paraguay, and Uruguay. Mate is served in a hollow gourd and sipped through a silver spoon (a *bombilla*) designed to filter the herb leaves. The custom calls for true friends to drink from a single gourd and *bombilla* passed around in a circle. I wasn't going to offend my hosts by declining to share the bombilla, but in a delicate gesture of cultural sensitivity, they handed me a fresh gourd and bombilla for my exclusive use. It was very touching and will never be forgotten.

The overall success of the venture in this story was based on following the guidelines provided earlier on how to connect effectively with other cultures. The intelligence-gathering process was successful because it combined:

- *Seniority*—to access the top echelons of industry and government
- *Cultural awareness and understanding*—to establish quick trust and rapport
- *Experience and ability to ask the right questions*—to uncover hidden agendas
- *Familiarity with the environments*—to gain acceptance in urban and rural areas

The factors contributing to the overall success of the business venture in this story are condensed in my *Ten Tenets for Business Success*, discussed later in this chapter.

Do More with Less

In keeping with the pragmatic approach to life and business presented throughout this book, you can practice your new mindset as you examine the challenges faced by international companies today. The examples shared throughout this chapter illustrate how executives and companies use new ideas and tools to increase awareness and understanding of their surroundings, clearing their minds to do more with less. This chapter also highlights one of the most important applications of the updated mindset proposed in this book: the acquired ability to expect the unexpected and to plan ahead for surprises that otherwise can create havoc in your strategic plans.

Although awareness, understanding, and knowledge are three important stages in adjusting your mindset, you also need to work at internalizing new concepts and ideas until you make them your own. This is best achieved through practice and after experiencing the benefits of the results, much like what professional basketball players do every day when learning new techniques. Their five-step process goes like this:

1. First, they have to buy into the idea of adopting a new technique. There has to be an incentive for them to change the way they have been shooting the ball up to now *(Part I—Awareness)*.
2. That incentive is related to personal reward and business success. Once they are convinced that adopting a new way of playing brings tangible benefits, they buy into it *(Part II—Understanding)*.
3. Understanding leads to willingness to learn specific and more difficult steps and maneuvers that will generate the desired results *(Part III—Knowledge)*.
4. Once they know and realize they can master the technique, they start unconsciously assimilating it as an integral part of the way they play *(Part IV—Internalization)*.
5. Finally, they deliberately seek to perfect the use of the new technique, practicing it until the motion is done consistently, with confidence, as an extension of their arm *(Part V—Practice)*.

Internalizing and intentionally practicing and mastering new strategies and techniques allows professional players to achieve more with less effort. It is how they become stars at their game.

In the business arena, however, it's still remarkable how many corporations don't take time to learn, assimilate, and put into practice more advanced ways of doing business.

Put a group of executives in a room to discuss and decide whether the company is ready to succeed abroad, and the most common reaction you're likely to get is a typical Alpha reaction—"Sure, we have done it before, we can do it again!" They enthusiastically jump right into the water, only to realize later they don't know how to swim and they either drown or are eaten by sharks.

Thinking outside the box is a rare skill. Companies are better at it when inventing something totally new. But when it comes to modifying what they have been doing for decades, original thinking plummets to near zero. Driven by the high purchasing power and sophisticated tastes of consumers in industrialized countries, multinationals have become used to adopting complex manufacturing processes to produce expensive products. Accustomed to building Cadillacs, they are now suddenly faced with cash-starved consumers in emerging markets who want to buy good-quality bicycles and scooters.

This is a serious problem for multinationals, because local competitors are able to manufacture quality products at affordable prices and thus capture substantial market share. At best, Western companies operating abroad may be able to manufacture cheaper goods locally for exportation to their home country, but they still have trouble making goods cheaply enough to get a solid foothold in local markets.

They need to simplify their processes, but unfortunately *simplicity* is not a word you will find in the operating manuals of conventional Western companies. It's a daunting proposition to reverse decades of complexity and high operation cost. For one thing, Western engineers are proud of their sophisticated designs. They are generally over-qualified and unable or unwilling to generate simplified products better suited for emerging markets.

Service companies face a similar situation. They also need to manage the reality—or perception—that their services are overpriced, and they risk losing business not only to local competitors but also to the growing pool of competitors operating across emerging markets (see the discussion on South–South trade in Chapter 4).

New Markets—Problem or Opportunity?

It depends on the corporate culture:

- Companies entrenched in their ways will plunge ahead and hit their heads against a wall of smart competition.
- Companies investing in educating the consumer on their benefits have a greater chance of succeeding.
- Companies doing both—educating and adjusting their business model—stand to be the most successful.

At the beginning of Chapter 7, I mentioned that simplicity is not a beginning but a destination; we achieve simplicity rather than start with it. Simplicity is the crowning reward of our development process.

That may be exactly what we are starting to see in the global market today: The most innovative and self-confident companies are achieving and embracing simplicity. Instead of resisting change, we see them avidly learning from their foreign counterparts and local services about the best ways to lower costs to conquer new markets. Take, for example, the case of the way Unilever approaches low-income African consumers:

Unilever, an Anglo-Dutch consumer goods company with global operations, became aware that the emerging middle class in Africa had a taste for brands but was suspicious of new products advertised through mass media. A society that makes decisions based on personal relations and trust required a localized approach to marketing.

Instead of handling the situation directly, Unilever built an instant support system by working with Creative Council, a company specializing in what is called "below-the-line" or "door-to-door" marketing, which is better suited to accessing African consumers. Creative Council organizes "Zonal Champions," regular local citizens who literarily go from home to home informing consumers about the benefits of particular products. Because local consumers have little disposable income, they are wary of making mistakes and need the kind of personal assurance that comes from people they know or can relate to.[1]

Unilever went back to basics and adopted simplicity, setting aside any concerns about using the door-to-door approach, to achieve the market penetration they sought to win. They successfully used the ABCs of Simplicity:

1. **Accept Complexity as a Constant in Life.** Unilever accepted the fact that the African market was different from other markets and required a new approach. Embracing instead of fighting the new reality, Unilever kept an open mind and was able to find a creative way to address the new challenge.
2. **Build a New Support System.** Working with a company like Creative Council, Unilever adopted the new concept of Zonal Champions and gained immediate access to a segment of the market that traditional advertising would have missed.
3. **Capitalize on A and B.** Instead of starting from scratch, Unilever achieved simplicity by taking advantage of a local system with proven results. They bought into the idea that the old door-to-door selling technique was exactly what they needed to conquer the African market. They are doing more with less—that's simplicity!

What Smart Companies Do

A good but still small number of smart, agile companies (such as Unilever, GE, PepsiCo, and IBM) are taking an aggressive look at the way they do business. They don't hesitate to listen, learn, and integrate with local markets, becoming local players looking out rather than foreign players looking in. When it comes to defining business strategy and tactics, most companies tend to consider their strengths, but rarely their weaknesses. Successful companies, however, take a close look not only at their strengths and weaknesses but also at the strengths and weaknesses of their local counterparts, uncovering opportunities for valuable and profitable collaboration.

> Being in the black in three years
> is not a strategy, it's a goal.

Through partnering with local enterprises, smart companies develop new co-innovation and co-exporting models to serve local markets, but they also serve the world from emerging markets into other emerging and developed markets. These companies do some or most of the following:

- Aggressively look for ways to simplify their traditional operations.
- Listen to and learn from local strategic partners.
- Seek partnerships with local governments to improve infrastructure conditions.
- Develop localized products and educate consumers about existing products.
- Adjust their pricing model to reach lower-income customers.
- Develop and adopt lower-cost manufacturing models on a global basis.
- Redistribute decision making to get closer to the point of contact.
- Hire local talent (as available) to lead or help run local operations.
- Create a local leadership pipeline and invest in local education and training.
- Invest in local excellence and efficiency programs.
- Have local R&D centers lead innovation for emerging and developed markets.
- Expand their footprint in diverse markets.
- Adopt local practices for financing local customers.
- Develop co-innovation and co-exportation models to serve the world from emerging markets.

But the number of companies resisting change remains too high, and many continue to incur high investment costs with little or no return. To be fair, a good number of emerging challenges are out of any single company's direct control—such as arbitrary government policies and preferential treatment of local competitors, or a lack of physical and institutional infrastructure.

These areas represent a growing opportunity for collaborative efforts among companies to campaign for, and in many cases share the costs of, improving local conditions for the betterment of all involved. Paying for infrastructure in exchange for leniency on certain local competition regulations represents that next level of development, and some of the most innovative companies are already engaged in this collaborative approach.

Visualize, for example, mining companies that have traditionally developed communities and infrastructure around their operations to provide their workers what they need. Today, these companies are extending their community improvement programs to protecting the environment. Granted, these measures are not necessarily voluntary, but rather required by local authorities and community leaders; still, they offer a model for a collaborative approach to elevating the quality of other local industries.

Most challenges, however, are related to companies' internal corporate cultures. The next section describes common mistakes that Western companies are prone to make when entering new markets.

Ten Common Mistakes When Entering Emerging Markets

1. **Information Saturation Paralysis.** A high level of white noise surrounds today's global market risk and opportunities. An excess of information makes it difficult to sort out what is truly relevant and can have a paralyzing effect on those responsible for defining and guiding a corporation's entry and expansion strategies. The challenge starts with how to decide which emerging markets should make it to the short list and how to prioritize. This lack of clarity slows down the decision-making process, because executives attend endless meetings without resolving which path to follow. Frustration escalates as otherwise capable executives keep going in circles and delaying action. Companies able to effectively manage the white noise and separate the right signals from the inconsequential ones stand the best chance of succeeding.

2. **Overconfidence.** Companies that believe they can easily export their products and services to foreign markets are still living in the last century—a time when developing countries were eager to attract Western products, know-how, and investment and when local manufacturing was unable to compete with imported goods. None of this is the case today. First, governments in emerging markets now understand the leverage they have to negotiate favorable terms and conditions with foreign entities seeking to capitalize on a new consumer base. Second, thanks to global communications, emerging consumers are more sophisticated and demand localization—that is, products designed to satisfy their specific needs and budgets. Third, local manufacturing and service companies are more competitive and can operate at lower cost, thus providing attractive alternatives to local consumers.

3. **Lack of Confidence.** Companies reticent to enter new markets and wait for others to pave the way find it increasingly more difficult to gain market

share later on. They miss out on the opportunity to learn and gain experience early in the game and allow others to establish a solid footprint among the local consumer base. In fast-evolving markets, delayed action places a company behind the curve, and the cost of trying to pull alongside and surpass well-established competitors may prove prohibitive. They also falsely believe that entering a new market simply requires high initial costs that can be paid for by the first wave of entrants. In reality, the first companies to enter a market learn lessons not easily gleaned by future entrants, who will stumble regardless of when they attempt to enter the market.

4. **Overlooked Industry and Capability Gaps.** Based on my experience working with senior management in Fortune 500 companies, I've noted that many companies overlook the reality that emerging markets are still in the process of building the kind of physical and institutional infrastructure we take for granted in the U.S. and elsewhere. This leads to the assumption that what works at home will work equally well abroad. However, any missing link in the local industry infrastructure may cause significant interruptions to the company's process. Management often realizes too late that their trusted capabilities may be inadequate to get the job done. Fixing capability gaps after the company has started operations in the field is the most expensive way to approach a developing market.

   Companies are better off uncovering ahead of time the hidden missing links that exist in the local industry and budgeting for solutions from the start, as illustrated by the food-industry story at the beginning of this chapter. Winners anticipate and verify breaks in infrastructure at the industry and country level and are willing to critically assess their own capability mismatch relative to local market conditions. By doing so, they turn obstacles into opportunities and bridge broken paths by adding, modifying, or reengineering the way they operate before making substantial, irreversible commitments.

5. **Irrelevance.** I am a strong advocate of companies finding ways to be relevant to the local market in which they wish to operate. More than ever, the best business deals and subsequent successes depend on advancing value propositions, which are hard to turn down because they effectively address the interest and needs of key stakeholders. In today's highly competitive environment, success belongs to companies that understand the importance of being relevant to the local market and go beyond just taking care of business.

   Foreign corporations are expected to be active participants in and contributors to improving conditions on the ground, not only by protecting the environment but also by stimulating economic development through investing in local infrastructure, financing local capabilities, and contributing to communities by hiring and educating the local workforce. In markets with traditional collectivistic practices, establishing a collaborative relationship with local governments and local communities distinguishes long-term, serious partners from opportunistic, short-term players.

6. **Corporate Isolation.** I encourage senior Western executives and managers to leave the comfort of their local offices or luxury hotels and walk the streets, meeting local leaders and employees on their own turf. In the last century, it was common practice to avoid integrating into the local community, but today that's a practice no company or successful executive can afford to ignore. Local markets are changing so fast that executives need daily access to relevant intelligence and information that can help them make timely adjustments to their strategy and local operations. They need to become an integral part of the local business society in order to learn how to anticipate changes that can affect their business. This interaction also allows them to influence outcomes and steer their companies to safety, not only during normal business periods, but also through times of sociopolitical unrest and business down cycles.

   Companies that tend to focus solely on the end customer fail to recognize and address the needs of the wide range of stakeholders essential to their success. These include local leaders, movers and shakers in business and politics, social groups and communities—each of which represents strong circles of influence.

7. **Insufficient Leadership Skills.** Traditional leadership qualities (vision, intelligence, determination, and resilience) are often insufficient to succeed in emerging markets, where personal relationships tend to precede business relationships. Successful global leaders learn to exercise emotional intelligence: the ability to understand the emotional makeup of other people, manage relationships, build networks, reach common ground, and build rapport.

   Lack of emotional intelligence results in isolation and virtually guarantees failure. Non-industrialized countries rely heavily on personal interaction and trust. Therefore, Western executives who practice isolation instead of integration are not only left clueless about the market changes but are excluded by local prospective partners who consider personal rapport an essential factor in accepting and collaborating with new business partners.

8. **Aloofness and Resistance to Change.** My research and interaction with multinationals consistently shows that successful companies are those that embrace change as part of their culture. They are flexible and agile enough to quickly adapt to market demands both at home and abroad. These companies also understand that they cannot operate in emerging markets from a distance and are assigning senior decision makers to run

local operations, thus significantly shortening the time it takes to adopt measures that keep them ahead of the pack.

This is an essential quality in emerging markets, in which local competitors continue to acquire global capabilities and are rapidly getting ahead in the game. On the other hand, Western companies capable of localizing and reinventing themselves are well positioned to succeed in today's global market.

9. **Resilience Deficiency.** Resilience is the name of the game when it comes to entering emerging markets. One successful campaign is not enough to succeed, just like one failure is not enough to fail. Acting quickly or slowly is not as important as acting based on reliable insight and information. Smart companies use precise market intelligence conducted by individuals with meaningful multicultural experience, and they then use this information to adjust their plans according to market conditions. At times they may take baby steps to test market behavior and then capitalize on their own field experience.

   Both strong initial investment and patient discovery help companies act with confidence by making use of first-hand knowledge to arrive at better decisions and consolidate their market presence more effectively and efficiently.

10. **Lack of Ingenuity.** The level of survival instinct and ingenuity demonstrated by local players in emerging markets never ceases to amaze me. Lacking the security of the economic prosperity, orderly political and institutionalized business, and legal environments that characterize industrialized countries, local companies rely on ingenuity to come up with low-cost solutions to satisfy customer needs.

    By contrast, Western companies are highly sophisticated and thus bogged down by the high cost of their complex mixes of products and services. Smart Western companies are pushing aside sophistication in favor of ingenuity in order to come up with good-quality products and services at a fraction of the cost of their more complex counterparts. These companies benefit from entering new markets with high consumer interest but still limited purchasing power.

Even though emerging markets are more structured today than they were 25 years ago, they're still in the developing stages and lack many of the advanced systems we take for granted in industrialized markets. It all goes back to the ABCs of simplicity:

1. Accept complexity as a constant in life.
2. Build a support system that helps fill gaps in local conditions.
3. Capitalize on A and B by going back to basics in the way you do business abroad.

Case Studies in Simplicity

The examples below further illustrate how some companies have embraced the ABCs of simplicity:

Case #1:

- **Accept Complexity / Problem Statement.** Governments in emerging markets are unable or seemingly unwilling to come up with consistent regulations that allow us to plan our businesses. China is well known for arbitrarily changing the rules to favor local competitors.
- **Build New Support Systems / Option Statement.** The Chinese government is unaware of the way industrialized countries have solved these problems. Let's work with the government to help them understand the benefits of our system, and let's partner with it to help develop the infrastructure needed to support future growth.
- **Capitalize on A and B / Action.** IBM opened an innovation center in Beijing to participate in the country's ambitious high-speed rail construction plans. It also made a small investment of $3 million in the city of Wuxi[2] so it could open a data center for local software firms, managing the IT operations of those firms and hosting their software as a Web-based service. Both projects involved government funding and opened the door to accessing a larger portion of China's two-year stimulus package of over $600 billion, launched in 2008.[3]

One may argue that only multinationals with mighty resources have the luxury of offering help to governments in the way IBM did, but keep in mind that not all emerging markets are as powerful as China. Even in China, local government agencies exist that can benefit from the experience of smaller Western companies. Selecting the right target market should include an assessment of the company's ability to influence change in the local market and the local government.

Some of my colleagues have successfully established a dialogue with governments to bring attention to laws that interfere with normal business. As a result, they have been invited to team up with these governments to help develop new laws. Small companies and individual consultants that have a particular expertise are also in position to help local governments at a municipal level. They may consider joining forces with other individuals or small firms to gain strength in numbers and broaden their expertise and resources.

Case #2:

- **Accept Complexity / Problem Statement.** Every country has different tax laws, and it's a nightmare for our tax specialists to comply with such a wide range of tax regulations. We are doing our best to minimize tax payments related to cross-border transactions.

- **<u>B</u>uild New Support Systems / Option Statement.** Tax evasion by multinational companies has attracted the attention of finance ministers of the 20 most powerful countries (the G20). In 2013, the G20 asked the Organization for Economic Cooperation and Development (OECD), a group of mostly wealthy countries, to come up with a comprehensive global tax system that closes loopholes for multinationals.[4]
- **<u>C</u>apitalize on A and B / Action.** GE supports the G20 and OECD on the basis that a comprehensive global tax system will bring stability to the market. William Morris, GE's senior international tax counsel, who is liaising between business and the OECD on the overhaul, explains the company support: "There is considerable instability [in the market], and instability is the enemy of business and investment."[4] In other words, simplicity is the ultimate destination for successful global business.

Ten Tenets for Business Success

Throughout the course of my career, I have been exposed to a diversity of situations and challenges related to doing business abroad. With experience comes the ability to take a big-picture perspective to confront new challenges, helping to differentiate between issues that must be managed internally and those that can be delegated or contracted out. The decision of Unilever to utilize the services of the local Creative Council is a good example of contracting out the need to adopt a localized approach to below-the-line marketing. The ability to identify and build trust with the right people is essential to form alliances and select reliable vendors who help implement the corporate strategy.

In the process of doing business abroad, I have identified ten tenets for business success (illustrated in Table 8.1). These ten tenets are divided into:

Table 8.1 Ten Tenets for Business Success

Survival ▶ Perspective ▼	Need to Know	Need to Do	Need to Manage	Need to Anticipate	Need to Relate
Mindset					
Strategy					
Tactics					
Connection					
Adjustment					

Five Tenets for Business Perspective

1. Mindset
2. Strategy
3. Tactics
4. Connection
5. Adjustment

Five Tenets for Business Survival

1. Need to Know
2. Need to Do
3. Need to Manage
4. Need to Anticipate
5. Need to Relate

The Five Tenets for Business Perspective Are:

- **Mindset.** Update your mindset to look at the world according to today's realities. Discard preconceived ideas and obsolete business practices. Strive to develop new common sense and innovative thinking. Practice putting yourself in the shoes of your prospective partners or your local competition to understand their needs and interests and how they make decisions. This will allow you to come up with value propositions that take into account everyone's needs and interests.
- **Strategy.** Lead with a well-thought out strategy and maintain control of its execution. Make sure that results match the original intent. Resist the temptation to lose perspective by going into tactical mode when the pressure builds to make things happen fast.
- **Tactics.** Simplify selectively. Delegate wisely to free up your time so that you can think strategically and anticipate changes. If you are setting up operations abroad for the first time, learn to identify trustworthy specialized services that can help you get started with tactical activities that are common to any business, such as leasing office space. Consult with your company's regular banking and legal services to get recommendations on hiring local banks and law firms.
- **Connection.** Learn to connect with people on a personal as well as business basis. Personal and business relations are at the heart of your success and at the center of the updated mindset needed to succeed in this century. If you don't know anyone, volunteer (or ask an employee to volunteer) to join the leadership of a local professional organization as a way to integrate into the community.

- **Adjustment.** Agility and flexibility are the names of the game. Changes are happening at high speed. You and your business need to stay agile and in constant motion. Make anticipating and adjusting to change part of your corporate strategy. A company, regardless of size, should have a risk management officer accountable for establishing and overseeing regular risk evaluations throughout the enterprise.

The Five Tenets for Business Survival Are:

- **Need to Know.** You can't run the business from the board room. Integrate into the local environment to make the right decisions.
- **Need to Do.** Take a critical look at the company's capabilities and culture. Innovate to match local demands.
- **Need to Manage.** Strategy alone will not take you across the finish line. Adopt a hands-on style to effectively manage field operations.
- **Need to Anticipate.** Risk management is the key to success. Don't let complacency set in. Anticipate and train people to deal with disruptions.
- **Need to Relate.** Participate in the local community at all levels. Don't be an outsider looking in.

These Tenets for Business Perspective and Business Survival represent the company's strategic and tactical cultures. They are interconnected and directly influence the actions the company and its leadership need to take to achieve success. This matrix interaction is shown in Table 8.2 (on next page).

Following are four examples (shown numbered and shaded in Table 8.2) on how to best integrate the use of the Ten Tenets for Business Perspective and Survival.

Note that the Ten Tenets for Business
Success is NOT a function-driven but rather a
mindset-driven approach to business.

---

[1] Mindset / Need to Know:

Local Environment from the Board to Ground Level. A fresh, updated mindset helps you understand the local environment, all the way from the boardroom to the ground level. Picture yourself as a local player. The aim is to think, talk, and walk like those you want to do business with. Get into their heads to understand how they do business: what values are at play, and what factors influence their decision-making processes? Is there compatibility between their approach to business and yours?

Table 8.2 Ten Tenets for Business Perspective and Survival

Survival ▶ / Perspective ▼	Need to KNOW	Need to DO	Need to MANAGE	Need to ANTICIPATE	Need to RELATE
Mindset	Local Environment from the Board to the Ground [1]	Address Industry and Company Capability Gaps	Match Strategic Intent with Results [2]	Enterprise Risk: Financial, Political, Economic Safety	Get to Know Stock and Stakeholders at Home and in Host Country
Strategy	Market Intelligence From Diverse Sources	Innovate in Technology and Corporate Culture	Financial, Political, and Human Capital	Global Trends, Business and Political Cycles [3]	Develop a Diversity of People Skills
Tactic	Operations, Management, and Borderless Negotiation	Master the Art of Developing Value-Driven Propositions	Global Workforce, Change and Innovation [4]	Emergency Preparedness, Infrastructure, and Employee Protection	Practice and Fine-Tune Newly Acquired Personal Skills
Connection	Who is Who in Business, Politics, Community, and Social Circles	Integrate into the Local Community; Know and Be Known	Broad and Meaningful Relationship Building and Trust	Political and Business Cycles Local Perception of Company Value	Build a Diverse Base of Supporters at Different Levels
Adjustment	Corporate Capability and Cultural Gaps vis-à-vis Local Environment	Form Mixed Teams to Address Company and Local Environment Gaps	Continuously Evaluate and Adjust Programs and Processes to Achieve Desired Results	Changes in Market Conditions Affecting Overall Strategy	Continuously Review the Reliability of Sources of Information

[2] Mindset / Need to Manage:

Match Strategic Intent with Results. You know that designing an annual corporate strategy or allocating capital is not enough. You need to become a hands-on executive who manages the day-to-day changes occurring abroad so you can make timely adjustments. You can no longer delegate execution to those on the ground. You need to be involved and strike a balance between centralized and localized decision making.

[3] Strategy / Need to Anticipate:

Global Trends, Business and Political Cycles. Economic and political cycles are not new, and there is much to be learned from past cases. There is no excuse for being caught unaware.

I met with Domingo Cavallo, Argentina's Minister of the Economy, in the mid-1990s, when his country's economy was soaring at an annual 5.5 percent growth rate. Cavallo had pegged the peso against the dollar to control an inflation of 5,000 percent in 1989 down to 7.4 percent in 1993, but signs that things were about to change started to become more evident a few years later, including[6]:

- The country's significant debt burden (near 50% of GDP)
- The brief recession caused after the 1995 Mexican financial crisis
- The Asian crisis of 1997
- The IMF warning Argentina of an Asian-style meltdown
- Russia, Brazil, and Turkey enter into crisis

Conventional Reaction: In December of 2001, Argentina finally defaulted on its debt and froze bank accounts, and many Western companies fled the country at great losses.

Unconventional Reaction: We, at a Fortune 200 company, had anticipated the outcome and were ready. Deciding to stay put, we restructured our clients' debt, collected payments as the system allowed, and recovered all payments within two years, when the economy rebounded.

---

[4] Tactics / Need to Manage:

Global Workforce. When managing a Middle Eastern workforce, I found that the concepts of "cause and effect" or "a sequence of steps or processes" are not easily understood. You explain the sequence of steps required to accomplish a goal, and employees will gladly execute the first step and stop.

In their minds, the next steps are not their responsibility. You actually have to explain again the need to take the second step for anyone to take action. Here is what happened when making a transaction at a local Saudi Arabian bank:

I was in a rush to make a withdrawal, so the first thing I asked the clerk was how long it might take to get it done. She told me it wouldn't take more than 15 minutes, which was fine. The clerk did the paper work efficiently and pushed the request for money through a window, and went about other chores. After 45 minutes of waiting, I managed to grab her attention and asked for the reason behind the delay. She didn't know, was not at all concerned, and offered no explanation. When I reminded her that she had said the transaction would take no more than 15 minutes, her proud response was: "Yes, and I did what I had to do in less than 15 minutes!" Again, no other comment or concern about why the process was taking so long. To guide her through the next step I asked: "Couldn't you help me find out what is going on?" To that she answered, quite surprised: "Why? I have nothing to do with it."

Her responsibility was to request the money. In her mind it was someone else's responsibility to actually produce it. I added: "Would you do me a favor and try to find out how long I have to wait?" She smiled and said: "Yes, I'd be glad to do that!" It took another ten minutes to finalize the transaction and I left pulling my hair!

But the experience taught me a valuable lesson. I learned that she was not incapable of helping or unwilling to help. If I wanted things to happen efficiently, I had to adjust and guide the process. I took the lesson to heart and used it later in my daily interaction with Saudi nationals. It was one of the secrets behind my success in getting my team do things faster than anyone else.

Smart Strategies

The pressure to generate short-term results plus the fluidity of the new global environment is forcing C-level executives to modify the way they guide their businesses. Chief strategy officers, for example, are not only designing strategies but taking a hands-on approach in the day-to-day execution of strategies and adjustment of business plans. Chief financial officers (CFOs) are increasingly expected to have a deeper understanding of operations across the enterprise. They also are expected to become more involved in understanding day-to-day operations at home and abroad to uncover hidden and high-cost land mines.

While co-leading a brainstorming session on this topic with several CFOs of multinational companies, I heard one explain that, at a particular time, the only reason he had been able to take an educated financial risk in Brazil was because he had worked in the country before and could understand the cultural nuances surrounding the proposal. Stricter and more complex regulatory and global environments are also expanding the role and increasing the accountability of chief risk officers.

The downside of the increasing demands that global conditions exert on traditional roles is the temptation to focus on tactical issues, leaving leaders with less and less time for strategic thinking and thoughtful evaluation of alternatives. In many cases, nobody takes clear responsibility for helping the company navigate the rough waters resulting from a global economy and increasing sociopolitical unrest. Even those responsible for evaluating enterprise risk focus mostly on financial risk, leaving a wide range of risks undetected and unattended—to the detriment of the company's success.

The higher the demands, the more leaders must resist the pressure to operate in tactical mode instead of strategic mode, and the more important it becomes to adopt simplicity as a way to do more with less. More time should be spent identifying and developing new support systems that help delegate the extra weight. I am not referring to outsourcing, which can be detrimental to the company's future if overdone, but to forming smart partnerships in which two sides learn from each other and accomplish more than either would acting independently.

One example of how to do this is the co-innovation and co-exportation models mentioned earlier in this chapter. By recognizing that others outside the company also have the capability to innovate, smart executives and professionals are teaming up with local talent to jointly address the demands of the new global market.

By establishing joint manufacturing centers abroad and increasing education and training, companies are also sharing the burden of servicing the global market. Pride aside, these steps are increasing these companies' probability of success while also elevating the local infrastructure and living standards, in effect making it easier to do business in the future.

Leaders that know how to do more with less have time to stop and search the horizon before setting the sails.

Commoditizing International Business

Remember the days when you had no choice but to hire a lawyer to incorporate your first company? That practice was significantly simplified when templates for incorporation became available in regular stores and sold directly to the general public. All you had to do was fill in the blanks on a form and mail it to your state office of incorporation. Today it's even simpler to incorporate online at the state government website. The process of incorporating a company has been commoditized, and it is worth paying attention to this trend as it permeates other areas of life. Investopedia offers a simple description of commoditizing:

> Commoditizing is "the act of making a process, good, or service easy to obtain by making it as uniform, plentiful, and affordable as possible. Something becomes commoditized when one offering is nearly indistinguishable from another. As a result of technological innovation, broad-based education, and frequent iteration, goods and services become commoditized and, therefore, widely accessible.
>
> "In the past few decades, previously 'modern' things such as microchips, personal computers—even the internet itself—have become essentially commoditized. Combinations of commoditized products such as computers and business software have in effect commoditized many processes, such as business accounting and supply chain management. In a truly capitalist society, the ability to commoditize anything is seen as a benefit to all, and opens up resources that can be put to better use on innovative enterprises."[7]

The advantage of commoditizing the routine side of business is that it frees experienced and specialized professionals to handle new problems brought about by globalization. Service companies, including large consulting and research firms, have long adopted the practice of commoditizing their services.

A common business model consists of hiring recent college graduates to perform routine tasks. College graduates are smart, enthusiastic, and energetic, and they can work long hours; more importantly, they are paid less than older, more specialized personnel. On the down side, college graduates lack corporate experience and, without a frame of reference, they tend to think linearly and abstractedly about real-life business problems.

Cleverly, companies have solved this problem by generating detailed blueprints to guide inexperienced individuals through the thinking process. This frees time for experienced and specialized consulting executives to deal with new and sophisticated problems requiring leading-edge thinking. The disadvantage of this approach is that by commoditizing routine analysis, these companies have created a "blueprint-driven" culture to address recurring problems encountered in business at the expense of a "thinking and innovation-driven" culture, which is essential to developing new leaders and making the company sustainable in the future.

Handled wisely, commoditizing routine tasks is favorable and can be applied to dealing with the global market. Although the market is still fluid and new business models are still in their initial stages, there are ways to simplify certain aspects of doing business abroad. This is true for large corporations, but particularly so for small and medium-sized companies with more limited resources. Many sources of commoditized techniques have been around, mostly ignored, for years.

For example, it may seem obvious, but I am still surprised by how many executives are not aware of the exporting services available through the U.S. government. When visiting a country for business purposes, executives tend to go solo and don't consider contacting the local office of the U.S. Department of Commerce or the commercial section of the U.S. embassy or consulate in that country.

The U.S. government is not the only one that has commoditized initial efforts to identify opportunities abroad. Countries depend heavily on exporting activities, so they have systems in place to support exporters at a reasonable cost. Government agencies are good sources of general information and provide a platform for personal introductions to prospective partners, vendors, and customers in a target market. They have commoditized market outreach efforts.

Whatever you do, pay attention to routine tasks that can be delegated or contracted out to others, so you can free up your time to pay attention to strategy and developing personal relationships.

Examples of information you should consider gathering, directly or indirectly

- Overview of legal and regulatory landscape
- Political risk insurance
- Documentation and product requirements
- Trade finance and insurance information
- Trade problems, including intellectual property
- Search for prospective partners, buyers, and sales representatives
- Introductions to government and industry officials
- Country and industry reports
- Customized market research
- In-country promotion patterns
- Diplomacy for advocacy and dispute resolution
- Updated global payroll data and practices
- Updated global tax regulations
- Overviews of global employee benefits
- Sources of financing
- Update on safety and emergency preparedness

Many of the items above can be handled by outside individuals or institutional specialists for a fee. For example, you might approach the Multilateral Investment Guarantee Agency (MIGA) to learn about political risk insurance. MIGA, a member of the World Bank Group, is dedicated to promoting foreign direct investment in developing countries.[8]

As global business continues to evolve at a fast pace, solutions to common challenges become more easily available through institutionalization and commoditization of services.

In 2013, the Ernst & Young's Global Payroll: Myth or Reality[9] Survey of 161 global senior payroll leaders showed that 85 percent of multinational companies want improvements in their payroll practices and are demanding comprehensive global solutions with local flexibility from current payroll vendors. It's only a matter of time before these services become routine.

What not to commoditize:

Although commoditizing routine aspects of business is useful and saves time, some aspects of the business should be handled internally by the company or by hiring professional experts. These include activities that relate to your unique operations and provide critical information needed to develop your strategy and help identify and manage hidden risks:

- Review of company readiness to enter a target market
- Local industry infrastructure assessment
- Specific competitive analysis
- Specific customer assessment
- Partner selection
- Government relations
- Business relations
- Company branding
- Contractual agreements
- Customer satisfaction
- Vendor selection

A New Kind of Global Leadership

Back in 1946, then Lieutenant General Barton Kyle Yount, Commanding General of the U.S. Army Air Training Command, saw a growing demand for international executive talent and created the American Institute for Foreign

Trade, today known as the Thunderbird School of Global Management, the first business school focused exclusively on international management,[10] one of the top-ranked schools of management in the United States. This kind of global vision was instrumental in helping advance American presence abroad during the last century.

Unfortunately, over the last few decades, we haven't invested enough in building a global business culture among the younger generations of Americans, which is one reason companies increasingly hire and train local talent to run their foreign operations.

In the 2000s, while teaching international business to college and executive students, I was witness to a novel initiative in which global corporations approached American universities to identify the best foreign students attending business schools in the U.S. They offered scholarships and guaranteed jobs to those who qualified if, upon graduation, they agreed to return to their country of origin and work for the sponsoring company. That initiative grew rapidly, and the practice of hiring Western-educated foreign nationals became a norm.

Later, while working in the Middle East, I came across global companies that approached foreign universities and offered to collaborate on curriculum improvement at the undergraduate level. One model provided lecturers to teach students the basics of the sponsoring company's industry. The goal was to identify the best students and, upon graduation, hire those who already had a basic knowledge of the industry. It was a clever way to reduce in-house training.

The greatest beneficiaries of these initiatives are foreign nationals who receive an excellent education and job security, thanks to the lack of Western personnel with strong global business education, training, and exposure. Nobody today questions the growing demand for global executive talent, and while it's laudable to educate and train local talent in emerging markets, we must be careful not to neglect to educate and train our own at home.

> Global business expertise is the currency of the
> 21st century. The more global you become,
> the wealthier you will be.

Inefficiencies in education systems are not limited to secondary and undergraduate schools; they also extend into executive graduate programs. My years as an associate professor made me particularly aware of the limitations of Executive MBA (EMBA) programs touted specifically as having a global or international focus.

For example, an EMBA program is typically classified as international, not because its curriculum teaches executives to be global leaders, but because the program includes a trip to one or two foreign countries at the end of the program. Or, it includes week-long lectures conducted in four or five countries over a period of two years. While in a foreign country, students participate in field trips to observe the operations of local companies and attend cultural briefings and events.

The implication is that these international MBAs are helping create global executives. In reality, however, they provide only a thin varnish of what a global executive could and should be.

On one occasion, I joined an EMBA class on a trip to Asia. The program consisted of visiting local plants and landmarks, attending cultural events, and visiting local shops and restaurants to get a feel for the local culture.

The president of a local manufacturing company arranged for the group to have lunch at a nearby restaurant. The display of food was impressive, and he took the time to introduce the local delicacies offered. To my dismay, several students refused to try food that looked unfamiliar and unappealing. One went as far as insisting that he only be served steamed rice.

There was no obligation for students to attend these programs or to report on their experience. The learning was optional.

These programs offer no systematic learning about international issues and the global market. There is no accountability for acquiring and applying new knowledge after returning home. Left to their own initiative, students who are indifferent or reluctant to engage in and understand the local environment can do so at will and still receive, at the end of the program, a certificate that is meaningless in terms of international understanding.

International programs should be designed to include all five aspects of the global leadership learning process:

1. Awareness
2. Understanding
3. Knowledge
4. Internalization
5. Practice

What Companies and Academia Could Do:

- Executive students sponsored by a corporation are exposed to living and working in a foreign market through well-defined internships or joint programs with local companies.
- Exposure to other markets would be for one month at a time for a total of six months over a period of two years.
- Upon return from each trip, students share experiences with their peers, professors, and corporate co-workers, thereby building on each other's experiences while analyzing challenges and rewards experienced during the process.
- The program includes materials, tools, and activities conducive to developing a global mindset in addition to understanding global markets.
- Students are rewarded for identifying and developing a community business plan, which, when implemented, will result in a measurable increase in the standard of living of the local community where the sponsoring company operates.

Corporations are and should continue to be highly interested in hiring graduate students who bring a fresh, updated approach to global business. I believe the best formula to accelerate global expertise and corporate success involves matching young graduates with experienced professionals and foreign workers familiar with the needs of their local communities.

Close collaboration between academia, industry, and local communities allows all parties involved to be in the driver's seat of a new era of progress, redefining the composition of the workforce of the future and creating the new kind of human capital needed to succeed in a global economy. It also helps to eradicate poverty through smart partnerships and collaborative education.

Finally, companies today have to address not only educational gaps in the global workforce, but also generational gaps that show significant differences in opinion about the future role of business among college students and CEOs of international companies.

In early 2010, IBM Global Business Services published an executive report entitled, "Inheriting a Complex World."[11] The report presented the results of an opinion survey conducted among 3,600 students in over 40 countries. Among the participating students, 68 percent were mostly 20–25 years old, 52 percent were undergraduates, and 27 percent were non-MBA graduates. The report compared responses provided by the students with those obtained from CEOs surveyed in an earlier study on the same topics.

Although the comparative study showed that students and CEOs agreed on their outlook of new economic environments, it also showed that many students greatly disagreed with CEOs on the future roles of public and private organizations:

- Students and CEOs were significantly divided in their view of globalization—"47 percent of students, compared to 31 percent of CEOs, said that organizations should optimize their operations by globalizing rather than localizing, or doing both, to meet strategic objectives." Students further believed that "globalizing allows organizations to create new value."
- Students' views also differed from CEOs when it came to factors that impact the organization—"Twice as many students than CEOs selected globalization and environmental issues as one of the top three factors to impact organizations."
- In North America, more than in any other region, students' views diverged from those of CEOs on issues of sustainability—"Students were almost three times as likely as CEOs to expect scarcity of natural resources to have a significant impact."
- Also in North America, "60 percent more students than CEOs anticipated that customer expectations for social responsibility will increase significantly."
- Students and CEOs were also divided in their perception of the importance of interconnectivity. Students demonstrated higher intuition and acceptance of the fact that "economies, societies, governments, and organizations are made up of interconnected networks."

Ragna Bell, Global Lead for Strategy at the IBM Institute of Business Value at William & Mary's Mason School of Business, put it this way:

"What these students are saying is that they understand the complexities inherent in a world that's getting smaller and more interconnected all the time, and the implications of those changes for their careers."   —Ragna Bell

---

The 2010 IBM study also uncovered important shortcomings in educational systems around the world. According to the study:

- A gap exists between the quality of education being imparted today and business expectations.
- When asked how well their education had prepared them to face the complexities of the world today, six out of ten students said they believe that universities have not prepared them to deal with global issues.

- As many as six out of ten students polled in 40 countries believe that universities do not prepare them to deal with issues of sustainability and benefit from the growth in emerging markets.
- In China, only four out of ten students believe that their education has prepared them to become global citizens, and in Japan, only 17 percent— lower than any other region—believe their education helps them benefit from the growth in emerging economies.

The results of the IBM report strongly suggest that it's time to bring "globalized education" to center stage. This requires innovative academic programs in both content and activities, including meaningful field trips abroad and hands-on, real-life activities while students are still in college and organized in conjunction with global corporations.

Risk Management—A Mirage

Studies conducted by *The Economist Intelligence Unit*[12] show that most companies recognize political and economic risks as the most threatening to their success, yet half of them fail to adopt an internal formal approach to managing this kind of risk. Although 80 percent of companies engage in due diligence before investing in a foreign country, once the investment is made, complacency sets in. Only 30 percent of companies report doing risk analysis on a regular basis after the transaction, and 14 percent report conducting political and operations risk management solely on an ad hoc basis.

Emerging markets are intrinsically volatile, and conditions that prevailed prior to the investment are subject to change at any time. If not anticipated through regular risk analysis, these changes can prove disastrous to investors and to a company's survival. For the most part, companies use external sources to stay informed about risks, but not on a regular basis. Outside sources of information used by corporations, ranked in order of preference, include:

- Economic analysts (66%)
- Political analysts (53%)
- Shared intelligence with other companies, including competitors (47%)
- Risk consultants (42%)
- Government organizations in host countries (40%)
- Trade associations (38%)
- Insurance companies (36%)
- Local communities in host countries (27%)
- Non-government organizations (27%)

Political risk is mentioned by 65 percent of companies as the main force behind cancellation of planned investments, consistent with a due diligence process in place prior to investment. Only 26 percent of companies indicated that they have cancelled existing investments due to political risk.

One of the Five Tenets for Business Survival is *What You Need to Manage*. At the top of the list of things to manage is *Match Strategic Intents with Results*. Unfortunately, when it comes to risk management, the task of achieving the desired results is often left unattended.

Nearly 70 percent of companies surveyed by *The Economist Intelligence Unit* don't assign specific roles and responsibilities in risk management, and only 43 percent indicated that they are confident they are capable of reporting risks to key executives in upper management. Fifty-nine percent placed the responsibility for risk management with the C-suite: chief executive officer (36%), chief risk officer (15%), risk committee (15%), regional directors (10%), and chief financial officer (8%).

The problem with this approach is that the C-suite is generally removed from day-to-day operations on the ground, where the first signs of trouble can be identified in a timely way. In addition, companies don't provide specific risk management training to employees lower in the corporate hierarchy. Unless companies start training their employees and creating a risk management culture from the bottom up, critical information may never reach the C-suite, because nobody has that responsibility or the training to spot sources of risk.

In addition, for the most part risk management policies and procedures are designed to ensure compliance with existing regulations. Functions usually assigned a role in risk management are: finance, legal, tax, human resources, and IT, which support the compliance process of the company's divisions. Other functions, such as internal audit and risk management compliance, are responsible for monitoring and reporting. Companies also engage a wide range of external specialists to help them manage risk: enterprise risk management specialists, internal auditors, compliance officers, fraud investigators, quality inspectors, and others.

Yet no one inside or outside the company is specifically responsible for the performance of foreign joint ventures and partnerships. This is incomprehensible when one considers that:

- Sixty-three percent of companies surveyed prefer to distribute risk and limit investor exposure by establishing joint ventures and strategic alliances with local companies in emerging markets.
- More than $2 trillion are spent on corporate acquisitions every year.[13]
- An estimated 70–90 percent of mergers and acquisitions are consistently reported to fail.

If history repeats itself and the unexpected always happens,
how incapable must man be of learning from experience.

— George Bernard Shaw[*]

The results of the GE Global Innovation Barometer corporate survey discussed in Chapter 4 included specific opinions on partnership management.

Under the headline, *"Lack of Trust and Policy Protection Underpins Much of the Anxiety over Business Collaboration,"* the survey included these results:

- We don't know how to attract potential partners (31%)
- We don't have time to allocate to managing the partnership (28%)
- I don't know if my company is ready or able to be working in partnership (28%)
- We don't have time to allocate to meeting possible partners (22%)
- Their company is bigger than ours (22%)

What's striking from these responses is that they exist at all. Imagine that the topic was not risk management but finance and investment. The equivalent list would look like this:

- We don't know how to attract potential investors.
- We don't have time to allocate to taking care of our finances.
- I don't know if my company is ready or able to be working with financial institutions.
- We don't have time to allocate to meeting possible investors.
- The investment firms are bigger than ours.

Because we are a finance-oriented society, we would never hear the statements on the second list; however, we let such attitudes prevail when it comes to the operating performance of joint ventures and partnerships in emerging markets. This occurs because of a lack of recognition and attention given to the post-deal process, where most of the costly and debilitating risks are hidden.

> What leaders need to realize is that their companies are consistently losing value because they fail to properly recognize and manage how people affect the bottom line.

This is a classic shortcoming of the traditional due diligence process: After the deal is closed, no operations team is allocated the responsibility for making sure the partnership is properly integrated and works smoothly. When

---

[*] George Bernard Shaw Quotes. BrainyQuote.com, Xplore Inc, 2018. https://www.brainyquote.com/quotes/george_bernard_shaw_163236, accessed February 10, 2018.

the strategic intent doesn't match the expected financial gains, the failure is usually pegged to external factors outside the company's control.

In summary, a large number of companies still choose to operate in emerging markets at their own peril. In spite of the talk and worries about risk, in the end nobody is in charge and nobody is responsible. Companies engaged in mergers and acquisitions (M&A) should update their traditional due diligence by adding a rigorous post-M&A process designed to identify and manage risk in all its forms. In addition, they should create a new role—a Chief Partnership Officer—responsible for identifying and taking appropriate measures to help stakeholders in the partnering organizations buy into the process and integrate to full capacity. This would enable the company to achieve the intended benefits of the investment.

Until that happens, for most traditional players, the concept of risk management still remains a mirage in the overall corporate strategy. These players can't even pretend to check the box.

Free Fall—From Boardroom to Ground Floor

Another blind spot companies have when operating in emerging markets is the preference for a high-rise view of the world, referring to the tradition followed by old-fashioned C-suite executives who do business from the comfort of the board room, high up and removed from the realities of street-level realities. In Chapter 7, we discussed how the CEO of PepsiCo defied this tradition by walking the streets of China with gusto, dragging behind some of her top executives through shanty homes in poor neighborhoods.

For safety reasons, I recommend staying in reputable, usually five-star hotels, when traveling abroad. But this precautionary practice should not lead to the practice of conducting business in the comfort of the hotel to the exclusion of interacting with the local population. Because these hotels are in areas that city officials build and maintain specifically to attract tourism and investment, it's tempting to believe that the rest of the city and the country are just as beautiful and advanced.

The pictures in Figure 8.1 show common scenes in the business centers of Shanghai and New Delhi. This view-from-the-top can be dangerously deceptive.

These are the scenes that conventional Western executives are likely to see as they travel abroad. Modern cities, posh restaurants, and clean cities create an illusion that progress is well spread throughout the country.

As casual tourists, we delight in the unexpected culture clash between the new and the old—the worker sweeping the street clean with an old-fashion broom in Shanghai, the policeman manually directing traffic in New Delhi, or the Chinese motorcycle driver delivering mattresses.

21ST CENTURY CITY, SHANGHAI, CHINA

POSH HOTEL, NEW DELHI, INDIA

CLEAN CITIES, CHINA

TRAFFIC CONTROL, INDIA

LOCAL DISTRIBUTION SYSTEM, CHINA

Figure 8.1   Modern cities, plush hotels, and charming scenes in the street may be deceptive. (*Source for all photos*—© Z. Kraljevic.)

Now look at the same scenes through the eyes of an investor: What do you see? Instead of charming scenes, you may see a precarious motorcycle-based distribution or supply chain system bound to create havoc in your business model. You may also infer that in a city of over 20 million people, as is Shanghai, the man with the broom may indicate a severe lack of modern waste management control, and the policeman directing traffic in New Delhi may make you wonder about the level of *actual* technological advancement in the country.

Conditions on the ground in emerging and developing markets may be far from what we might expect or see at first glance, particularly when it comes to physical infrastructure.

CARPOOLING TO WORK, INDIA

LOCAL ELECTRICAL GRID, THAILAND

CROWDED CITY, CHINA

PRECARIOUS FAMILY LIFE—
CHILD STEERING THE WHEEL, INDIA

SELLING PRODUCTS IN THE DESERT,
SAUDI ARABIA

Figure 8.2 Actual conditions on the ground may impede doing business effectively. (*Source for all photos*—© Z. Kraljevic.)

The pictures in Figure 8.2 illustrate some of the surprises that optimistic companies may uncover, too late, as they rush to establish operations in frontier and emerging markets. Lack of preparation leads to last-minute emergencies that cost the company significant time and money and ultimately may ruin a business that otherwise could have enjoyed significant success.

Actual conditions on the ground may seriously affect a
company's capability to do business cost effectively.

Ten Checklists for Planning and Execution

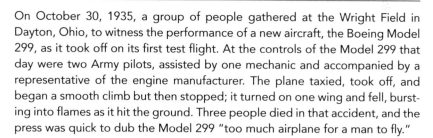

On October 30, 1935, a group of people gathered at the Wright Field in Dayton, Ohio, to witness the performance of a new aircraft, the Boeing Model 299, as it took off on its first test flight. At the controls of the Model 299 that day were two Army pilots, assisted by one mechanic and accompanied by a representative of the engine manufacturer. The plane taxied, took off, and began a smooth climb but then stopped; it turned on one wing and fell, bursting into flames as it hit the ground. Three people died in that accident, and the press was quick to dub the Model 299 "too much airplane for a man to fly."

The investigation identified "pilot error" as the cause of the accident, but it didn't end there. Pilots got together to find a way to make sure that no errors were made in the future. They came up with not one, but four detailed checklists to ensure that nothing was overlooked or forgotten. The "pilot's checklist" then became standard use. As it turned out, the Model 299 was not "too much airplane for one man to fly"—it was simply too complex for any one's man's memory.[14]

Likewise, entering new markets is not too complex for any company to accomplish successfully, but it does require several checklists to make sure nothing is overlooked or forgotten.

If I had an hour to save the world, I'd spend 59 minutes thinking about the problem and one minute thinking about solutions.

— Attributed to Albert Einstein

Keep in mind that the airplane accident at Wright Field in Dayton happened not because the mission was impossible, but because it was approached using a traditional way of thinking. Model 299 was new and demanded a new way of thinking, one that was not anticipated but only reengineered after the tragedy.

Just like the Model 299, the reason the majority of joint ventures and partnerships stall and fall down is because companies still go about the process of due diligence using a traditional approach.

They have checklists for assessing risks and return on investment, and if the result is favorable, they decide to invest (takeoff). Then resources are committed, and the new venture is under way (climbing). Then the process stops (stalling).

There are no checklists and no crew at hand to monitor the health of new relationships, the success of a post-acquisition integration, and the buy-ins down the hierarchy of the partnering organizations.

No pre-landing checklist exists: That is, the list that prepares the company to adjust to new conditions or change course as necessary, to adjust altitude, or verify that conditions remain favorable for a soft landing. Once the company is on the ground in the target market (landing) there is no "post-landing" checklist to prepare the operation to continue to strengthen and get ready for new flying plans.

Avoid "human errors." Make sure that you and your team brainstorm and constantly think outside the box to identify all the steps involved, but not in the traditional due diligence way. You need a new, more robust due diligence process that is all-inclusive, that is not only transaction driven but also transformation driven.

I use no less than ten checklists to assist strategists and those responsible for executing strategies in addressing issues that can make or break a new venture:

1. Checklist #1—Know Thyself
2. Checklist #2—Know Thy Market
3. Checklist #3—Know Thy Competition
4. Checklist #4—Own Country Selection Metrics
5. Checklist #5—Mitigate Costly Disruptions
6. Checklist #6—Extend the Due Diligence Process
7. Checklist #7—Keep Adding Value
8. Checklist #8—Build New Support Systems
9. Checklist #9—Search for Landmines
10. Checklist #10—When Relationships Break Apart

Because every company and every project is different, checklists are more effective when customized by the team responsible for the project. Using the airplane example, you wouldn't like to use checklists prepared for a Boeing 787 to fly an Airbus 380.

To illustrate the use of checklists, I have next expanded on the top three listed above: Know Thyself, Know Thy Market, and Know Thy Competition. Use them as a guideline to build your own according to your company's plans and objectives.

Make sure to plan not only for the start of the business but also for building a sustainable, "crash-free" business.

Checklist #1—Know Thyself
▪ What are the concerns of the company to expand abroad? Strong competition, access to sourcing, distribution channels, consumer preferences, other?
▪ Is the company's leadership risk-averse? Are employees resistant to change? Is the company a first adopter or a follower?
▪ Is the company seeking long-term steady growth or fast, riskier growth?
▪ Is the corporate culture agile enough to embrace changes in the way the company does business?
▪ Has the company assessed its capabilities vis-à-vis the capabilities needed to succeed in the target market?
▪ Is the company willing to invest in new capabilities to cover for missing links in the local industry and address the convenience and needs of local customers?
▪ Will employees unwittingly boycott the company's efforts because they lack understanding and training? Are buy-ins secured at the lower levels of the corporate hierarchy?
▪ Has the company assigned team training and responsibility for building meaningful relations with local key players at all levels?

Checklist #2—Know Thy Market
▪ Is the company using standard metrics or developing its own metrics to select target markets?
▪ Is the offering a match to the needs of the local market? How well known is the local consumer profile?
▪ Are conditions in the local market acceptable? Is the company engaged in assessing a broad range of risk?
▪ Who are the key players in the local industry, including both the private and public sectors?
▪ Does the company have a strong image in the target market? If not, is it ready to educate the market on the benefits of its offerings?
▪ Does the company conduct risk analysis on a regular basis to determine the health of current investment and assess where to invest/divest?
▪ Has the company sent qualified and reliable people to collect market data on the ground?
▪ What measures is the company taking to verify the information provided by new third parties?

Checklist #3—Know Thy Competition
▪ What's the real value the company is planning to offer its new target market?
▪ What are the internal barriers the company faces to expand abroad—liquidity, talent, commitment, technology, obsolescence, or other?
▪ Is the product or service elastic or inelastic? Can prices be altered without losing out to the competition?
▪ Is the company ready to outsource or acquire local companies to complement its activities and products in local markets?
▪ Has the company conducted a thorough value chain analysis of the local industry to identify potential disruptions in its business model?
▪ How well does the company understand political stability, foreign exchange, technology, and obsolescence, and how prepared is it to deal with them?
▪ Is the company prepared to match the innovative and entrepreneurial spirit of local competitors?
▪ Where does the company stand on social responsibility? Is it ready to partner with local municipal or state governments to help develop the local community?

Next, *Chapter 9, Real-life Anecdotes from a Business Globetrotter,* describes a diverse set of personal anecdotes accumulated over years of international travel. I selected them to illustrate how to put into practice the concepts discussed in this book.

The stories include some life-threatening situations and are offered as a frame of reference for when you are training others to expect the unexpected. By sharing these stories, I hope to help you visualize unexpected situations and show you how to feed your brain with actionable information you can use to make better on-the-spot decisions.

PART V
PRACTICE

Practice: To Do Something Again and Again in Order to Become Better at It*

---

* Merriam-Webster Dictionary

Chapter Nine

Real-Life Anecdotes from a Business Globetrotter

This chapter is a collection of real-life anecdotes that I have had the good fortune to experience while doing business abroad. They are not uncommon, and all add something to helping you increase awareness about your surroundings and develop the skills and knowledge that may come in handy as you meet strangers in unfamiliar territory. At the end of each story, you will find a summary section with questions that may help you internalize the message.

> *Like all great travelers, I have seen more than I remember,*
> *and remember more than I have seen.*
>
> — Benjamin Disraeli[*]

> *To travel is to discover that everyone is wrong about other countries.*
>
> — Aldous Huxley[**]

> *The traveler sees what he sees, the tourist sees what he came to see.*
>
> — Gilbert K. Chesterton[†]

---

[*] https://www.brainyquote.com/quotes/benjamin_disraeli_108147
[**] https://www.brainyquote.com/quotes/aldous_huxley_108145
[†] https://www.brainyquote.com/quotes/gilbert_k_chesterton_100091

A Whimsical Glimpse into Chinese Nature

One summer, I was in Shanghai leading a group of American senior executives visiting the region. Loyal to my golden rule, I had set aside time to wander on my own around the city to get a feel for the local culture and the sociopolitical mood of the day. Here is what happened the day I joined a group of tourists visiting a most beautiful landmark.

Figure 9.1   Chinese old state. (*Source:* © Z. Kraljevic.)

An elderly man stared at me from a distance. He appeared while I was visiting an old estate once belonging to a rich and prominent Chinese family. Over time, the estate had been transformed into a public museum. The formidable tall and stark wall surrounding the estate looked foreboding. Its top had been designed to resemble a giant dragon protecting those living inside by keeping malevolent spirits away.

Once inside, however, the estate was a peaceful, beautiful paradise dominated by a large lagoon, which provided the calm waters that surrounded the many one-story buildings that made up the estate. Interconnecting the buildings were the most graceful multicolored wooden bridges that I had ever seen. Each building was a labyrinth of corridors leading from room to room.

Each room featured a veranda on the left overlooking the lagoon, and a window on the right that perfectly framed an inner garden delicately designed around a particular theme. I learned that every plant, tree, and pond in each garden had a particular meaning and was designed for reflection, relaxation, and peace as well as happiness and joy. It was impossible to stop at a window and not feel an intimacy with the garden outside. I could experience the peace but also imagine the muffled laughter of mischievous children at play, perhaps risking the wrath of strict parents.

In contrast with the simple interiors, the exterior of each building was exquisitely ornate; each roof displayed curious gargoyles designed and positioned to protect the house from bad spirits and fire. A wooden veranda with a waist-high rail ran along each building on the lagoon side.

Standing by the rail of one veranda, I decided to take a moment to admire the view of the lagoon. It was extraordinary; the harmony between simplicity, practicality, and beauty was striking. On impulse, I brought my camera to my eyes and started to take pictures, slowly moving from right to left. Through the lens, I saw the veranda of a building in front of me, some 100 yards across the pond, and was startled to discover an elderly man sitting on a bench by the rail; he seemed to be looking straight at me. His stare made me pause. It was neither a friendly nor an unfriendly stare, but came across as being stern and cold.

To my eyes, he was clearly a Chinese man; a regular visitor, perhaps, taking in the history of his ancestors. For a moment the thought made me feel like an outsider, invading his right to be in "his" house, at peace. He must have seen that my camera had stopped dead the moment the lens discovered him.

Behind the camera, I took a closer look at his facial expression: inquisitive with a touch of patience, understanding with a touch of resignation. His demeanor was dignified, and his stare was not as hostile as I had believed at first. I was mesmerized by having found an individual who, judging from his external image, seemed to be such a perfect representation of China's present and past.

Aware that in many cultures picture-taking is an invasion of privacy, I slowly lowered the camera and looked directly at him, challenging him to react. He waited, motionless. At that point I was intrigued and decided to test my theory that every person, as harsh or intimidating as he or she may appear

Figure 9.2 The Chinese man across the pond. (*Source:* © Z. Kraljevic.)

on the outside, has an inner human nature that can be revealed as just the opposite. Deciding to take his picture, ever so slowly I brought the camera to my eyes again, giving him time to turn his back or leave. He didn't flinch. He surely knew what I was about to do, and when he straightened his shoulders, I knew he was game. I focused and clicked.

After taking his picture, I lowered my camera, looked at him again and bowed my head in his direction, slowly and reverently, thanking him for allowing me to capture a glimpse into the heritage of which he seemed to be so proud.

And then, the unexpected happened. He sort of smiled, and to my astonishment, he brought to his face his own camera, which up to this point had been hidden from view on the bench. Realizing that he wanted to take a picture of me, I lowered my camera and stood still. After he took the picture, he in turn lowered his camera and bowed in my direction. It was a most magic moment. We both then smiled widely, acknowledging and enjoying the "trick" we had taken turns playing on each other.

The Chinese, like the walled estate I was visiting, sometimes seem hard to read on the outside but can be harmonious, peaceful, and friendly on the inside. Personal connections, anywhere in the world, start with a show of respect, providing an opportunity to get a glimpse of each other's inner soul and ignoring preconceived ideas that spoil the moment and keep us ignorant of others. On that day, I corroborated once again that the human touch is the most valuable and effective skill that nature has given us to reach out into any culture.

This story illustrates the impact of respect on a relationship with others, in this case with a Chinese national. It would be naïve, however, to interpret the response of the elderly man with the camera as a sign of acceptance, and that a hypothetical business negotiation will easily follow.

The Chinese don't want to lose face, and neither do they want you to lose face. From that perspective, a show of respect is appreciated and indicates the type of person you are. It is a good beginning of what will probably be a difficult negotiation.

As is always the case, the success of the negotiation depends on the value that the parties bring to the table. It would be erroneous for a Western executive to confuse smiles, compliments, and friendliness with an easy negotiation and quick agreements.

- What would have been a typical reaction of a Western tourist faced with the same opportunity?
- What concepts or golden rules described in this book were put into practice to react to this new situation?

- How would you explain the old man's reaction to the situation?
- Does this kind of experience help increase understanding among people?
- Have you or would you try a similar approach given the opportunity?

The Monkey at My Car Window

In the mythology of Hinduism, India's majority religion, Hanuman is the monkey commander of an army of monkeys. As recounted in the great Hindu Sanskrit poem the Ramayana ("Romance of Rama"), Hanuman led his army to help Rama—an important Hindu god—recover Rama's wife, Sita, from the demon Ravana, king of Lanka.[1]

Figure 9.3   Hindu temple, Singapore. (*Source:* © Z. Kraljevic.)

Since then, Hanuman, the monkey army commander, has been upheld by Hindus as a model for all human devotion. By association, all monkeys are indulged and even venerated in India. Considered sacred, they roam villages, temples, and public places at will, unmolested. But not all monkeys are the same.

India's langur monkeys are aggressive toward other, more common monkeys. For this reason, langurs have been trained as security guards to work alongside the police to help maintain order and discipline among mobs of stray monkeys that cause havoc around cities.

In New Delhi, for instance, the population of stray monkeys is getting into the hundreds of thousands. They have been known to bite people and terrorize public and government buildings and hotels, as well as upper-end residences built near the forest that surrounds the city. As urbanism reclaims the monkeys' natural habitat, Indian authorities have been on high alert to control them.

In October 2007, the BBC reported[2] that Deputy Mayor of New Delhi, S.S. Bajwa, age 52, reportedly died from head injuries after falling from the terrace of his private residence while fighting off the attack of a pack of monkeys. Since then, public opinion in India has slowly started to turn against monkeys.

I was unaware of this situation when a monkey jumped and perched itself outside my car window (thankfully closed) when I was traveling through rural India. Its sudden appearance startled me, but my first reaction was to be amused by the curious way the monkey was looking at me. It seemed that I was just as big a novelty for him as he was for me. It didn't cross my mind then that this was the beginning of what could have been a dangerous situation.

The night before, I had made arrangements with the hotel to provide a reliable car and driver to visit Agra, home of the Taj Mahal, a five-hour trip one way. Because my colleagues and I had agreed to leave the hotel at 6 PM to go to the airport and catch a plane home, I had to leave around 6 AM to be back on time. Graciously, the hotel manager offered to provide a box with breakfast and lunch for the trip. I sat behind the driver with the boxes neatly arranged next to me. As is my habit even at home, I made sure the windows were rolled up and the doors were locked.

My Indian driver turned out to be an attentive young man, but being from the interior, his English was rather broken. As we left the hotel, my interest turned to observing the transition from urban to rural life. In this country of over one billion people, the sights on the streets can be both enchanting and overpowering. The sheer number of people around us at any time was surreal. Heavy traffic and large crowds seemingly going in every direction at once made the scene highly chaotic.

Judging by the rundown look of the housing and shops that lined the main road, the rural villages we crossed were very poor, a rather common occurrence in even the largest cities of India today. Buildings were mostly in disrepair, either half demolished or half constructed, as if they had been abandoned after an earthquake or another natural disaster. The shops—selling everything from fruit, water, and soft drinks to wooden artifacts and car repair services—were as small as they were numerous.

Yet, on closer inspection, one could see normal, peaceful events taking place among the mayhem, such as a group of children being herded by parents anxious to get them to school. Considering the environment, these children seemed oddly out of place: well-groomed, well-scrubbed faces, hair still wet and glistening, wearing black pants, white shirts, and yellow ties.

Further down, a group of five school girls wearing white skirts and blouses along with white sneakers and white mid-calf socks were traveling on a tricycle, the local equivalent of the school bus.

Figure 9.4   Local "school bus," India. (*Source:* © Z. Kraljevic.)

Down the road, I saw a tuk-tuk, the most popular form of transportation in India. It consists of a motorized tricycle encased in a metal cabin, and the one I saw was giving a ride to another group of school boys. Designed for two people and a driver, this particular tuk-tuk was carrying at least eight young children, with their backpacks precariously hanging from the frame and dangling wildly as the tuk-tuk-turned-school-bus made its way through the crowd.

On the other side of the road, amidst hundreds of people walking or driving at a fast pace, there was another oasis of calmness. A tall, thin man was going about his business as if he was the sole inhabitant on Earth. He was a barber and had set up shop in the median between two roads.

His "shop" consisted of three "walls" made of white pieces of cloth forming a "room" that could barely contain a chair, a mirror (apparently hanging from thin air), and of course the barber who, being tall and skinny, seemed to occupy no space at all. His client was sitting on a flimsy chair facing the mirror, and he seemed equally oblivious to the outside traffic. I was fascinated by the ingenuity and contrast of it all.

It was approaching the middle of the day, and the air was hot and humid. Stray dogs and sacred cows were the only unmoving beings as they rested under the shadow of trees. It was then that my driver announced that he was making a quick stop at the center of this populous and entrepreneurial village to buy a product you could only find in this place.

I agreed, and pulling a book out of my purse, decided to take a rest from the hectic surroundings. But it wasn't meant to be. Soon after the chauffer left to be swallowed by the crowd, I heard a loud thump; lifting my head, I saw a monkey perched outside my car window. It was as unexpected as it was funny, and the way the monkey looked at me made me reach for my camera and snap a shot.

Figure 9.5 The monkey at my car window, China. (*Source:* © Z. Kraljevic.)

It was then that I noticed that the animal was on a leash, and two men were quickly approaching my side of the car; knocking at the window, they started to ask for money. The monkey's appearance had clearly been staged for that purpose, and I suspected they now wanted me to pay for the photograph I had taken. I thought their trickery was preposterous.

Being alone in the car, experience told me to stay calm and not to acknowledge them in any way, a means to avoid encouraging them. I went back to my book and pretended to read, impervious to the increasing force of the knocking on the window. I didn't move a muscle, except that my eyes darted to the doors to make sure they were locked. The back doors were, but not so the driver's and the passenger door.

At first, the men were unsure of what to do and I gained some time. After a while, however, they started to bang on the roof of the car. The driver was nowhere in sight. I figured it was just a matter of time until they realized that the front doors were unlocked. But the fact that they hadn't noticed this already told me I wasn't dealing with trained criminals, just people improvising and wanting to take advantage of a situation.

Their next move was to start rocking the car. It was a gentle motion, perhaps a product of my imagination, and I was considering my next move when the driver came back, sporting his infectious smile, and seemingly unconcerned. As the driver returned, the men quickly took the monkey and withdrew back into the crowd. Not a word was exchanged, and as calm was restored, I decided to emulate the driver and not make much of the event.

Looking back at this situation, I am sure that had I been inclined to open the window and either give in to the men's demands or try to negotiate, the situation could have been much worse. A show of vulnerability, particularly from a lone woman in a large crowd, can have tragic consequences. Indifference, on the other hand, is unexpected, intriguing, and at the end, intimidating. They weren't sure what to make of it, and their actions, even if loud, were tentative. Had they wanted to do something, they would have had plenty of time to do it. The deterrent worked.

- How many clues can you identify in this story that helps you better understand India and its citizens?
- What would you have done in my place—and why?
- Have you ever been in similar situations? Where, why, and how did you handle it?
- Are you likely to travel through the countryside in countries you visit for business? If so, why?
- Do you prepare yourself in the event something similar happens to you in a crowded city or in your hotel?
- What would you do if attacked by a pack of monkeys, as the Deputy Mayor of New Delhi once was?
- Did the story provide you with new ideas on how to react to unexpected situations?
- Would you decide never to go to India because of this story?

A Woman's Success in Male-Dominated Societies

Paternalistic attitudes toward women in the workplace are common in collectivistic societies, and managing paternalism in business is a challenge for any woman. The respect for seniority observed in these traditional societies usually results in authoritarian and centralized decision making in both life and business.

The oldest man of the tribe is the head of the tribe. He's also the head of his family unit and the head of his office environment, large or small. There may be a council of elders, but the head of the tribe rules. As such, they expect and demand obedience from all, but particularly from women. Such attitudes are observed across continents from Latin America to the Middle East and beyond. Below are three examples of how paternalism is expressed and what you can do to address it.

While working in Saudi Arabia, I met an Arab man who, like many Arabs in senior positions, had been educated in the United States. His English was excellent and his demeanor polished and professional.

More important, he was a good, gentle man; a good father and husband and a good provider for his family. He was also friendly, and several times he invited my husband and me to visit him and his family at his beautiful home. We always had a good time, not only because Arab hospitality is excellent, but also because there was friendship and mutual respect.

Surrounded by his family, it was obvious that he was the "paterfamilias." When coming into the room, his children, good-looking young men and women who seemed content with their lives, would show him respect by kneeling in front of him and kissing his hand. His wife was well educated and an active member of the local society. She clearly had her own opinions and was not afraid of expressing them. They would joke and laugh easily.

But at work, the situation was different. His management position demanded that he be authoritative and stern. He was expected to display a harsh attitude toward subordinates—men and women—and so he did. As it happens, I was a senior Western female executive working side by side with him. This was a hard situation for my friend to deal with, not because he doubted my capabilities, but because he needed to maintain his public image in front of his male colleagues and superiors. This put a strain on our relationship, but we both did our best to reach middle ground.

I could see that he was torn between the private person he was and the public person he was supposed to be. While he endured the fear-based respect that the local custom imposed, he also yearned to be his normal friendly self. During a conversation in which he and I compared leadership styles used around the world, he admitted that he wished he had learned to deal with men and women in a more relaxed environment and thus develop a management style more in line with his personality.

This story helps illustrate that people react the way they do for different reasons. External behavior may or may not reflect the true character of an individual, or even imply a deliberate personal attack. The next story illustrates another set of circumstances that gives insight into the reasons behind common attitudes observed in the workplace.

When working in the Middle East, I was the only female member of the executive team headed by the president of the company, a Saudi national, and composed of 10 Arab men of different Middle Eastern and North African nationalities. As such, the opposition to my presence there was strong and quite obvious, and I became the center of lively discussions about what my role meant to the rest of the team. These were well-educated men who nonetheless shared the belief that a woman's role was to stay at home and obey men's directions. Their concerns were evident at every executive meeting. Five minutes into his agenda, the president was invariably interrupted by someone saying some version of, "I cannot concentrate on what you are saying because I don't understand what 'she' is doing here."

The first time this happened, I was surprised. I had never been in a situation in which people would complain about someone in such open and blatant fashion. Western business tradition calls for airing displeasure about others in private. Instead of being offended, I found it utterly refreshing to see them speak so openly about their discomfort with having a female as part of the team. Knowing first-hand what was on their minds was valuable information.

The outburst became so predictable that the president and I developed a routine: Each time this happened, he would smile benevolently and asked me if any of those present were reporting to me. Following his clue, I would use a friendly tone to respond: "Not to my knowledge." He would then proceed to explain my role and to make it clear that my responsibilities did not include supervising them. This scenario was repeated at every meeting over a period of six weeks.

The open discussion helped me discover that their rejections were deeply rooted in the terrifying notion that, because of my American education and global experience, they might end up reporting directly to me. Clearly, this notion was impossible to bear in their environment and kept them awake at night. With this knowledge, I initiated a communications campaign, inviting my colleagues to attend a series of meetings at which I would share the objectives of my program and the strategy I was developing. The move helped identify early supporters, who in turn helped convince the rest of the group that I wasn't the threat they had perceived me to be. This is not to say they all supported me enthusiastically, only that those remaining skeptical would give me the space required to build a collaborative environment.

This is what I learned: I learned new ways to deal with adverse situations. From experience, I knew that success in company-wide, high-visibility projects requires strong support from the top leader in the organization; thus, having the backing of the president was essential.

The only way to maintain that backing, particularly in an adverse environment, was to generate results beyond expectations, the kind of results that nobody could refute or claim could be achieved by just anyone. As in any other environment, it was important to earn the respect of my peers, so instead of taking offense, I established a higher level of communication with them to ease their discomfort.

I specifically learned that humor can be an effective weapon to help diffuse tense business situations. Every time someone complained about my presence in the room, the president adopted a bemused stance and engaged me in light, friendly dialogue to send his message. My contribution was to match his mood in responding to his questions but never adopt the same approach when addressing my fellow team members. It would have been out of place for me to make light of the problem.

When I called for meetings with my Arab colleagues, I anticipated that most would not listen or even come. My strategy was to convince one colleague at a time. At the first meeting, I identified one strong supporter and one strong opponent. The majority were unsure. By connecting with them one-on-one, I was able to gradually increase support and have others help convince the most reticent ones to reach the level of comfort that allowed us to work together.

Stories about how members of traditional societies, not only in the Middle East, try to influence the role of women in the work environment are numerous.

My friend Anna, a successful business woman with international experience, found herself working at a large corporation in a country that by all standards was modern and economically successful. The country exhibited a large number of women in high-level positions, above the regional norm, but some sectors of the society still held on to the characteristics of a traditional collectivistic society, including paternalism among senior executives.

To Anna's surprise, one morning she received an email from the Office of the President, sent to all employees, announcing a new company policy in which all female personnel were required to wear dresses or skirts. Pants were prohibited. Utterly offended, Anna defied the policy and continued to wear pantsuits. She was not fired for defying the policy, but she felt the pressure to conform and eventually decided to leave in search of a different environment.

Anna's experience is from the late 1990s, and mine is from the late 2000s; both indicate that executive women are still affected by similar experiences when working in collectivistic societies. However, international organizations and social media are helping change societal behavior in favor of women's equality. Foreign students graduating from Western universities are exposed to individualistic societies, and as they return home they bring with them a more diverse set of values and preferences, which may also favorably influence the role of women in their countries.

Because of this behavioral transition, it's best not to generalize when interacting with foreign nationals, but instead to take into account that, although individualistic behavior may be present, it is likely to be combined with traditional behavior.

It pays to keep in mind that not everyone behaves the same way and, therefore, to give everybody a chance to express their personal positions.

- What would you have done had you been a Western woman in that same situation, in each of the examples described above?
- What would you have done had you been a Western man and a member of the president's team in both examples?
- What do you think was the main factor that prompted my first supporter to speak up?

Mindset Alert—Managing Kidnapping Threats

Safety requires a significant mindset adjustment, because most of us are not used to dealing with threatening situations. We are still surprised when protests, street riots, sudden violence, and insurgence erupt in our or other countries. Once we accept that these types of disruptions are unlikely to disappear, we can prepare to face them as best we can. The story below includes several clues to think about and help you act calmly should you ever find yourself in a similar situation. See if you can identify the clues as you read; a summary of them follows the story.

In July 2000, President Bill Clinton signed into law a military aid package to help the Colombian government fight local guerrilla groups involved in drug trafficking and political unrest. The package was worth $1.3 billion, at the time the largest U.S. aid package outside the Middle East. "Plan Colombia,"[3] as it became known, incensed local guerrilla groups such as FARC (The Revolutionary Armed Forces of Colombia) and ELN (The National Liberation Army.) At a later time, when President Clinton was expected to visit Bogotá, U.S. intelligence picked up credible threats of imminent kidnapping attempts against American citizens in the country.

At that precise time, I was an American citizen working in Bogotá at a high-profile American company. My team and I had plans to stay in the country for another week, but the afternoon before the official presidential visit, an urgent email showed up in our inbox just as we were getting ready to return to the hotel. The email was an order for all American citizens to leave the country as soon as possible.

What do you do in such a situation?

For some, the first reaction might be to run back to the hotel, close the account, and grab a taxi to the airport—only to find that there are no flights available until the next morning. Acting out of fear, some people may get boisterous, raising their voices at the airline personnel, demanding an immediate solution. I have seen it happen. The only thing they gain is to call undue attention to themselves and make their situation worse by becoming self-made targets.

The reaction of veteran travelers, on the other hand, is to stay calm. While still in the office, find out about flight availability. If there are no flights scheduled that evening, go back to the hotel as usual, avoid talking about the situation with strangers, and avoid public places. The thing to remember is that the information about possible kidnapping of Americans comes from U.S. authorities directly through your company; even when it may be paramount in your mind, it is not public knowledge and you should not be the one that publicizes it.

From the office (or the hotel), confirm a seat on the first flight out the next morning. In the morning, pay your bill and leave for the airport. Seasoned travelers stay in reputable hotels that are likely to take effective security measures because they understand the need to avoid the bad publicity should any harm come to their guests.

Our hotel had a security policy in place. As we approached the hotel that afternoon, we saw a ring of well-equipped paramilitary personnel surrounding the building, a planned response to the U.S. presidential visit. My colleagues and I had dinner at the hotel and agreed to reconvene the next morning in the lobby.

In the lobby the next day, I noted my colleagues had chosen to dress in dark business suits and ties, with dark expressions to match. They had also secured what seemed to be an armored jeep and a security guard to take them to the airport. This isn't a bad option but it's not the only one. I pictured them standing at the airport as a group of well-dressed business people with a sign over their heads that said, "Kidnap me!"

I didn't join them. As a believer in blending with the local crowd, I had chosen to dress as if I were a local going on vacation: slacks, blouse, and a sweater over the shoulders, complemented with flat shoes, sunglasses, and a big smile.

I closed my account and asked for the same hotel taxi driver that I had used before. The taxi driver recognized me, and we had a nice chat on the way to the airport. Then I switched my train of thought to the airport facilities. The night before in my hotel room, I memorized the map of the airport that the company had attached to the email; it showed emergency routes at different levels of the building. It wouldn't do to wait to study a map while trying to run away from kidnappers!

- What clues can you identify in the story above that would be useful to remember if you are faced with a similar situation?

Here are some ideas to keep in mind in case of an emergency like the kidnapping threat of the story:

- **Stay calm.** Understand the situation, and plan your next move before you act. In the case described here, running to the airport without contacting your airline and securing a seat was not the best plan of action. You will be more secure spending the night at the hotel than at the airport, which closes at night because of slow or no traffic at all. Once you realize you are alone, you are already at risk of being singled out for an attack. Learn to survive on your own, and be a leader rather than a clueless follower.
- **Keep a low profile.** Take note that the email in the story was sent only to American citizens in that particular office. There was no need to disclose this information to strangers or call home from the hotel, as some people do when they get nervous, but without considering that they may be overheard.
- **Keep your situation close to the chest.** If you believe you cannot handle the situation alone, talk privately with people you trust and who are in a position to provide advice and specific help. (Trusted friends or colleagues may invite you to stay in their homes until you can leave the country.)
- **Dress for the occasion.** If you are leaving the country, you are not going to a high-level meeting, so do not dress as if you were. Some people believe that dressing well demands respect. Although this may be the case in normal situations, it isn't a good idea when well-dressed people may be the intended targets. Only James Bond can escape a kidnapping attempt while impeccably dressed!

- **Behave normally.** This is the time to be cool, calm, and collected. Panic is your worst enemy.
- **Be aware of your surroundings.** This doesn't mean taking furtive looks right to left every other second. It means to be prepared ahead of time by identifying alternative routes to safety should you need to use them.

Common Mistakes Westerners Make Abroad:

- Jogging or taking a walk at night around the hotel or office building in a foreign city because that is what they do at home.
- Traveling without enough cash to buy a ticket home in case of an emergency.
- Leaving their passports at the hotel, making it impossible to flee in an emergency.
- Wandering into isolated parks or streets looking for unique photographs to text/send home.
- Carrying a wallet without a list of emergency numbers to call for help, such as supervisors and local co-workers who know the area, and the numbers for local police and hospitals in case of accident.
- Opening a map when walking down the street, calling attention to themselves as naïve foreigners.
- Crossing busy streets distracted, expecting cars to stop as they do at home.
- Overdressing for a meeting and then walking the streets instead of taking a taxi cab.
- Wear the company logo on their lapels.
- Being loud in public places, annoying everyone and attracting undue attention.

Grandma and the Stock Market

The financial crisis that took the world for a spin in late 2008 traveled instantly to every country, affecting not only every stock market and business, but also every household in cosmopolitan cites and small rural towns. With just a few exceptions, citizens of all nationalities became quickly and painfully aware of the ramifications of the sudden and significant drop of stock value driven by a paralysis of industrialized economies.

During the past century, regular citizens were generally unaware of the ups and downs of the stock market. My favorite aunt was one of them. I doubt that she even bothered to find out what the stock market was. But this century is different, and regular citizens the world over follow stock markets and global financial news on a regular basis to take action and protect their individual investments.

The popularity of this activity hit me right between the eyes shortly after the financial crisis, when I was doing business in Hong Kong. I was killing time at the modern and beautiful Hong Kong International Airport and had decided to walk around the airport to stretch my legs between international flights. It was easy to observe the many wi-fi stations enabling travelers to access the internet while waiting for their flights. A number of young people, alone or in groups, appeared to be fully immersed in their virtual worlds, while others kept looking for a free station.

I was taking in this local scene when I came across a peculiar situation. I spotted an older woman, clearly Asian, perhaps Chinese, standing at one of many public access computer terminals. She first grabbed my attention because she did not seem to be a regular traveler. She was not a business woman, or at least she was not dressed as one. Her clothes were rather plain and comfortable, the kind of clothes that a mother or grandmother might choose to wear while preparing a big meal in her kitchen. She was not young, perhaps in her 70s or even older, and yet there she was, as fully immersed in her virtual world as the youngest person in the crowd.

I found it odd that she was actively, I might even say furiously, typing on the workstation's keyboard. Clearly, she was glued to the computer and giving no signs of leaving any time soon. I couldn't read the information on her screen, but I could see that it was changing from one full screen to another at the speed of light.

Curious, I got closer, and to my astonishment realized that she seemed to be playing the stock market. Not wanting to interfere with her privacy, I approached her at an angle, so she could clearly see me standing nearby. She looked at me briefly, but ignored me, clearly not wanting to break her concentration.

She quickly studied page after page of tables of numbers on the screen, apparently related to different stock accounts. She would observe a particular set of data, and then go back and forth between sheets of information. In some cases, she appeared to make decisions and send instructions.

After a while, she looked at me and gave me a huge smile. I thought she might inquire if I needed to use the terminal. Instead, she showed me a screen and said:

"I [sic] addicted to stock market. We all are. . . . [we] . . . like to see stock go up and down. Sometimes we lose lots of money but sometimes not. I cannot have enough of this."

She smiled again and went back to following the stock, moving from account to account faster than my eyes could make sense of it all. I must confess that I had not expected to see an older woman, likely a grandmother, so hopelessly addicted to the virtual world of financial transactions.

- What does this story tell you about the impact of technology on regular citizens?
- Are your current assumptions still valid when interacting with regular citizens around the world?
- How does that translate into your interaction with local nationals around the world?
- Have you taken the time lately to simply observe people in their own environment?
- If so, have you made an attempt to talk with them and engage them in conversation or make yourself comfortable among them, so they approach you as the older woman did with me?

Sociopolitical Unrest—Awareness Keeps Panic in Check

On January 4, 2011, Mohamed Bouazizi died, finally succumbing to self-inflicted wounds.[4] Mohamed was a 29-year-old Tunisian fruit street seller who had been trying to make a living from odd jobs since he was a kid. As a street seller, he was often harassed by local authorities; but one day, the harassment proved to be too much to bear. This time corrupt inspectors asking for bribes had confiscated his goods, for which he had pre-paid $200, a debt he now had no means to repay.

Desperate, he went to the government authorities to complain and demand the return of his produce; but his demands were ignored. Desolated, Mohamed self-immolated. Three weeks later he died from the severe burns that covered most of his body. Shocked by Mohamed's misfortune, many ordinary citizens gathered in the streets in anti-government protests. Many were arrested, and riots rapidly intensified; by January 14, the Tunisian government had been overthrown.

The force of the protests and the resulting collapse of the government reached the news wires and spread around the world in a flash. Protests immediately erupted in Algeria and Egypt, and within a month, on February 11, 2011, the world was shaken again when the powerful Egyptian president, Hosni Mubarak, was forced to resign after 30 years in power. The Arab Spring movement had been born.

The Arab Spring movement continued to spread throughout the rest of the year. It affected Libya, Yemen, Lebanon, Morocco, Jordan, Iraq, Iran, and Syria and spilled over into 2012. Countries of the Gulf region (Saudi Arabia, UAE, Qatar, Kuwait, Bahrain, and Oman) either have been free of protesters or protests have been quickly squelched. Other pockets of sociopolitical unrest and clashes among religious groups have occurred in Central and Southeast Asia, Africa, China, and North Korea, while ethnic tensions are on the rise in Europe.

The safety of company employees and their families is a top concern for any company doing business overseas. Significant money and effort are invested in preparing for such emergencies, and manuals on safety policies are readily distributed to all employees.

Is this enough? No, it isn't. If anything, this well-intentioned and necessary practice also creates a false sense of security, because individuals subconsciously believe: "The company will take care of me." In reality, the chaotic nature of the situation may prevent a company from reaching its employees.

Thus, as in every aspect of life, you are ultimately responsible for your safety and that of your family. This means you need to have a plan, and to develop such a plan, you need to not only be aware of your surroundings but also have knowledge of the situation on the ground. One effective way to prepare involves building a support system that includes local people with whom you have established solid personal relations.

When working or visiting another country, preconceived ideas often lead to overlooking personal contacts. We tend to keep to ourselves and avoid mingling with people we don't immediately understand. Keep in mind that local citizens are used to political protests and insurgencies and have developed the skills and instincts to survive by staying out of the way. Making friends among local people pays off when you find yourself in any emergency—be it political, medical, or during the aftermath of a natural disaster.

Remember that not all citizens believe in violence and unrest, as was the case in the killing of Christopher Stevens, the U.S. Ambassador to Libya (and three others), on September 11, 2012. A number of Western newspapers published a picture of Libyan citizens gathering on the streets with posters that read: "Sorry people of America. This is not the behavior of our Islam and prophet."

- In your opinion, are you doing enough to integrate and internalize the local environment to allow you to act like and blend with the local population in case of an emergency?
- When you arrive in a new city/country, do you take a tour to get acquainted with the area? Do you ask the tour guide smart questions to get a crash course on the culture and the safest places to visit?
- Do you take the time to question the concierge in your Western chain hotel for tips on where to go and what kind of transportation to use? Remember that the hotel's reputation would suffer should anything happen to you during your stay.

- If you cannot afford the best hotel, have you thought about walking into one as if you belong and gathering this information anyway? After all, your survival is at stake. Be clever, not naïve.
- Do you set time aside, regardless of how busy your business agenda may be, to follow the crowd during the day and see the world the way they see it? Are you convinced that this is helpful to understand the world around you? If not, do you have a better plan?
- Once you have established residency in a city, or if you plan to stay for a while, do you take special (and genuine) interest in building a network of local friends and friendly co-workers who can extend a helping hand in case of an emergency? Do you carry their contact information with you at all times?
- In preparation for an emergency, do you carry your passport, credit cards, and sufficient cash with you at all times?
- Do you register with your local U.S. embassy or consulate to let them know you live in the country in case mass evacuation becomes necessary?
- If so, do you trust that help will come when you need it, or do you allow for unforeseen circumstances that demand you be prepared to take evasive action on your own?

What most Westerners also fail to realize is that local citizens in emerging markets are not new to political activism. Local college students are notorious for taking to the street in anti-government demonstrations, willingly engaging in confrontations with local police and security forces. Even in progressive emerging countries, there may not be a single day without a political demonstration; and yet, local citizens continue to go about their business as usual. This is because they are not shocked by demonstrations in the same way that Westerners may be. Familiarity with these situations has taught regular citizens to stay calm and take the necessary steps to avoid being involved in the conflict. Therefore, local people are an excellent source of insight and information. A lifetime of uncertainty has hardened citizens against violent chaos in countries most subject to political unrest.

Through experience, they are better prepared to sustain uncertainties than those in the secure environment of industrialized societies, and you will benefit from learning through their experience. Part III discussed how to develop trustworthy relationships with local citizens in any country. This is one of the reasons why it's important to build mutual trust and stay connected to the local community.

Those who live in a vacuum die alone.

Minimum Emergency Preparation Includes:

- Awareness of how local citizens react to sociopolitical events.
- Identification and verification of options (e.g., alternative routes) to get out of harm's way.
- Familiarity with the area where you live and work in order to minimize making wrong turns.
- Keeping contact information at hand so you can communicate with local friends to exchange information and organize support in case of any emergency.

Other considerations:

Televised news tends to report demonstrations that have turned violent and are out of hand (after all, it's what makes news). In some cases, such as the Syrian situation in 2013, television broadcasts carried scenes of a declared civil war spreading throughout the country, resulting in the death of several thousand people.

But civil wars are rare, and they don't happen overnight, so it's important to have the ability to judge the degree of danger that you might be in at any point in time. Television news should be seen as a first warning that the country may be entering an unstable sociopolitical situation; but panic is the last emotion you want to experience. As a rule, however, conditions on the ground are less violent than they initially appear on the news.

From personal experience, I have learned to look for patterns and clues to discern real versus perceived danger. Some clues to look for: If the news shows only violent scenes occurring during the night, it may indicate that revolts are isolated and controlled, because people are still going to work, and schools continue to operate. This is not to say that you should wander around to learn more, but stay in close communication with your office, colleagues, and friends to keep your finger on the protest's pulse.

Again, the message here is not to panic. Generally speaking, industrial and residential areas are far from government districts and rarely affected by political demonstrations. These are useful bits of information that help distinguish between localized protests that may erupt and disappear at any given moment and the beginning of an extended revolution or civil war that requires taking further precautions.

During the 2011 Arab Spring protests in Cairo, for example, the situation turned serious, and some foreign citizens were evacuated. A friend of mine worked for a European diplomatic agency, and she and her family were evacuated. In these tense situations, you are asked to grab your children, minimum personal belongings and documentation (e.g., passports), and follow instructions to the letter. You may be directed to a safe hotel until everyone is gathered and ushered out to the airport.

Emergency procedures were the topic of conversations while I worked in Saudi Arabia, and we were advised on what hotel to go to in case of emergency if we were outside our home. Generally speaking, your best alternative is to let your embassy know that you are in the country. That way, they know to look for you in situations involving evacuations. But evacuation efforts may take time, and the best way to handle the waiting is to stay at home or inside your hotel.

For the most part, political unrest remains limited to specific areas that may or may not affect the normal conduct of business. While I was meeting with an executive in India in 2011, he confirmed that, two weeks after the beginning of the Arab Spring movement in Egypt, his company's operation in that country was working normally.

But that wasn't the case in Egypt two years later, when, in August 2013, the government imposed a curfew, and companies such as IBM, Royal Dutch Shell, Toyota, Electrolux, GM, Heineken, Suzuki, and BASF closed their operations—primarily those located in 6th of October City, in the Cairo suburbs—telling thousands of employees to stay home.[5]

Here is some additional advice to consider when faced with sociopolitical unrest:

- **Respect curfews.** If the local government imposes a curfew, it means that the violence has escalated to a level requiring strong control or repression. You don't want to be caught in the middle. Stay at home during curfew hours and even longer if you can. Although curfews can be established for full days at a time, normally they are called from dusk to dawn. This was the case in Egypt in 2013, when the provisional military government established a dusk-to-dawn curfew for a full month. Checkpoints are established at those times of day, and you don't want to risk accidentally alarming security forces who are already on edge.
- **Don't engage in political debate.** It's never wise to share political opinions with citizens in a foreign country, especially during times of sociopolitical unrest. Even when local nationals may engage you in political discussions, you will quickly find out that the moment you agree with their pleas, they turn against you. Why? It's an unspoken rule that criticizing local governments is a luxury and a right reserved for local citizens, and taboo for foreigners like you.

That Elusive Fourth Dimension

Time has different meaning to different societies. My Swiss cousin, Beate, for example, is a stickler for punctuality. You can set your watch by the time she shows up just to have an ice cream. Needless to say, Beate doesn't have much tolerance for people arriving one minute late to anything.

But the majority of societies around the world are not like my Swiss cousin. My husband is also European, but he grew up in Latin America and has a distinctively Latin soul. He delights, for instance, in telling everyone willing to listen that, "Time is a concept invented by man to make life miserable."

When traveling abroad for pleasure or business, at one point or another, we're bound to come across societies for which time has a different meaning from our own. The unfortunate "mañana" concept is widely spread around the world, usually frustrating Western managers to no end. To be fair, some emerging countries respect punctuality, but even then, it's not necessarily enforced in the way it is at home.

For example, if you are late for a business appointment, you may be "penalized" by having to wait the same amount of time you were late. The people you are meeting may be in full view but "unavailable," a tactic devised to point out that your delay was disrespectful. These same individuals might not think twice about being late to their appointments and offer no apology for it.

Games of this kind are more indicative of a sense of self-importance than anything else. It's a reflection of the ego that manifests in believing that some people are more deserving of respect than others. Bottom line: Don't be late, but be prepared to wait for others to show up.

On the plus side, different perceptions about time don't necessarily mean that things don't get done when they should. The personal anecdote below serves to illustrate how the impossible can indeed be accomplished at the very last minute.

My experience in the Middle East was as rewarding as it was enlightening in terms of how differently people go about achieving a particular goal, giving the concept of project management a totally different dimension. Rich oil-exporting countries, that is to say the Gulf countries, as opposed to North African countries, are so rich that they're able to compensate for tardiness by putting enormous resources behind an important project at the very last minute. It could be said that project management relies on a mixture of fear of higher authorities and incredible monetary and labor resources at hand.

On this particular occasion, I witnessed the process followed by the organizers of an event featuring a special Saudi speaker. They had decided that the auditorium at which the event would take place needed a complete makeover. The auditorium was less than two years old and looked fine, but once the decision was made, everything came down in a hurry. From walls to floor carpet, seating chairs, audio visual equipment, and lighting, everything had to go and be replaced. Considering the few days available, it was hard to imagine finishing such a complete remodeling on time. On the evening before the special event, a friend and I walked into the auditorium to assess the situation.

What we witnessed left us speechless: The new walls and lights were in place, but that was about it. The auditorium was empty—really empty. We saw no carpet and no chairs on the floor, and no audiovisual equipment in place or the connections to make it work even if it was. We returned one hour later and learned that, at the very moment the carpet finally arrived, the construction crew was given the green light to triplicate the number of working hands. The sight in front of us was dreamlike, buzzing with activity. Like ants building tunnels, workers were everywhere, affixing the carpet from wall to wall. As the carpet was put in place in one section, another crew showed up and started bolting the chairs in place. The new auditorium was coming to life right in front of our eyes, as in a fast-rolling movie.

When late that evening we finally went home, the audiovisual equipment had yet to be installed and tested, because the IT technicians were on hold until the carpet and chairs were in place and the room had been vacuumed clean. When the program started the next morning at 7 o'clock, all special guests had arrived and were seated in the new chairs, including my friend and me. Everything worked perfectly, and the event was a huge success. The world had literarily been transformed overnight!

Suppose you are the person responsible for the success of such an event. It is your special speaker who will be talking next morning:

- Would you take control of the situation and direct the crews to get the job done on time?
- Would they listen to your instructions and appreciate your efforts?
- Would you be willing to take full responsibility for the situation? Or would you play the role of a neutral observer?
- Would you relax and let the local teams come up with their own solutions?
- What would you do the next morning if the place was unfinished?

Welcome to the Guerrilla Path

According to a bibliography by David S. Palmer and Thomas A. Marks entitled *Guerrilla Insurgencies in Latin America*,[6] the term *guerrilla* gained currency in Spain in the early 1800s, during the campaign by patriots to harass Napoleon's forces. These groups used terror and violence to try to overthrow the government, protect illegal businesses, or both.

They were most active in Latin America, from Cuba to Uruguay, in the 1970s and well into the late 1990s. Today, however, guerrilla-type groups are less prominent. Some have entered into negotiations with governments to reach middle ground[7] or evolved into political parties that participate in general elections.[8] The story below may give you a glimpse of the wide range of surprises you may encounter when leaving the relative safety of urban locations.

In the 1990s, I was in a small country known to have active guerrilla groups. I was leading a five-person negotiation team seeking to secure contracts with perishable food suppliers. Our final destination was in a remote rural area that could only be reached by single-engine planes and required we cross the country from coast to coast—which is not a rare occurrence in the field of agriculture.

Because we had good access to local government officials, we had been able to secure two planes with experienced pilots said to be in the presidential pool. Our flight across the country was uneventful, except for unnerving turbulence that left us with the impression that the plane was jumping from cloud to cloud. We had no luggage, because the planes couldn't afford the extra weight or space, and we were due to return the same day. As we landed, our primary local contact was waiting for us with a van and a truck.

As the leader of the American team, I was given preferential treatment, which in this case meant riding shotgun in the leader's truck while the rest of the team followed in the van. We soon encountered a bridge, and the vehicles stopped. Those in the van were instructed to step out and let the van cross the river empty, with the passengers following on foot. The concern was that the old wooden bridge might not support the weight of a van full of people. With that exercise out of the way, we all got back into the vehicles and continued to travel deeper into the jungle.

The trip was certainly spectacular in many ways, starting with nonexistent roads. The truck regularly hit big potholes that splattered mud all over the windshield. I was told it had been raining almost non-stop for several days, and the only way to make it across the field was to drive as fast as the driver would dare. We finally arrived at our destination and stopped in the middle of a narrow trail, barely wide enough for vehicles to pass. Then the local leader declared: "We're standing in the middle of a guerrilla path, but we haven't seen them in about a week, so don't worry, we are okay."

Surrounded by jungle, only a large structure on the side of the road stood out. It had four flimsy walls and a pointed roof seemingly made of local vegetation. The place was large enough to house the 50 individuals that had already arrived and were waiting to hear our value proposition. We sat in the plastic chairs at the table facing the 50 men, whose chairs were arranged classroom style.

I was the only woman in the room. As the leader of our delegation, it was up to me to make the presentation with my team ready to support the Q&A segment as needed. The presentation, made in Spanish with no audiovisuals (I had anticipated limited technology), went smoothly, evidenced by the fact that the audience's attention never wavered. Once I finished, however, a roar erupted in the audience, with everyone talking at once as they discussed the proposal and what it meant to them.

They discussed and argued among themselves for a while and then asked questions, followed by more discussion and deliberation lasting about an hour. The leader suggested a brief break, after which we all sat down again as they continued the deliberation.

At one point it became clear that all the questions had been answered and the audience was just going in circles as they revisited each provision of the deal, lowering the intensity of the discussion to a normal conversational tone. Attempts to get them to make a decision were handled with apologetic gestures of indecision. After some time, the leader asked me to join him outside the room. There, in the privacy of the jungle, he told me, apologetically but in no uncertain terms, that the suppliers liked the proposal and wanted to do business with us.

The reason they were holding back in making a decision was that accepting our proposal meant abandoning their traditional buyer, described as a powerful company. The move implied uncertainty and, frankly, they expected to be unofficially compensated for taking such risk. Their proposal, as genuine as it may have been, could be easily interpreted as a call for us to sweeten the deal—under the table—to gain access to that particular market.

I thanked him for being so straightforward and explained that American laws are very clear in prohibiting American business from engaging in certain kinds of activities, and we would be withdrawing our offer. He went back inside to caucus with the group as I gathered my team and explained the situation. We all agreed to withdraw our offer, and in five minutes the meeting was over. We said our friendly goodbyes, both sides lamenting our inability to do business, and we were driven back to the small landing strip. No harm done on either side.

But our adventures didn't end there. As the two single-engine planes flew back to the city, the radio operator told the pilots to be on the alert for another plane in our vicinity that had lost contact with the tower. The pilots took the right action. They eased the planes toward the nearby mountain to their right to protect that side from a possible collision and we all concentrated on scouting the horizon to our left. Since this wasn't the first time I had flown over rural areas in a single-engine plane, I wasn't worried. I knew that experienced pilots like to fly along the mountainside to ride the thermals. In the end, the lost plane made contact with the tower, and we all relaxed and landed safely in the city, our lives several notches richer for the entire experience.

- If your project's success depended on it, would you have been willing to take this trip?
- What was the key factor helping us secure reliable transportation and safe passage through the area?
- What would have been your reaction to the counter-proposal presented by the suppliers?
- Why do you think the suppliers respected a woman being in charge of the team?

When Face Saving Gets Sticky

The most commonly known characteristic of collectivistic societies is the need to save face. Public embarrassment is unbearable and avoided at all costs. When dealing with these societies, the need to save face deserves all kinds of considerations. It's also one of the hardest to keep in mind for Western individualists, not because they don't suffer when they lose face, but because they are not as aware of its consequences. Individualistic societies allow people to shrug this off and move on, so the experience is not nearly as traumatic as it is for those in collectivistic societies.

Saving face involves covering up for mistakes made by the individual or the group. This generates some absurd situations resulting from lack of transparency in communications that frustrates and can become unbearable for Westerners accustomed to a direct approach. Fatalism, a sense that life events depend solely on the will of God, is a widely held belief in many societies, particularly in the Middle East. Fatalism plays a role in daily decisions and also in the concept of saving face. Those who believe they have no control over the outcome of simple day-to-day activities see no need to anticipate and plan for contingencies. Here is a story that illustrates how complicated a simple task can become.

While working in Saudi Arabia, I often hosted Western visitors who came to speak or provide services. One such visitor was a European business expert scheduled to deliver an important lecture. To account for contingencies, we had suggested that he arrive the day before the event. When visiting Saudi Arabia, it's easier to travel first to the neighboring kingdom of Bahrain, which offers a larger selection of international flight connections.

On such occasions, it was customary for us to send a driver to pick up our visitors at the airport in Bahrain and drive them to Saudi Arabia using the causeway over the Gulf connecting the two kingdoms. It's not a long distance, but because borders are crossed, the trip involves customs, immigration, and insurance verification on both sides (seven stops) and takes between two and four hours, depending on traffic.

My visitor was scheduled to arrive in Bahrain at 9 o'clock in the morning. I had been warned that drivers often missed visitors for one reason or another, so I asked my assistant to call the driver to verify the visitor's arrival. She happily reported that the driver had indeed verified arrival and had indicated that the visitor was comfortably resting in the hotel for a couple of hours before continuing to Saudi Arabia.

The stay in the hotel was necessary at the time when visas to enter Saudi Arabia were preferably processed at the embassy in Bahrain, with the passport provided by the visitor in person. The hotel was used to allowing the visitor to rest while the visa was being processed. (I understand this intermediate step is no longer in practice).

An Arab colleague of mine familiar with local customs overheard the confirmation delivered by my assistant and shook her head, skeptical. Curious, I asked her why and she said: "Until you hear the visitor's voice on the phone and he confirms his arrival, he has not yet arrived." I was puzzled by her conviction but followed her advice and called the visitor on his mobile number. No response. The driver was also unavailable.

One hour later, as we were setting other options in motion, I received another phone call. It was the European visitor enthusiastically announcing that his plane had been delayed but had finally landed in Bahrain and wanted to know how to get hold of the driver!

We instructed the visitor to wait where he was while we located the driver. The driver, having been exposed on his false story, confessed that the 9 o'clock plane had never arrived and he had no information on where the visitor was. Instead of explaining his situation, he pretended that everything was under control as planned and was hoping for some kind of miracle to save him from the embarrassment of losing his customer.

- What part of the story will you remember the most the next time you deal with foreign nationals?
- What lessons can be learned from the story about ways to anticipate situations that are seemingly simple but may become complicated in a matter of minutes?
- Would you have paid attention to the comment of the skeptical colleague or would you have dismissed it as an exaggeration?

Overcoming Inhibitions

Lack of familiarity with other countries and their societies can affect people's behavior in many ways. Some may become obnoxious and act aggressively, usually to mask their shyness and feelings of inadequacy. Others may be truly shy by nature, a condition exacerbated when confronted with new people, particularly with powerful high-ranking officials.

Not too long ago, I was invited, along with others, to moderate a panel at an international conference in an emerging market. It was one of those high-visibility events inaugurated by national political and industry leaders and attended by executives and professionals from all over the world. The host country was an emerging economy attracting significant attention, and everyone was happy to take part in a number of official programs offered by the organizers. The hotel facilities were spectacular, the crowd was massive, and the atmosphere was filled with excitement.

Our panel consisted of powerful senior leaders in government and industry in various countries, each with impressive résumés. A member of our team was a Western professional who had just been promoted by his firm and charged with opening and heading a new regional office. This conference offered him the perfect opportunity to personally meet the leaders he would soon be doing business with. By all measures he was a successful executive, but this was his first assignment outside his home country and he was clearly uncomfortable.

Worried about not making a good impression, my colleague couldn't sleep the night before the program. He missed breakfast with the panelists, and when he finally showed up, he was nearly paralyzed by nervousness. He could not think straight, he told me, and begged to excuse himself from the program. What a wasted opportunity this was—and all because he lacked familiarity with foreign environments and couldn't handle the level of anxiety it generated. Lack of awareness, understanding, knowledge, internalization, and practice with foreign cultures had kept him from taking advantage of a setting ideally designed to establish a personal connection with regional leaders in his industry on neutral ground.

- Have you ever experienced stage freight when confronted with large audiences?
- How do you prepare to step out of your comfort zone and meet high-level officials in foreign countries with confidence and enthusiasm?
- Have you planned or are you planning to put the advice presented in this book into practice to increase your familiarity with people of other cultures?

Connecting the Dots

This last story differs from the previous ones in that it's not a personal experience but an anecdotal-style history of the world. This book has emphasized the similarities that exist among peoples of the world, and in doing so it has touched on a wide range of viewpoints that offer perspective on the world's complexities and the advantages of simplifying life. Here is yet another angle.

I invite you to join me on an imaginary tour that shows how interconnected we are with people all over the world. This narrative will describe some unexpected relationships that started to form centuries ago among people in countries apparently as dissimilar and as far apart as:

- Spain and the Philippines
- Portugal and India
- Portugal and China
- China and India
- India and Singapore
- Latin America and China
- The Arab World and Latin America

We believe that the Chinese are very different from Arabs and Arabs are very different from Latin Americans. They in turn are different from Indians and Africans. It's difficult to believe that these dissimilar cultures can be related in any way. The narrative below helps shed some of those unfounded beliefs and will add a different perspective to the way you look at the world and the commonalities that exist among its people.

Connecting the dots opens a new door to
understanding people around the world.

The stories below are real and historically well documented, but this particular narrative is not intended to be a rigorous analysis. It's a practical way to help you get a quick grasp on just how easy it is to break the world into manageable pieces we can understand.

Grab a map or use Google Maps to connect the dots as we follow the travels of our ancestors who, guided by a desire to discover a new world and increase commercial trade, cross-pollinated the globe and gave birth to a world population that is now more similar than they could have ever imagined.

Consider this:

The history-based affinity between the United States and the United Kingdom is unquestionable, and we know that a large number of Americans are of European descent. This occurred because European immigration began in the 16th century in what was to become the U.S. with the arrival of the Spaniards, who were then followed by the English, Dutch, Scots-Irish, and others. Similarly, we know that with the exception of indigenous people, the majority of Latin Americans are of Spanish descent, whereas Brazilians are of Portuguese descent. On average, however, our knowledge of the inter-connections between other regions of the world is less fresh in our minds.

Let's take a look at other historical ethnic interfacing around the world.

Spain and the Philippines

The numerous sea explorations in search of the Indies initiated in Europe in the 16th century, between 1498 and 1555, had tremendous influence on the creation of a new world.[9] Everyone knows that Italian-born Christopher Columbus discovered America, but few may know or remember that in addition to Columbus, there were numerous Portuguese explorers of the same era, such as Ferdinand de Magellan, Vasco da Gama, and Alfonso de Albuquerque.[10]

Magellan was the first Portuguese explorer to lead a fleet that circumnavigated the planet, sailing from Spain to the West and returning to Spain from the East. After leaving Spain, Magellan landed in Brazil (1519–1520), which had been discovered in 1500 by an earlier Portuguese explorer, Vicente Yáñez Pinzón. The Portuguese presence in Brazil helps explain why Brazil is the only Portuguese-speaking country in South America. By the same token, if Columbus was Italian, why is Italian not the official language of Latin America? As it happens, Columbus lived in Spain most of his life, where he learned Latin and Castilian Spanish, and never wrote in his native Italian language.

Back to Magellan: From Brazil, Magellan continued south searching for a passage (what is now known as the Strait of Magellan) from the Atlantic Ocean into what Magellan would name the "Pacific Ocean" because of the calm waters it offered to tired sailors as compared to the treacherous waters of the Strait and the Atlantic.

Once on the Pacific, Magellan reached the Philippines, named in honor of Philip II, ruler of Spain and Portugal. The Spanish ruled the Philippines for over 300 years, influencing its culture and society, which explains why many Filipinos have Spanish surnames and have incorporated some Spanish vocabulary into their language.

While in the Philippines, Magellan was killed in a political battle while defending the local government. The fleet, now under the command of Sebastián del Cano, continued the voyage, reaching Borneo, Sumatra, Siam (now Thailand), China, Vietnam, and Japan before returning to Spain on September 6, 1522.

Portugal and India

Vasco da Gama reached India in 1498, landing on what is today the state of Kerala. In 1510, Alfonso de Albuquerque also landed in India and established a permanent settlement farther north, in the region known as Goa, which became the headquarters of Portuguese India and the seat of the Portuguese viceroy, charged with governing all Portuguese possessions in Asia.

The Portuguese influence in India spread throughout the country, from coast to coast, and for centuries influenced politics, religion, and trade. Goa, in particular, was under Portuguese dominance from 1530 until 1961, when it was liberated and merged with the Indian Union. This helps explain why citizens in some areas of India, such as Chennai (formerly Madras), Kerala, and Goa have names of Portuguese origin.

Portugal and China

The history of Macau, today a Special Administrative Region (SAR) of the People's Republic of China and a near neighbor of Hong Kong, dates back more than 5,000 years. In the 5th century, Macau became a port of call for traders traveling from Southeast Asia to Guangzhou. In 1513, Portuguese traders settled in Macau, marking the beginning of almost five centuries of Portuguese political control and influence. The city became an important center for the development of Portugal's trade along three major routes: Macau-Malacca-Goa-Lisbon, Guangzhou-Macau-Nagasaki, and Macau-Manila-Mexico.

Macau remained a Portuguese colony until as recently as 1999, when it was handed over to China under SAR status. Both Chinese and Portuguese languages are official in Macau, although today most people speak English. Hong

Figure 9.6 Chinese New Year in Portuguese, Macau. (*Source:* © Z. Kraljevic)

Kong was handed over to China by Britain in 1997 under much-publicized circumstances. Under SAR status, both Hong Kong and Macau maintain their monetary, legal, and passport systems, while China controls foreign relations and defense.

While on business in Hong Kong, I visited Macau, just a short distance by ferry from Hong Kong. Walking down the streets, I shot a photo (see Figure 9.6) of a sign displaying a Happy Lunar New Year message in Portuguese.

China and India

In the 19th century, two beautiful white jade statues of Buddha were brought into China from Burma (now Myanmar) by sea at a time when Burma was a province of India and part of the British Indian Empire.[11] The statues, representing a sitting and a reclining Buddha, were housed in an old temple built in 1882, later destroyed when the Qing Dynasty (1644–1912), the last imperial dynasty of China, was overthrown in the 1912 revolution.

The statues were saved and moved to the Jade Buddha Temple in Shanghai, built in 1928. While the original reclined Buddha statue is slightly less than one meter long, the statue that calls most attention from visitors is a four-meter reclining Buddha statue (below), brought in from Singapore in 1989.

Figure 9.7   Reclining Buddha, China. (*Source:* © Z. Kraljevic.)

But how did Buddhism penetrate China?

The history of the development of Chinese religion is long and complex, and there is a diversity of theories and legends describing the introduction of Buddhism to China. There is agreement that Buddhism was founded by an Indian prince, Siddhartha Gautama (Gautama Buddha or the Supreme Buddha) around 556 BC. Over time, missionaries and traders traveling the Silk Route between China and Europe helped spread Buddhism.

But Buddhism didn't spread significantly among the common people of China until the end of the Han Dynasty (202 BC–220 AD), which had embraced Confucianism as a primary religion. In the period following the Han Dynasty, Confucianism declined and gave way to the strengthening of Taoism (Daoism), which has a high level of compatibility with Buddhism. It was then that Buddhism expanded throughout China, particularly once the "sutras" (scriptures or oral teaching of Gautama Buddha) were translated into Chinese using terminology borrowed from Taoism.[12]

India and Singapore

About 77 percent of Singapore's 5.5 million people are of Chinese origin, primarily descendants of the Han Dynasty.[13] The other 23 percent is divided primarily between Malaysians and Indians. Geographic proximity helps explain both the Chinese influence and the Malaysian presence; but why so many Indians?

It started in 1919 with the British initiative to establish a base of operations in Singapore to facilitate trade between China and India. By doing so, the British hoped to undermine the dominance that the Dutch exerted in the region and their imposed restrictions on which ports the British could use to trade with China.[14] And so it was that Indian nationals started to work in Singapore, in time joined by relatives, which helped establish an Indian presence there.

The majority of Indians living in Singapore today are Hindu, and when you are visiting Singapore, you can walk by the market and visit the Hindu temples commonly found in the Indian sector of the city.

Figure 9.8   Indian market, Singapore. (*Source:* © Z. Kraljevic.)

Figure 9.9   Hindu temple detail, Singapore. (*Source:* © Z. Kraljevic.)

Latin America and China

Chinese influence in Latin America started with commercial ties linked to the silver trade dating back to the 1600s.[15] At that time, China was an aggressive importer of silver, a commodity in great abundance in the southern cone of South America and Mexico.

Did you know that Argentina derives its name from the French word *argent,* which means silver? The commodity was much appreciated in Europe and Asia, and Spanish traders were quick to establish a silver route directly to Europe, and from there to Asia through European merchants. They also established a more direct route from Acapulco (in what is now Mexico) and the Philippines. The famous "Manila Galleon"[16] was a Spanish vessel that made an annual round trip (one vessel, one trip per year) across the Pacific between Manila, in the Philippines, and Acapulco during the period 1565–1815. Galleons were the sole means of communication between Spain and its Philippine colony, and they served as an economic lifeline for the Spaniards in Manila.

As international commerce flourished in the mid-1800s and early-1900s and Latin America started to develop, Chinese sailors started to venture into Latin countries, in some cases establishing permanent residence after experiencing the similarities between the two cultures. Both Asian and Latin American cultures are collectivistic societies that favor respect for authority and the elderly; these societies prefer top-down decision making over individualistic empowerment. Face saving is another common and important trait shared by both Asians and Latin Americans.

In modern times, a Chinese business man passing through the Latin American southernmost country of Chile decided to leave the ship and establish a business in the Northern part of the country, where a well-established Chinese population already existed. He adopted a local name, José, which the locals quickly translated into the endearing version of "Pepe" or "Pepito."

He tried his luck by opening a butcher store supplying local restaurants, and over time he became a successful businessman. He also met and fell in love with a local Chilean girl by the name of Teresa—a tall, slender, and mischievous young woman with big gray eyes, and a descendent of recent Spanish immigrants from Salamanca, Spain. Teresa happens to be my grandaunt, and I had the fortune of meeting Pepito when I was four years old.

Figure 9.10 Family picture, 1953, Chile. (*Source:* © Z. Kraljevic.)

My earliest memories include Pepito chasing my sister and me around the house and playing hide-and-seek with us. It also includes finding Pepito in the kitchen skinning an octopus with extreme dexterity. This experience made a huge impression on me, and it is as vivid today as it was then.

In the family picture above: my grandmother (right), my grandaunt (left) and Pepito (in the middle).

It should be noted that Japan has also played a role in increasing the Asian presence in South America. Notably, in the 20th century, Brazil imported Japanese citizens to develop their agricultural industry. As a result, Brazil became home to the largest population of Japanese living outside of Japan at the time. When visiting São Paulo, it's quite striking to find people with clear Japanese features who speak native Portuguese. Today, nearly two million Brazilians of Japanese origin live in Brazil, and a walk through the Liberdade district of São Paulo will easily transport you to Tokyo.[17]

The Japanese also had a presence in the northern part of Chile, where a few of my relatives on my mother's side learned to speak Japanese. My mother was nicknamed "Yoto"—presumably a Japanese adaptation of her name, Yolanda or Yola. True or not, this factor likely contributed to my curiosity about different cultures.

The Arab World and Latin America

Using history as an ally, we continue our quest to connect the dots between regions of the world and travel from Spain to the Middle East. Did you know that there are over 4,000 words in the Spanish language that are of Arabic origin? Why?

The Arab tribal rebellions erupting in 632 after the death of Muhammad, the founder of the religion of Islam, resulted in a territorial expansionist campaign led by Muhammad's successors as a way of reestablishing political and religious control. Between 633 and 711, Muslim forces conquered neighboring empires, in some cases for several years. These empires include the area we now know as Syria, Iraq, Palestine, Turkey, Persia, Jerusalem, and Egypt. Raids also targeted Sicily, Rhodes, and Cyprus, which negotiated a peace agreement and became neutral territory.

Eventually, the Moors, a mixed group of primarily North African Muslims, crossed the Strait of Gibraltar into Spain, which at the time had been significantly weakened by internal political discord among the Visigoths. By 718, most of Spain and Portugal were under Moorish domination.

The Moors established a strong caliphate in the city of Córdoba but failed to establish a central government and were continuously attacked during the wars of the Reconquista, which lasted over 750 years. By 1085, the Moors started to lose ground. Córdoba surrendered in 1236 to Ferdinand III and joined the Christian kingdom of Castile. The last Moorish city of Granada fell to Ferdinand V and Isabella I in 1492.[18]

The Moors' influence in part of the Spanish culture, customs, architecture, science, and language is, perhaps, best illustrated by the splendid development experienced by Córdoba, the capital of Muslim Spain. In 785, its ruler, Emir Abd-al-Rhaman of Damascus, initiated the construction of the Great Mosque, considered a jewel of Islamic civilization.

In the 10th century, Córdoba was the most populated city in the West, and its level of development was comparable to that of Baghdad and Constantinople in the East. The Great Mosque (known in Spanish as *La Mezquita de Córdoba*) was later converted to the Christian faith and renamed the Cathedral of Córdoba, but those attending mass today still may say "I am going to *La Mesquita*."[19]

The Great Mosque is as distinctive to Córdoba as the Alhambra Palace is to Granada and the Giralda Tower is to Seville. Not surprisingly, today there are over 4,000 words in the Spanish language that derive from the Arab language.

Later, the Spaniards colonized Latin America (except Brazil), bringing with them their Arab-influenced language and customs. Were you to look for them, you might find many similarities between Arabs and Latin Americans. Of course, each region has developed and evolved at a different pace and been affected by different religions, historic events, climates, education, democracy, and international trade. But you can find similarities in their predilection for an authoritarian and paternalistic management style, certain negotiation tactics, and the ever-so-important face-saving practice. The chemistry that exists between the two cultures makes business interaction much easier than you might anticipate.

Knowing that Latin America reflects the Spanish culture, which in turn reflects part of an earlier Arab civilization, is extremely useful in business. It means that your experience working in Latin America is transferable to working in the Middle East. Because of the interconnectivity described earlier in this section, experience working in Latin America is also transferable to many Southeast Asian countries.

While working in the Middle East, I met a number of Arab citizens from both the Northern African countries and the Gulf region. Among the most affluent were many Spanish-speaking Arabs, and I enjoyed lively conversations about their experiences in Spain, which turned out to be one of their favorite destinations for pleasure travel. I also had the opportunity to confirm that the Spanish and Arabic languages share several common words—but, as expected, this similarity is more noticeable in North African countries, and less so in Gulf countries.

As a general rule, Spanish words that start with "a" and "al" are likely to derive from Arabic words, and are part of the common language, or slang, of Northern African countries. For example:

-aceite (al-zait; oil)
-azúcar (sukkar; sugar)
-arroz (roz; rice)

Other examples include:

-almohada (pillow)
-alfil (bishop on a chess board)
-asesino (assassin)

-alfiler (pin)
-aldea (village)
-alcachofa (artichoke)
-aceituna (olive)
-adobe (mud)
-algodón (cotton)
-algoritmo (algorithm)
-alquiler (lease)
-arrecife (reef)

Other Spanish words derived from Northern African Arabic include[20]:

-ojalá (hopefully)
-carcajada (laughter)
-hazaña (feat)
-jaqueca (migraine)
-tarifa (tariff)
-hasta (…la vista baby; until)

Closing Remarks

The concepts, guidelines, and stories shared in this book were chosen to highlight the wide spectrum of circumstances that you may face when traveling around the world for pleasure or business.

The common thread throughout the book has been to help you visualize the many opportunities available to help raise your level of awareness, understanding, and knowledge of the world today.

You may never face the threat of kidnapping or the uncertainty of political unrest, but reading about these situations increases awareness of the benefits of staying alert and being better prepared to face unexpected situations.

The more you travel and put these concepts into practice, the more you will internalize the similarities that bring people together. Understanding the interconnectivity that exists among the people of the world will make it easier to understand what drives them when making personal or business decisions.

Just the realization that, wherever you go, you have myriad opportunities to meet new people and assess their intrinsic value as human beings will help you surround yourself with those no-longer strangers, who can contribute to your professional success, personal safety, and a more enjoyable life in today's world.

Notes and Bibliography

Preface

1. The *About Water* video is no longer available on YouTube due to a copyright claim by the David Foster Wallace Literary Trust. It's a beautiful piece, and hopefully it will be allowed to air in the future. The actual commencement speech is also on YouTube (audio and text, https://www.youtube.com/watch?v=8CrOL-ydFMI). Published on May 19, 2013, it is entitled *Commencement Speech to Kenyon College class of 2005, written by David Foster Wallace.*
2. It must be emphasized that the narrative used in this book is based on the *About Water* video and reflects the author's interpretation of the scenes shown in the video. They are not intended to represent David Foster Wallace's exact words, and for those the reader is encouraged to listen to Wallace's speech, now posted on YouTube.

Chapter 1 Lost but Not Alone

1. Bianchi, Constanza C., and Enrique Ostale, Lessons Learned From Unsuccessful Internationalization Attempts: Example Of Multinational Retailers In Chile, *Journal of Business Research,* Vol. 59, No. 1: pp. 140–147. July 2004.

2. Landler, Mark, and Michael Barbaro, Wal-Mart Finds That Its Formula Doesn't Fit Every Culture. *New York Times,* August 2006.

3. *The Home Depot Closes Seven Big Box Stores in China.* Press Release posted by Reuters and Global Atlanta, September 2012.

4. Rein, Shaun, CNBC Contributor, Managing Director, China Market, Why Best Buy Failed in China, CNBC, March 2011.

5. Foreign Direct Investment—The China Story, *The World Bank News,* July 2010.

6. Isadore, Chris, U.S. Companies Dump Billions into China, CNN Money, January 2011.

7. The fDi Report: Global Greenfield Investment Trends, fDi Intelligence, *Financial Times,* 2013.

8. Coy, Peter, Give Me Your Yuan: Chinese Are Eager for U.S. Assets, *Bloomberg Businessweek, Global Economics,* August 2013. See also: Russia's Outward Investment, *Deutsche Bank Research,* 2008; and Chatterjee, Sumeet, India's Capital Outflow Controls Seen Hurting Overseas Drive, *Reuters,* March 2013.

9. Badkar, Mamta, China Is About to Take a HUGE Step Toward Internationalizing Its Currency, *Business Insider,* March 2012.

Chapter 2 The World Is Hyperventilating— Bring on the Brown Bag!

1. Schumpeter: A World of Trouble, *The Economist,* January 12, 2013.

2. Poverty Analysis—Overview, World Bank, 2013.

3. *Rich World, Poor World: A Guide to Global Development,* Center for Global Development, 2002.

4. de la Torre, Augusto, and Jamele Rigolini, MIC Forum: The Rise of the Middle Class, World Bank. For additional commentaries on the rise of the global middle class, See The New Global Middle Class: Potentially Profitable—but Also Unpredictable, Knowledge@Wharton, July 09, 2008.

5. *Number of Active Users at Facebook Over the Years,* Yahoo News citing Associated Press, May 2013.

6. Twitter Ranked Fastest Growing Social Platform in the World, *Forbes,* Jan 2013.

7. 200 Million Users? LinkedIn is Just Getting Started, *Forbes,* April 2013.

8. Suddenly, Google+ is Outpacing Twitter to Become the World's Second Largest Social Network, *Business Insider,* May 2013.

9. YouTube Statistics, 2013.

10. The Gated Globe, Special Report World Economy, *The Economist,* October 2013.
11. Begbie, Yolanda, Born in Burundi, This Angel of Africa Built a Village and Saved Thousands of Children, Social Enterprise & Philanthropy / Spotlight, Africa.com blog posted June 19, 2013, http://www.africa.com/blog/angel-of-africa/
12. See also: The Future of Social Enterprise and the Future of Individual Philanthropy, *The Centennial Global Business Summit Report,* Harvard Business School, 2008.
13. Maslow, Abraham, A Theory of Human Motivation, published first in *Psychological Review,* 1943, Vol. 50, no. 4. This article has been amply cited, and today there are a number of sources on this topic, including a book by the same title that can be found online or in bookstores.
14. Hicks, Jonathan P., Bridgestone in Deal for Firestone, *New York Times,* March, 1988.
15. Bebar, Jill, Dow, Nasdaq, S&P Cap Phenomenal Year, Decade at All-Time Highs, *CNN Money,* December 1999.
16. Clapper, James R., Director of National Intelligence, *Statement for the Record, Worldwide Threat Assessment of the US Intelligence Community,* Senate Select Committee on Intelligence, March 12, 2013.

Chapter 3 They Did What?

1. Developing Countries to Receive Over $410 Billion in Remittances in 2013, The World Bank, Press Release, October 2, 2013. For other enlightening reporting on this topic See: Ratha, Dilip, Workers' Remittances: An Important and Stable Source of External Development Finance, *Global Development Finance,* World Bank 2003; and de Haas, Hein, International Migration, Remittances and Development: Myths and Facts, *Third World Quarterly,* Vol. 26, no. 8, pp. 1269–1284, 2005.
2. For additional levels of remittance, See: Mohapatra, Sanket, Dilip Ratha, and Ani Silwal, Outlook for Remittance Flows 2012–14, *World Bank Migration and Remittance Brief,* 17, 2011.
3. Data adapted from: Migration and Remittances: Recent Developments and Outlook, Special Topic: Return Migration. World Bank Group, Knomad. Accessed at http://www.knomad.org/sites/default/files/2017-10/Migration%20and%20Development%20Brief%2028.pdf
4. The World at Six Billion, United Nations World Population Data, Population Division, 1999; See also: Roudi, Farzaneh (Nazy), Population Trends and

Challenges in the Middle East and North Africa, *Population Reference Bureau Policy Brief,* funded by the Ford Foundation, October 2001.

5. For more information on MENA countries See: MENA Population: 1950, Now, 2050, Middle East Strategy at Harvard, John M. Olin Institute for Strategic Studies, Harvard University, March 2008; and the keynote speech by El-Badri, H. E. Abdalla S., OPEC Secretary General, The MENA Region in the International Arena, the Middle East & North Africa Energy 2012 Conference, *Investing for the Future in Turbulent Times,* Chatham House, London, U.K, 30–31 January 2012.

6. Who Invented the Lightbulb?, The Museum of Unnatural Mystery (www.unmuseum.org); See also the Humphrey Davy's biography at the Chemical Heritage Foundation website (www.chemheritage.org).

Chapter 4 Up, Down, and Sideways

1. Trying to Pull Together: Africans Are Asking Whether China Is Making Their Lunch or Eating It, *The Economist,* April 2011; and Benard, Alexander, How the US Can Out-Invest China in Africa, *The Christian Science Monitor,* August 2012.

2. Kissinger, Henry, *On China,* The Penguin Press, 2011.

3. Sempa, Francis P., *The Geopolitical Containment of China,* The Mackinder Forum.

4. South-South Trade Monitor, United Nations, UNCTAD, June 2012.

5. Jagtiani, Sunil, and Unni Krishnan, Maersk Lured by $1.5 Trillion in 2020 Asia-Africa Trade: Freight Markets, *Bloomberg Businessweek,* September 2011.

6. World Trade Developments, International Trade Statistics, World Trade Organization, 2012.

7. Free Trade Agreement Will Help Boost UAE-India Economies, *Gulf News,* July 2011.

8. Gulf Arab Investors Target Asia as U.S. Ties Wane, Reuters, March 2007.

9. China Investment Deal, Library of Congress/Law Library of Congress/Global Legal Monitor/ASEAN/China, August 2009.

10. GCC-EU Free Trade Agreement Must Be Saved. *Financial Times,* July 2012.

11. Singapore Government Official Web site /FTA/ The Gulf Cooperation Council (GSFTA).

12. GE Global Innovation Barometer: Global Research Findings and Insights, January 2013.

13. Goleman, Daniel, *Emotional Intelligence—Why It Can Matter More than IQ,* Bantam Books, 2005.

Chapter 5 In Search of the Human Fractal

1. Sub-regional classifications can be found in regular reports issued by the CIA World Factbook, the Center for Strategic and International Studies (CSIS), the World Bank, the United Nations, and others.
2. How We Classify Countries, The World Bank Data, the World Bank, 2013.
3. Mandelbrot, B. B., *The Fractal Geometry of Nature,* IBM Thomas J. Watson Research Center, W. H. Freeman and Company, New York, 1982.
4. The full transcript of the *NOVA* program can be found at http://www.pbs.org/wgbh/nova/physics/hunting-hidden-dimension.html
5. Mandelbrot, B. B., How Long Is the Coast of Britain? Statistical Self-Similarity and Fractional Dimension, *Science,* Vol. 156, pp. 636–638, 1967.
6. Fractal Geometry, Icons of Progress, IBM100 (http://www-03.ibm.com/ibm/history/ibm100/us/en/icons/fractal).
7. *How does the nervous system work?,* The U.S. National Library of Medicine, March 12, 2012.
8. Körding, Konrad, Decision Theory: What Should the Nervous System Do?, *Science,* Vol. 318, No. 5850, pp. 606–610, October 2007.
9. Gold, J. I., and M. N. Shadlen, *Annu. Rev. Neurosci.* Vol. 30, p. 535, 2007.
10. Yang, T., and M. N. Shadlen, *Nature* Vol. 447, p. 1075, 2007.
11. Krulwich, Robert, Daniel Glasser, et al., *Mirror Neurons,* PBS program directed by Julia Cort, aired January 25, 2005.

Chapter 6 First Impressions—Skewed and Backwards

1. Hofstede, Geert, National Cultures in Four Dimensions, *International Studies of Management and Organizations,* 1983 (See: scholar.google.com/citations).
2. Pareto, V., *Cours d'Economie Politique,* Droz, Geneva, 1896; and Luigi Amoroso, Vilfredo Pareto, *Econometrica,* Vol. 6, No. 1, January 1938.

Chapter 7 Simplicity—A New Way of Life

1. Einhorn, Bruce, Pepsi's Indra Nooyi Focuses on China, *Global Economics, Bloomberg Businessweek,* July 2009.
2. Kraljevic, Zlática, *Born to Succeed (or How We Graduated to Toddlers),* Blog first published on www.zk@zkraljevic.com/Blog, 2012.
3. Asimov, Isaac, *The Relativity of Wrong,* Kensington, 1995.
4. Ostrofsky, Marc, *Get Rich Click!* Razor Media Group LLC, 2011.

Chapter 8 Expect the Unexpected—A New Kind of Leadership

1. Elliott, Leonie, How Big Brands Reach Africa's "Next Million" Shoppers, CNN, May 2013.
2. Greenberg, Andy, IBM's Chinese Cloud City, *Forbes,* July 2009.
3. *China Stimulus—China's Big Bang,* Thomson Reuters, 2010.
4. Thomas, Leigh, OECD Drive Against Tax Avoidance Gets Fresh Backing, Reuters, May 2013.
5. Argentina Didn't Fall on Its Own, *Washington Post,* August 3, 2003; and Erin McCarthy, Emerging-Market Currencies Extend Selloff U.S., China Pressures, *The New York Times,* June 2013.
6. Definition of *commoditize,* Investopedia.
7. Multilateral Investment Guarantee Agency (MIGA), World Bank Group.
8. *Global Payroll: Myth or Reality?,* Ernst & Young, April 2013.
9. Thunderbird's History, Thunderbird School of Global Management (www.thunderbird.edu/about-thunderbird/thunderbird-history).
10. Inheriting a Complex World: Future Leaders Envision Sharing the Planet, IBM Institute for Business Value Executive Report, IBM Global Business Services, May 2010. See also: Education Lags in Preparing Students for Globalization and Sustainability, Facebook, 2010.
11. Operating Risks in Emerging Markets, The Economist Intelligence Unit, *The Economist,* 2006.
12. Christensen, Clayton M., Richard Alton, Curtis Rising, and Andrew Waldeck, The Big Idea: The New M&A Playbook, *Harvard Business Review,* March 2011.
13. Schamel, John, History of the Pilot's Checklist—Why Checklists Now Help Ensure Flawless Execution (www.checklists.com.au/personal/history; History of Checklists); others cited: James Gilbert, *The Great Planes,* 1970; Edward Jablonski, *Flying Fortress,* 1965; Lloyd Jones, *U.S. Fighters,* 1975.

Chapter 9 Real-Life Anecdotes from a Business Globetrotter

1. Hanuman, *Encyclopedia Britannica.*
2. Monkeys Attack Delhi Politician, BBC News, October 2007.
3. Serafino, Nina M., Colombia: Plan Colombia Legislation and Assistance (FY2000–FY2001), Congressional Research Services, Library of Congress, July 2001.
4. Inspiration for Violent Protests in Tunisia Dies, CNN News, January 2011.

5. Robin Wigglesworth and Henry Foy in London and Richard Milne in Stockholm, Foreign Companies Close Offices Amid Fears of Violence in Egypt, *Financial Times,* August 2013.

6. Palmer, David S., and Thomas A. Marks, Guerrilla Insurgencies in Latin America, in *Political Science,* published online November 2011, Oxford Index, Oxford University Press.

7. Colombia Peace Talks with FARC Rebels Suspended, France 24 News Wire, August 2013. The efforts on both sides to end decades of bloodshed have been going on since the 1980s, and the last round of negotiations fell apart in 2002: Colombian Negotiators Meet with FARC in Cuba, CNN, November 2012.

8. Torregrosa, Luisita Lopez, A Woman Rises In Brazil, *The New York Times,* September 2010.

9. There are a number of sources that describe European exploration from 1400 to 1600. Suggested reading: (a) James Voorhies, *Europe and the Age of Exploration,* Department of European Paintings, The Metropolitan Museum of Art, New York; (b) Emma George Ross, *The Portuguese in Africa—1415–1600,* Department of Arts of Africa, Oceania, and the Americas, The Metropolitan Museum of Art, New York.

10. Da Gama, Vasco, and Ferdinand Magellan, History (www.history.com). Also, George Comet, Geneviève Dermenjian, and Vincent Sevin, The Age of Discovery, The Map as History (www.the-map-as-history.com); Amerigo Vespucci in www.history.com; and When Worlds Collide (www.pbs.org).

11. *Burma: 1930–1947,* British Military History Online (www.britishmilitary history.co.uk).

12. There are a variety of different theories and legends on the topic of Buddhism spreading from India into China. Some are included here: Yijie Tang, *Confucianism, Buddhism, Daoism, Christianity, and Chinese Culture,* The Council for Research in Values and Philosophy, Cultural Heritage and Contemporary Life Series III, Asia, Vol. 3, Edited by George F. McLean, The University of Peking, 1991; *History of Chinese Religion,* ReligionFacts.com; and *Buddhism in China,* AsiaSociety.org.

13. There are numerous articles on Chinese migration spanning over centuries: (a) Joyce Ee, Chinese Migration to Singapore, *Journal of Southeast Asian History,* Vol. 2, No. 1, March 1961. Also quoted in this paper are: Owen Lattimore, *The Mainsprings of Asiatic Migration in Limits of Land Settlement,* edited by Isaiah Bowman, p. 129, New York, 1937; T. H. Montague Bell and H. G. W. Woodhead, *The China Year Book,* p. 17, London, 1916; and Ken Pomeranz and Bin Wong, China and Europe: 1500–1800, *China and Europe: 1500–2000 and Beyond;* and *What is Modern?* Asian Topics in World History, Columbia University, 2004.

14. *Singapore, Founding and Early Years,* Library of Congress.

15. South America: 1600–1800 A.D., *Heilbrunn Timeline of Art History,* Metropolitan Museum of Art, New York, 2013; Tignor et al., *Worlds Together, Worlds Apart: A History of the World from the Beginnings of Humankind to the Present,* Third Edition, W. W. Norton & Company, Inc., 2013.

16. Johanna Hecht, *The Manila Galleon Trade (1565-1815),* Department of European Sculpture and Decorative Arts, The Metropolitan Museum of Art, New York, 2013.

17. Veselinovic, Milena, Mixing Sushi and Samba—Meet the Japanese Brazilians, On the Road: Brazil series, CNN Travel, July 2013.

18. Reconquista, 717–1492, Christian Kingdoms of Spain versus Moslem Moors, Heritage History (www.heritage-history.com). Also, Islam and Europe Timeline (355-1291 A.D.), The Latin Library (www.thelatinlibrary.com/imperialism/notes/islamchron.html); Daniel Medley, The Moorish Invasion of Spain and the Hispanic Reconquest (http://staff.esuhsd.org/balochie/studentprojects/moorchristian/); and The Great Mosque of Córdoba: La Mezquita, *Spain Then and Now* (www.spainthenandnow.com/spanish-architecture).

19. Spanish Words Derived from Arabic (http://www.ctspanish.com/arabic/arabic.htm).

Index

UCLA. *See* University of California, Los Angeles
Ukraine, 38
unconventional reaction, 143
Understanding, 20, 26, 35, 110, 130, 150
understanding people's behavior, 93
unfamiliar territory, 84, 165
Unilever, 131, 132, 139
United Arab Emirates (UAE), 45, 48, 183, 210
United Kingdom, 194
United Nations Millennium Development Goals, 16
United States, 6, 24, 29, 40, 51, 90, 149, 174, 194
University of California, Los Angeles (UCLA), 77
University of London, 77, 78
University of Parma, 77, 78
unstable sociopolitical situation, 185
Uruguay, 129, 189
U.S. food industry, 126

V

value propositions, 75, 93, 135, 140
veteran travelers, 178
Vietnam, 38, 48, 195
Visigoths, 201

W

Wallace, David Foster, 207
Wall Street, 30, 31, 45
Walmart, 7–10, 127
Watanabe, Gedde, 29
weaknesses, 25, 32, 132
Wilde, Oscar, 6, 66, 125
William & Mary's Mason School of Business, 152
women in the workplace, 174
World Bank, 8, 16, 37, 40, 60, 148, 208–212
WorldCom, 45
World Economic Forum, 60
Wright Field, 159

X

Xian, 107

Y

Yemen, 182
Yount, Barton Kyle, 148
YouTube, 21, 207, 208

Z

Zonal Champions, 132

Printed and bound by CPI Group (UK) Ltd, Croydon, CR0 4YY

28/10/2024

01780233-0001